ISBN: 9781407749297

Published by:
HardPress Publishing
8345 NW 66TH ST #2561
MIAMI FL 33166-2626

Email: info@hardpress.net
Web: http://www.hardpress.net

LIFE OF LORD NORTON

Rt. Hon. Sir Charles Adderley K.C. M.G.
from a drawing by George Richmond R.A.
made for Grillion's Club

LIFE OF LORD NORTON

(RIGHT HON. SIR CHARLES ADDERLEY, K.C.M.G., M.P.)

1814—1905

STATESMAN & PHILANTHROPIST

BY WILLIAM S. CHILDE-PEMBERTON

AUTHOR OF "MEMOIRS OF BARONESS DE BODE"

WITH ILLUSTRATIONS

LONDON

JOHN MURRAY, ALBEMARLE STREET, W.

1909

PRINTED BY
HAZELL, WATSON AND VINEY, LD.,
LONDON AND AYLESBURY.

PREFACE

THERE can be no hesitation in claiming that the memory of Lord Norton—better known as Sir Charles Adderley—and of the great, if little known, services rendered by him to his country, deserves permanent record, for he was one of those Englishmen, of whom there have been many in the past (let us hope there will be many like them in the future), who, while entirely devoid of self-seeking or of desire for personal advertisement, have done much to shape the policy and ameliorate the social condition of their country. Lord Norton's special characteristics in this respect are set forth in Chapter I., and need not be repeated here.

It is hoped, further, that whatever throws light on his life, his surroundings, and his character, may be not without interest.

It was his practice from early youth—even from childhood—briefly to chronicle the events of his life, with meditations on them as to how they had affected his character and spiritual advancement. From these records he began at one time an autobiography of his early years, the object being, he tells us with characteristic modesty and sincerity, "firstly, to give myself a comprehensive survey of my past life, its whole meaning and tendency, with its defects while there is time to rectify them ; secondly, to leave any who may care for me, or for what my life may have been, a gift at parting. . . . The barest autobiography," he adds, "has an interest, as being, even if idealised, at least the thing a man has himself built up of what he would be. Every man's record of his own little part not only is a valuable observation for himself, but also helps in the general survey. In the comprehensive view it matters little whether the features of each individual observation be great or small, in so far as we are all the instruments of work God does through our hands for the same account, . . . to which indeed the widow's mite may be the greatest contribution."

As the years advance the autobiographical notes become terse and scanty, and but barely outline the events of his busy career. It has been the part of the editor to bring these rough notes and scattered diaries together, and to illustrate the life as fully as possible by his correspondence, and by additional information from various other sources.

Among his correspondence are included letters from many of the leading statesmen of the Victorian era. The compiler of this memoir desires to express his thanks to Lord Cobham (who inherited a large number of letters to his father, Lord Lyttelton, from Lord Norton); to Sir Arthur Godley and to Sir Thomas Dyke Acland, whose respective fathers were among Lord Norton's intimate friends; to Mr. Henry N. Gladstone; to Lord Salisbury; to Lord Rothschild, and Mr. Monypenny, who have allowed him to print some letters of Lord Beaconsfield, and to others for permission to print the letters of which they hold the copyright; to Mr. Hobbiss, of Saltley College; and to Lord Crewe for permission to publish a poem by his distinguished father, Lord Houghton.

W. S. C.-P.

October, 1908.

CONTENTS

CHAPTER I

CHAPTER II

CHAPTER III

CHAPTER IV

1832–35

CHAPTER V

1835 (continued)

CHAPTER VI

1836

CHAPTER VII

1837

CHAPTER VIII

1841

CHAPTER IX

1842

CONTENTS

CHAPTER XIX

1852 (*continued*)

CHAPTER XX

1852 (*continued*)

CHAPTER XXI

1852 (*continued*)

CHAPTER XXII

THE MAKING OF SALTLEY

CHAPTER XXIII

1853

CHAPTER XXIV

1854

CHAPTER XXV

1855

CHAPTER XXVI

1856

CHAPTER XXVII

1857

CHAPTER XXVIII

1857 (*continued*)

CHAPTER XXIX

1858

CHAPTER XXX

1859

CONTENTS

CHAPTER XXXIV

1867–68

CHAPTER XXXV

1868 (continued)–73

CHAPTER XXXVI

1874

b

CHAPTER XXXVII
1875

CHAPTER XXXVIII
1877

CHAPTER XXXIX
HAMS THEATRICALS
1862-1886

CHAPTER XL
1878

CHAPTER XLI

1878 (*continued*)

CHAPTER XLII

1879–84

CHAPTER XLIII

1884

CHAPTER XLVIII

1892

CHAPTER XLIX

1893-95

CHAPTER L

1895 (*continued*)

CHAPTER LI

1896–99

CHAPTER LII

1900–5

LIST OF ILLUSTRATIONS

Life of Lord Norton

CHAPTER I

OUTLINE OF CAREER

STATESMAN in all he accomplished, it is perhaps less as politician than as philanthropist that Lord Norton is revealed in the private note-books, papers, and correspondence which he has left.

Although from a strong inclination towards traditional institutions he was always a Conservative in name, he was, at heart, a Reformer in the literal and best sense of the word—an "Improver" is the designation which may best describe his attitude in relation to his Parliamentary work. As such he laboured in Parliament for sixty-four consecutive years—thirty-seven in the House of Commons (during which time he represented the same constituency without a break) and the remainder in the House of Lords—his own personal advancement being throughout a matter of no consideration to him, while his life-long ambition was not so much "to achieve great things, as greatly to achieve the thing in hand."

There was in him little or nothing of the partisanship usually associated with the name of politician. His independence of his party was, in fact, a disadvantage to him, if viewed from the standard of mere worldly success. It was certainly the cause of his not attaining a more prominent position among statesmen, and of his never receiving a seat in the Cabinet. "Adderley would be Adderley still," was the reason Disraeli gave for not putting him

I

in the Cabinet when President of the Board of Trade; and early in his career Adderley's refusal of a post in the Government, such as an ambitious man would have eagerly hailed, retarded his prospects of official prominence. This independence arose from a want of sympathy with any party. In this he resembled the great Lord Shaftesbury, who said he was neither Whig nor Tory.

Lord Norton's best work was done when no party feeling came in; and while he showed in office ability as an administrator, his most notable achievements in colonial movements were long before he held office, and it was with reference to these that John Bright said on more than one occasion Adderley's name "will go down to posterity," and Mr. Joseph Chamberlain has borne testimony that " he rendered great service to the State." It was not when he was in office that he drew up with Gibbon Wakefield the Constitution of New Zealand, for which his name is still gratefully remembered there; while the name of "Adderley Street," Cape Town, perpetuates his unofficial benefits to Cape Colony.

It is aptly said in a letter to Lord Norton by a distinguished correspondent : " It is one of the strong points in this country that its real work is often, perhaps generally, not done by official people in official ways. They are the ultimate mouthpieces of the policy adopted. But the real work of thinking out what the nation requires, of discussing it, of urging it in and out of Parliament, and of preparing the nation to adopt it, is done by men who, from public motives and interest in the subject, give their lives to it, often without ever holding office or passing a Bill." Although Lord Norton successfully held office in three Governments and passed many Bills, it is among such unselfish politicians that his name will always stand prominently forth, not only for his unofficial yet influential work in colonial matters, but also for his philanthropic labours in and out of Parliament on the subjects of education and of penal legislation and juvenile offences (it was truly said that the gaols would have been overflowing had it not been for his efforts in reformatory work); while among his other achievements may be reckoned his writings and essays on educational matters and on colonial history, of which Mr. Joseph Chamberlain has said that "he has left on record a statement of facts and principles which have been useful to all his successors." Nothing, indeed, is more remarkable than his attitude in his early parliamentary days with regard to the future of British Colonies, and the views which he advocated in advance of his contemporaries and almost alone among Imperialists. Few statesmen, if any, in the 'forties and early 'fifties of the last century, combined, as did Adderley, a policy of freedom for the Colonies in the management of their own affairs with a sense of Imperial unity which was to animate the whole British population all over the world. Cobden and the Radicals who joined with him in the formation of his Colonial Reform Association for the hastening of responsible government in the Colonies, cherished a policy of " snug little-Englandism " totally opposed to Adderley's Imperial conceptions, while the old Imperialists of those days stood aloof from Adderley's wide outlook, and his chief, Lord Derby, pronounced his young supporter's views " dangerous." Adderley consistently held to his ideals, and lived, as Lord Norton, to see the realisation of them.

His unfailing devotion to the Colonies was the more disinterested that he had no personal connection with them. He never set foot in a Colony, or had leisure to visit any. Nor did he, as a founder of the Province of Canterbury, New Zealand, ever buy an acre in it, when he might have reaped considerable profit by the purchase of land.

Lord Norton's habit of outlining the events of his life in rough notes with meditations and self-communings has been alluded to in our Preface. These trace, during fourscore years and ten, a life of high mental activity and industry; but more, they reveal a soul singularly lofty in its ideals, steadfast in the realisation of them, transparent in its truthfulness, steeped in religious feeling.

He tells us that, as a young man, he was led to his parliamentary career by a series of circumstances which he had not sought and little anticipated; and that, opening out for him as it did a field of work and usefulness at a time when he was in great doubt as to what plan of life he ought to pursue, he felt in it the hand of unseen Guidance leading him in the direction best suited for him to follow. It is not too much to say that the standard of conscience was the only one by which his actions were guided; and the path of duty—a path which he firmly believed opens out literally step by step before all who earnestly seek to find it—was the only one he ever desired to pursue.

Born to what he calls "perhaps the most fortunate position in life, that of a country gentleman," he was not hampered, as is too often the fate of men of large landed property, by mortgaged acres or a barren rent-roll. Inheriting in childhood a pleasant ancestral home, he was not dependent on the precarious income derived from agriculture, for he inherited at the same time valuable collieries in Staffordshire and property in the suburbs of Birmingham, which brought in a large and increasing revenue. Arrived at man's estate, he found himself in possession of an ample income, of which, however, he felt he was but the steward, to spend in accordance with his sense of duty and for the public good. His fortune and social position might have led him into a more costly manner of living, but all his life he wisely lived, whether at Hams Hall or in London, in the simple though hospitable style of a country gentleman of the early Victorian days, thus always leaving a large surplus to be given away in philanthropic and religious undertakings.

To hear that indolence and shyness were the qualities to which Lord Norton alludes as the banes of his early manhood, may surprise those who knew him, his active and industrious habits, and his constant contact with his fellow-creatures. Those who remember his social qualities, his genial hospitality,

and the pleasure he took in the society of distinguished persons—whether at the reunions at
Grillion's Club which he never willingly missed,
or in the country at Hams, or in his corner house
in Eaton Place—will be struck by the account he
gives of his extreme shyness. When, as an orphan
youth of evangelical upbringing, he was launched
in the London world by his uncle and aunt,
Sir Edmund and Lady Hartopp, as "the great
unknown," he shrank from uncongenial surroundings. He longed to retire into his shell, to the
unconcealed disgust of his relatives. But he early
foresaw the danger to character and prospects of
such a course, and forced himself to associate with
the world, even with the mammon of unrighteous-
ness, in accordance with the scriptural precept,
which, by the way, his aunt advocated, and in
which, if in no other, she firmly believed. "She
did me much good," he admits, "routing me out";
and he was later rewarded by reaping the benefit
of his brave struggle against this infirmity of
youth.

Again, those who know that work was the
predominant feature of his busy life will find it
remarkable that, in his early years, indolence was
his "special temptation." So averse was he from
a busy career, so drawn by nature to the merely
contemplative life that he felt himself unsuited to
active pursuits, and actually thought seriously of
retiring from the world before he had reached
middle age. But here, again, he determined to
conquer his inclination; and whether in Parliament, or administering his property, or leading his
"Volunteers," work became his constant aim. And
as time went on, when he felt himself carried along
in the full swing of useful work, it was the greatest
satisfaction and happiness to him that his lines
had fallen in a distinct and defined path of duty,
and one to which he felt he had been clearly
directed by spiritual guidance. Through all the
progressions of his career he invariably looked for
this in a special manner. In the ministrations of
guardian angels, appointed by the Supreme Being

as His messengers, and as instrumental in answer
to prayer to Him, he had a firm belief. Many a
time in the turning-points of his life he felt he
was upheld and directed by their agency. Prayer
was to him a very real force—" fuel to the fire," he
called it. " I have long realised," he noted, " the
fact that all the interests of life are the proper
subjects of prayer. Distinguishing between the
common objects of earth and matters of religion is
the greatest of all mistakes. Things 'above' and
things 'of the earth' are the same to men. It is in
the common aspects of life that men acquaint themselves with God." With this practical religion he
united an entire devotion to the Church of England,
and may be ranked with his intimate friends, Mr.
Gladstone and the late Earl of Selborne, among the
foremost in his generation of her leading laymen.[1]

These outlines of Lord Norton's characteristics
would be incomplete without allusion to the remarkable breadth of his sympathies, as shown in his
association and friendship with men holding opinions
totally different from his own. Illustrations of this
are to be found in his friendly intercourse with
Cardinal Manning and with Dr. Dale—two most
dissimilar personalities ; in his affection and esteem
for Bishop King of Lincoln, whose ritualistic
observances he did not like ; in his regard for
Cobden and Bright, with whose political programme
he usually disagreed ; and, above all, in his firm
friendship for Gladstone, which may be said to have
increased the more as each became in politics
opposed to the other.

Many will remember the pleasant companionship
of Lord Norton, his anecdotes of bygone celebrities, his pointed stories, told with racy but always
kindly humour. In congenial society his powers
of conversation and repartee continued up to
advanced age with undiminished vigour.

It is disappointing to find little in his notes
indicative of this social side so characteristic of

---

[1] Dr. Gore, Bishop of Birmingham, wrote : " Lord Norton was
among the very greatest and best of our lay Churchmen."

himself; and such stories as are introduced by the editor into this chronicle of his life have lost the freshness of their original colouring.

But what he has left us has a value of a different, of a higher and more instructive kind. We have before us the inner life of a statesman, who reveals his thoughts and ideals, lays bare his actions and efforts, and shows us human nature in its noblest aspect.

CHAPTER II

BIRTH AND ANCESTRY

CHARLES BOWYER ADDERLEY was born the year before Waterloo, on August 2, 1814. He was the eldest son of Mr. Charles Clement Adderley, who, not surviving to become the head of his family, was all his life the heir-presumptive to a childless uncle, Mr. Charles Bowyer Adderley, of Hams Hall, Warwickshire. This wealthy squire possessed, in addition to that family inheritance, collieries at Norton, Staffordshire, and property at Saltley, Birmingham. To these valuable and productive estates Lord Norton (then C. B. Adderley the younger) eventually succeeded, at the age of twelve, on the death of his great-uncle (C. B. Adderley the elder) in 1826. A remarkable fact, and one probably unique in the history of family properties, is that two owners only were successively in possession of Hams for 158 years, Lord Norton's predecessor having succeeded in 1747, in the reign of George II., and Lord Norton having lived till 1905.

The Adderleys have for centuries been settled in Staffordshire and Warwickshire, and are given a place in the late Mr. Shirley's list of the " Noble and Gentle Men of England," in which only the old aristocracy (untitled as well as titled) find mention. From a limbo of forgotten worthies three of the family stand forth more prominently than the rest. One Humphrey Adderley must have had remarkable powers of tenacity to have held, as stated in the genealogy, the honourable post of Gentleman of the Chamber to the Sovereign in four such dissimilar courts as those of Henry VIII., Edward VI., Mary, and Elizabeth. His record recalls that of the celebrated " Vicar of Bray " in a different age.

8

After the Drawing by J. P. Neale.

HAMS HALL.

p. 3

In the next century Sir Charles Adderley was Equerry to Charles I., as is stated on a monument to his memory in the Church of Lea Marston, the parish in which Hams Hall is situated. He planted the oak avenue, which is still the most noteworthy feature at Hams, and he married the heiress of the ancient family of Arden, who brought her Warwickshire estates into the Adderley family. Lord Norton, in allusion to his paternal descent from this ancestor and to his maternal descent from Oliver Cromwell (of whom there is a fine portrait in the hall at Hams), says in one of his early letters : " I'm happy to think my direct ancestor [in the male line] was in Charles's Court. I should certainly have been a royalist. I think the principle of submission to authority is always the right side to err upon. The resistance, however, I admit was blessed to this country." Sir Charles Adderley was fined by the Commonwealth for his services to Charles I. With reference to this Lord Norton used to say that one of his ancestors was heavily fined by another.

A third member of the family, in the time of William III., does not owe the perpetuation of his memory to personal merit ; but is rescued from oblivion by a humorous story related by Lord Norton, and recorded in the late Sir Mountstuart Grant Duff's Diaries.[1] The story was told at Grillion's Club as illustrating the difference between the manners of the seventeenth century and those of our own day :

" Captain Adderley and another gentleman had a quarrel, and agreed to meet in mortal combat. First, however, they adjourned to a tavern, where they got very tipsy. At last it occurred to them that they had better go and settle their little affair, which they proceeded to do in Pall Mall. The sword of one of them got lost, and his adversary helped him to find it. Presently the Watch came up, but so far from desiring to interrupt gentlemen in their pastimes, they held up their lanterns to enable the antagonists to see each other more distinctly. In process of time the little affair ended

[1] Grant Duff Diaries, May 20, 1889.

by Captain Adderley running his friend through the body, and the wife of the man who was killed duly attended to express her opinion that his opponent *had done nothing which did not become a gentleman.*"

Lord Norton's mother, through her maternal ancestors the Fleetwoods, had in her veins the blood of the great Protector. She was a daughter of Sir Edmund Cradock-Hartopp, Baronet,[1] who assumed the name of Hartopp in right of his wife, a considerable heiress. To Four Oaks Park the finely timbered place of the Cradock-Hartopps, situated on the edge of the Forest of Arden, Lord Norton was always greatly attached, associated as it was with his childhood and youth.

When Lord Norton first remembered Four Oaks, his childless uncle and guardian, Mr. Edmund Hartopp, afterwards the second baronet, was in possession, Sir Edmund and Lady Hartopp, Lord Norton's grandparents, having handed over the property to their second but eldest surviving son, while they themselves resided at Clifton (Bristol), where Lord Norton spent his early years near them, paying an annual visit to Four Oaks.

To return to Lord Norton's ancestors on his father's, Mr. Charles Clement Adderley, side :—the Christian name of Clement was derived from the Kynnersleys of Loxley Hall, his mother having been a daughter of the ancient house of Kynnersley now extinct in the male line. She was the sister and correspondent of the Baroness de Bode. Lord Norton was therefore a great-nephew of that remarkable woman, a record of whose courageous enterprises and wanderings during the French Revolution, and of her subsequent settlement in Russia, where the Empress Catherine II. granted her an estate, has been recently published.[2]

The story of Lord Norton's childhood is told in his own words.

[1] This gentleman was born Bunny, and assumed the name of his maternal ancestors the Cradocks ; while yet another change of surname was added by his eldest son, who assumed the name of Fleetwood.

[2] " Baroness de Bode " (1776—1803), by W. S. Childe-Pemberton. (Longmans.)

ANNE HURLOCK, WIFE OF SIR EDMUND CRADOCK
HARTOPP, FIRST BARONET (LORD NORTON'S
GRANDMOTHER).

ANNA MARIA, WIFE OF CHARLES CLEMENT ADDERLEY,
DAUGHTER OF SIR EDMUND CRADOCK HARTOPP,
FIRST BARONET, AND MOTHER OF LORD NORTON.

P. 44

CHAPTER III

EARLY MEMORIES

Autobiographical Memoranda [1]

At the age of three and a half I lost my father, in 1818. He died at the age of thirty-eight of consumption, at Cowes, trying to make his way home from Bonchurch to die at Hams. I can recollect (and have since tested my recollections) the features of both places. I can recollect the armchair in which he died at the Vine Inn at Cowes, and which is now at Hams; and the funeral packet to Southampton which crossed with his body on board. I remember my brother and my two sisters playing with me on the deck, and the very toys I had given me to keep me quiet on the sloop. What left a vivid impression on my memory was the tacking of the sloop from side to side—the great boom coming across at each tack, and her deck heaving first on one side and then on the other—and this is a significant recollection for me, looking back from these steam days, characterising the period of my life as spanning two widely distinct eras of the world's economic history.

My father was deeply religious in his turn of mind and life, at a time when such a character had

---

[1] Compiled in 1853 from early notes and diaries.

more ridicule than sympathy to meet with, even in the home circle. Men and women were ordinarily divided between an absolute worldliness and evangelical pietism, sincere or feigned.

All my father's scraps of manuscript, which are many, and notes in books, show earnest piety of sentiment and self-discipline ; and, though all his life having feared death, he died in the most assured and happy but humble faith, with cheerfulness repeating at the last moment the words : " For we know that if our earthly home of this tabernacle were dissolved we have abiding of God," etc. His chief friends were George Hartopp and Sir Thomas Acland, whom he was with at Oxford and afterwards travelled with abroad.

My mother was broken by this blow, and her grief for his loss and anxiety about her children developed the seeds of consumption which were laid in nursing my father. She was deeply religious, warm-hearted, very accomplished. Her water-colour drawings fill the saloon walls at Hams, and her exquisite music - I have still in my memory. I owe any taste I have for real beauty in Art or Nature to her. [Lord Norton inherited a taste for drawing and designing ; he was also an accomplished player on the violoncello.]

On my father's death I and my brother Edmund and two sisters were her charge, living at Clifton (Bristol) with our maternal grandparents, Sir Edmund and Lady Hartopp ; and every year posting a two days' journey to visit my old great-uncle and godfather, Charles Bowyer Adderley, at Hams, and my uncle, Edmund Hartopp, at Four Oaks.

In 1823, at eight and a half years old, I was sent

C. B. ADDERLEY (LORD NORTON) AND HIS BROTHER AND SISTER.

to a school of thirty or forty boys at Redland, near Bristol, under the Rev. J. Parsons, and commended to the care of a much older boy, McGeachey, who afterwards married my sister, Anna Maria.

I had then an inherited religious turn of mind, and had my share of ridicule and nickname for it; but otherwise got on well with the other boys, though, with more contemplative than active disposition, I was naturally indolent, and constitutionally weak, and thought to be consumptive.

In 1826, at the age of twelve, I was sent to a private tutor, the Rev. F. R. Spragg, at Combe St. Nicholas, near Chard in Somersetshire. The same year my great-uncle Adderley died, and left Hams as my future home and possession, giving me the advantage of fixed prospects and certain position or *métier* in life—that of a country gentleman, perhaps in England the happiest in the world.

It is a great advantage to any one to know early in the educatory part of life the sort of employment for which he is properly destined, and through life I have found myself in each stage looking to the next as in a natural and known course. From boyhood it seemed instructive to look on life as a practice in duties set before one. I find my notes and memoranda, which, like my father, I have always scribbled, show this habitual feeling [he was not yet thirteen]; and my first little printed pamphlet in adult life, "Happiness the practice of right intentions," was a record of my main idea.

The next year, 1827, my mother died of consumption, a disease which was fatal to her family. Her last words as she sank away were, "Oh! who will take care of them as I have done when I am gone ? God will, who never failed the widow ! " These words as a legacy and talisman have often through life recurred to my mind.

My guardian, Uncle Edmund Hartopp, left me entirely to my grandfather's superintendence, and I lived, with my brother and my two sisters, under the care of a governess, Miss Ollivant, sister of the Bishop of Llandaff, in a house in Clifton, near my grandfather.

To the beauties of Clifton scenery, the Avon Valley, the Downs, Blaise Castle (the Harfords' place), the Severn and Bristol Channel, I owe the love of landscape and whatever taste for natural charms I have enjoyed. Every summer in these years my grandfather took us to the sea-side, to Weymouth twice, and to the Isle of Wight. There, in 1830, one fine morning in July, walking along the shore from Ryde towards Bembridge, where my excellent holiday tutor lodged, I saw a memorable sight—Charles X., with the Dukes of Berri and Angoulême, etc., coming in three ships of war with tricolor flying, into the roads of Spithead—ejected after the " Glorious days."

Mine was a dull life during these years, and I saw nothing of the world or life. My tutor was a Low Church clergyman who had begun life in some wine merchant's house in Madeira, and had no great knowledge, but natural talent. He had the Wilberforces as his pupils, and amongst the five or six pupils always with him in my own time I made two or three friendships which lasted— Lord Powerscourt; Henry Ker Seymer, George Drummond.

My education may have been secluded from trials and temptations, but it offered no spur to natural indolence, and was of the most meagre kind in instruction or any good influence from others, though lavish in costliness.

The causes of this home education were firstly, my mother's dread of a public school; secondly, the old age of my grandparents on her death; and thirdly, there being no uncle on either side who could or would take me in hand. Perhaps it was all the better they did not. The result, however, was want of acquaintance, want of knowledge both of men, things, and books, and confirmed shyness and indolence, only relieved by a natural love of contemplation and a turn for some kinds of observation and thought. I loved natural history idly pursued. The first burst of nature and spring life was a recurrent period of pleasure, excitement, and interest to me. I had a friend in every insect and bird skimming the ponds or flitting through wood and sunlit field.

CHAPTER IV

OXFORD DAYS, 1832–1835

In October 1832 I went to Christ Church, literally knowing no one there. I fell in of course with my order of Gentlemen Commoners and Tufts—distinctions now happily abolished. They were mostly old Eton or Harrow friends, or had made acquaintance in the London world—all *terra incognita* to me.

My brother Edmund had, by what I think a mistaken notion, been sent to a different school from mine, and afterwards, at Christ Church, got as a *Commoner* in Chaplain's Quad into a totally different set from my villainous *Gentlemen Commoners* lot in Peckwater—both extremes bad and our separation mischievous, and a foolish distinction thus being created between us.

Another misfortune for him was his passion for the sea having been thwarted by our grandmother, Lady Hartopp, who would not have him exposed to the "wicked navy life." Consequently the instant he was free enough he spent his little means in hiring a rotten old yacht, nearly getting wrecked in Portland Race, and would never take to any profession.

During my three years at Oxford the set in which

I was thrown, with very few exceptions, spent their whole time in amusements, hunting, and gambling. Although mixing freely in their society, shyness and ignorance, as much as principle, kept me within bounds, and free from immorality. On my first arrival I had been so utterly without a single acquaintance that I strolled about the town alone, and at last resolved to call on a Balliol Tutor, Ogilvie, who had been civil to me when I came up to matriculate. He received me most kindly, gave me tea, of which he was fastidious, and, what was more valuable, a keepsake text from the thirty-seventh Psalm as a talisman : " Keep innocency, and take heed unto the thing that is right, for that shall bring a man peace at the last."[1] I have handed down this same talisman or amulet to all my sons and some nephews at the same period in their lives, and they have all thanked me for it afterwards. It exalts innocency over the youthful conceit of knowingness as the true test of wisdom and guard of virtue which, once broken through, can never be completely restored ; and there is peculiar force in pointing to the *last* issue from the *first* beginning—setting the goal in view from the starting-point, and putting life in its true aspect as *gathering along its course* and not gaining *at the end* the character of eternal future.

Another piece of advice of a very different character was given me on my arrival at Oxford by the man whose rooms I took, where I found a book-case filled wholly with top-boots, whips, and spurs. " Mind this, if you give up Sundays to

[1] This " talisman text " is now inscribed on the College Students' Memorial to Lord Norton in Saltley Church, Birmingham.

books and work, you may have the rest of the week for enjoyment."

I found books for the week and books for Sunday, and enjoyment with each. I attribute much of my escape from vice surrounding my noviciate at Christ Church to my thorough possession of the sense of Sunday's value and authority.

I read to a certain extent at Oxford, though my education had been so inefficient that I could not hope to keep pace with those who had had real training. I took a fancy, however, to mathematics, in spite of Dean Gaisford's sneers; and my tutor, Kynaston, thought me up to honours, had not my coming of age, just after taking my degree of B.A. in 1835, dissipated this ambition and diverted my mind to other thoughts. I afterwards regretted this much. The study, however, did me lasting good, giving a habit of close reasoning and forcing accurate method in thinking out, to a logical conclusion, any subject which required sustained attention, or, failing that, the Sisyphus alternative of having to begin again. My natural disposition being rather contemplative than active, the discipline was the more essential. I led a convivial life at Oxford, and made many friendships. Two only I inherited from Spraggs—Lord Powerscourt and George Home Drummond. But there was one acquaintance I made at Christ Church which had a great influence on my life—John Robert Godley, a man of strong mind, original thought, with an uncompromising, almost stern sense of duty, whom Gladstone long after described as ἄναξ ἀνδρῶν [a king of men].

In the autumn of 1834 I travelled with George

Home Drummond through Scotland, partly on foot with knapsacks—Blair Drummond being our headquarters. We had two escapes: one, a night in a fog on Loch Rannoch; the second, crossing in a storm in an open boat to the Orkneys. His sister, afterwards Duchess of Atholl, was the liveliest of her sex I had ever seen, and taught me to dance every night up till two or three in the morning. The Uncle Abercairny was an oddity; the father, the shrewdest of Scotsmen, a great improver, and in Parliament entrusted with all Scotch business, which he generally passed through its stages at midnight. Charley Home Drummond Moray, now owner of Abercairny, Blair Drummond, etc., is one of my best friends, but too seldom seen by me (1883).

CHAPTER V

McGEACHEY, at that time my constant friend and mentor, being four years older than myself, married my sister in 1834.

In the autumn of 1835, after I had taken my degree and come of age, I went with Acland to join them in Rome. His father, Sir Thomas Dyke Acland, had travelled with my father, after leaving Oxford, in Norway, during the Peace of Amiens (in 1802), and they got detained prisoners in Christiania at the rupture of the Peace.

Our journey is characteristic of the wide contrast in travelling then with what steam has now produced. We bought a britska in Long Acre, and had the front seat fitted as a book-case; and in the first week of December 1835 got across to Calais and slept at Dessin's Hotel of "Sterne" immortality. We thence posted with four horses day and night, sleeping in the carriage, open, with ice on our cloaks by morning, and only a box of cigars to comfort us. Along the Belgian frontier we had to pass through fortified towns often at night, our courier, Cardinali, having to knock up the porter at the gate, who asked, "Avez-vous des dépêches ? Non ? Eh bien, bon soir !"—light out. This repeated

till a *silver* key, swelled to fit the keyhole, finally
secured our admittance—the same process again on
leaving the town.

The crack, crack, crack of the postillions' whips
echoed through the rattling streets, lighted only
by oil lamps hung from ropes across them. Our
"rumble" having broken, we slept at Rheims.
Crossing the Rhine at Kehl and Strasburg, we
were robbed of our cigars, and had to take to
German tobacco. Across the Black Forest, postillions blew horns, a different tune in each little
state. From Ulm we passed up to the Lake of
Constance, and crossed the Splügen by the Via
Mala in five sledges: (1) containing body of
carriage, (2) wheels, (3) luggage, (4) ourselves, (5)
servant and courier—ours with four horses and one
postillion, guiding the leaders by his whip in frozen
zigzags, with two thousand feet of precipice sometimes sheer below the angles of turning. We slept
at Coire—the Macassar oil freezing in my dressing-
case—and next night we dug our way with twenty
men through three feet of snow over the Apennines
to Radierfani, where we thawed ourselves with a
cup of coffee boiled on a log fire.

We reached Rome on a lovely evening, my sister,
Anna Maria, and McGeachey meeting us a little
outside and lodging me in their house in Via Felice,
Monte Mario, Acland joining his father, who had
come by yacht, *St. Kilda*, and taken the Villa Aldo-
brandini. Three months in Rome, with the Vatican,
Sixtine Chapel, Forum, the Offices of Christina,
Carnival, Campagna rides, Laurentine Wood and
Ostia, opened the mind to new sensations, thoughts,
tastes, and ideas.

This summer passed in an excursion with Lord Clements [afterwards the Lord Leitrim who was murdered in 1878] round Sicily—full, to my mind, of Virgil, and realising my little store of classical recollections. We went on to Malta, living there a week with the 60th Rifles, and, coming back to Naples, found a vendetta prepared which might have anticipated my friend's murder.

I stayed a little at Rome, *en retour*, as the guest of Thorwaldsen, whose bas-reliefs now adorn the hall at Hams.[1] [A marble bust of Mr. Adderley by Macdonald was executed during this visit to Rome.]

I posted alone through the South of France and, by Paris, back to England about September 1836, after an absence of over nine months.

[1] Thorwaldsen, the great Danish sculptor, born at Copenhagen, 1770, lived the greater part of his life in Rome. He left it in 1838, two years after Mr. Adderley had been his guest, and returned to Copenhagen, where he died in 1844.

The following is a list of Thorwaldsen's works at Hams—the two first were gifts from the sculptor, the rest were done to order :

(1) Singing Genii ; (2) Playing Genii ; (3) Cupid awaking the fainted Psyche ; (4) Bacchus giving Cupid his first cup ; (5) Cupid's reception by Anacreon, wounded by dart of poetry in gratitude. These are all in marble. The terra-cotta frieze (6), round the cornice of the hall, represents the Triumphal Procession of Alexander the Great into Babylon—the same as in marble at the Villa Sommariva Como and the Quirinal, Rome. After seeing the latter, Mendelssohn, in his "Letters from Italy and Switzerland," wrote (March 1831): "Never did any piece of sculpture make such an impression on me. I go there every week and stand gazing on that alone, and enter Babylon along with the Conqueror."

FRIEZE BY THORWALDSEN IN THE HALL AT HAMS.

CHAPTER VI

1836

LAUNCHED IN LONDON

HAMS was still let to Lady Rosse, Lord Lorton's[1] mother-in-law. He was so charmed with the oaks at Hams that he sent sacks of acorns yearly to his splendid Rockingham Castle, Ireland. There he shewed me a few years later his " Hams Wood," and, what struck me more and has abode in my mind ever since, his village pulled to the ground under the protection of soldiers from the Castle, himself having assisted, with pistols at his breast, to disperse the mutinous tenantry.

I now began to live with my [childless] guardian Uncle Sir Edmund and Lady Hartopp at Four Oaks. She was the daughter of old Lord Henley[2]—

[1] Viscount Lorton, married Lady Frances Parsons, daughter and heiress of Lawrence, first Earl of Rosse, whose widow, the above-mentioned Countess of Rosse, rented Hams and died at an advanced age in 1838. Lord Lorton, who was a younger son of the second Earl of Kingston, died in 1854. His eldest son eventually succeeded as sixth Earl of Kingston, while his second son succeeded to Rockingham Castle and assumed the name of Harman in additional to the patronymic of King.

[2] Morton Eden (second son of Sir Robert Eden, Baronet), a distinguished diplomatist accredited to various Courts in Europe, was created Lord Henley in 1799 and died in 1830. His only daughter, the Hon. Mary Jane Eden, married Sir Edmund Cradock-Hartopp, second Baronet in 1824, and died childless in 1843.

" the last pig-tail," as he was called. At Four Oaks I renewed my early love of Sutton Park, the loveliest bit of old forest scenery remaining of the Forest of Arden. I owe to my uncle and aunt my first introduction into London Society. These were the days of Almack's. Balls and dinners were hateful to me.

My aunt, a formidable dame, called me " the great unknown." She was a fine-looking figure— *femme de caractère*, brilliant, accomplished, of great talent, woman of the world, sarcastic. She did me much good, shaking me out and introducing me to Society, and amusing herself in trying to make up a match for me. I wished she would think less of the vanities of life, but her mind was in and out imbued with them, so as not so much to blind her to higher things as, what was worse, to give a false view of them.

My uncle's influence was, as far as it went, to lead me to the profession of a man of the world ; but his influence was altogether remiss and *laisser-aller*, as he thought my constitution weak and that his trouble might very likely be thrown away.

When first I came to London from my nursery education, having seen nothing of the world but Oxford, and knowing, and known of, none, my shyness, pride, and indolence made me shrink from contact with Society, and from taking part in either London amusements or public action, and I found in reticence the best cover of my ignorance and inexperience. I tried to reconcile to myself the propriety of yielding to my inclination and retiring to the country. The Hartopps, half willing, half afraid, and utterly annoyed and disgusted, remonstrated; while partly pride and partly a sense of duty urged me to take my stand with other men of my position in life. Thus I got acquainted with most of the leading men of my own standing or among the Hartopp acquaintance, and, bored to death, danced in a few balls every year. . . . Do I now regret having taken that step into the gay world? Have I lost another and a better line by doing so? I do not think I condemn myself further than for having been careless and reckless of the attendant risks and contamination incident to a course which I still think I was right in pursuing. It is a question whether all must not upon entering life mix generally in Society in order to know themselves, their position, their duties to their proper friends. This is a great ordeal, and requires unusual care; but can it be avoided, especially in a case like mine? I had no friends, no acquaintances, no father since four years old, no mother since thirteen, no one to take their place. If I had had a profession, my line would have been clearer, but the line for a country gentleman with a certain amount of fortune was too indefinite without some knowledge of Society—the material of its action. How, besides, could I marry without some acquaintance? I am glad, on the whole, that I did not yield to the temptation of indolence and retire, though I know pride had as much as conscience to do with my effort.

How extremely conscientious was young Adderley, and how anxious as to the dangers besetting those who frequent London Society, is shown by a letter (of a somewhat later date) from Lady Leigh [1] (after-

¹ Wife of Chandos, first Lord Leigh of the second creation.

wards his mother-in-law). " Dear Mr. Adderley," she wrote : " I am vexed with myself for having said anything in our long discussion which gave you the impression that I could for a moment treat the subject you were so earnest upon with levity or deem it worthy of sarcasm. Believe me, it is far otherwise; for it is one on which I have thought much, and am perfectly aware of the difficulties, not to say dangers, which beset those who really enter into *all* the gaiety of a London life. Still I have yet to learn that its attractions *are* so powerful or fascinating. Of course I, who am no longer young (and who from taste and other circumstances have lived much out of the world since I married), cannot be a fair judge. Yet *I* think you may participate moderately in gaiety without *one* feeling of ' display, emulation, vanity, or frivolity'; and if I saw one of these feelings generated by going out I should strongly advise either man or woman to fly from pleasures which could make them forget all that is valuable in life, and give them a distaste for the only true sources of enjoyment, which are to be sought in the quiet of domestic life, when it is embellished with intellectual attainments and based on that true foundation which can alone support us under every circumstance of life. Without such ballast I should indeed think it dangerous to enter *at all* into the world. In the plan you have laid down for yourself I should think you would find every satisfaction that the feeling of a well-spent life can afford, and with the assurance that I received no false impression of your ' ideas,' and that they were by no means misunderstood by me, believe me, dear Mr. Adderley, ever truly yours, M. LEIGH."

But how I longed to lounge by myself at Hams, and on summer days to be at home on the river, then clear as crystal![1] I recollect the first peep I

[1] That was in the days when the Corporation of London used (regardless of expense) to get their fresh-water fish from the Tame for their own consumption, before the river was polluted and discoloured by refuse from Birmingham.

had at Hams I took by myself, riding from Four Oaks as far as my park gate; and I was invited for a night there by Anchitel Grey, Lord Stamford's brother, who rented it for a time. Old Lingard, a venerable bailiff and old soldier who had seen service, lionised me, and showed me all the old labourers who recollected my father and myself as a boy; and the old keeper, Mercer, whose son, now as old, was succeeding to his office. . . .

I had to get an Estate Act to remedy a bungling will [his great-uncle's], and this introduced me to the inside of Parliament, soon to be my home for life. Old Lord Shaftesbury,[1] with a stroke of his pen, greatly improved the draft Bill, though drawn by Tyrell, a first-rate draughtsman; and Lord Hatherton, coming by, said to me: "What! so soon at a job?"

I had troublesome questions about my Staffordshire Colliery with Ralph Adderley [his father's brother], the executor of my great-uncle's will. The three Adderley uncles were all out of my line. It would be unfair to say that all wanted to make something *out of* rather than *of* me, as they were all friendly and amusing. Arden, the Admiral, was most companionable afterwards to my brother; and the cleric, Bowyer, left his pretty place, Fillongley, at his death—which occurred after seventeen years of patient blindness—to my second son, Arden.

I noted in my locked book at this time the singularly educative variety of my property. Hams, a charming country home in central England; Saltley, a suburban town property, adjoining such a

---

[1] Cropley Ashley, sixth Earl of Shaftesbury, Chairman of Committees in the House of Lords.

busy place as Birmingham; Norton, a colliery and mining district, with another sort of manufacturing town near, at Uppingham; then Peterborough [a small property near], a fen district, requiring much draining and engineering. This variety forced me to get knowledge of each kind of property and people, not to say of many kinds of law. I note a resolution I formed not to seek to enlarge property, but to get all I had into good order, that when I died it might show good stewardship, materially as well as morally, and that I might leave my vineyard better than I found it. With this view it was that I engaged, while in London, in reading Blackstone with Robert Kenyon, in the dingy Temple, repulsive as it was to me. I also accepted a troop in the Warwick Yeomanry. I took this duty, in total ignorance of it, as a right work to accept, and learnt much from it; and for four consecutive years, during the Corn Law Riots, I had to take out my troop of Warwickshire Cavalry in aid of the civil power.

During the interval between travelling and getting into Parliament—that is, between 1836 and 1841—I passed half each year in London and half in the country. My various occupations were furnishing Hams; laying out grounds and terrace with Gilpin [landscape gardener]; estate management; law reading and agency work; Church incumbency; village schools; Norton entire parochial reconstruction and division into four districts; coal release on better system to same lessee as Sir G. Chetwynd; my brother and younger [invalid] sister's money arrangements—she living with a companion, he going with a friend to Rome.

It was a stirring time in London when I made my little début in 1837. I saw William IV.'s funeral at Windsor, at night; and I saw Queen Victoria's Coronation, in company with some who took part in the spectacle and festivities.

It was an epoch of great social changes in the country and in the world. Railways were beginning. It was a time of Church revival, from extreme Low Church to extreme in the opposite direction. Reform was the political order of the day.

Lord Norton used to relate how, when railways were first introduced and Stephenson was asked, "What was the greatest speed trains would go?" he said, "They would go fifteen miles an hour" (he thought if he said more he would not be believed). On hearing this an enterprising coach proprietor started a coach to go fifteen miles an hour—it only taking thirty seconds to change horses. He was ruined by the increased speed of railways, which he could not compete with, and went mad! Lord Norton saw him regularly in a lunatic asylum. Lord Norton used also to tell how Sir Robert Peel described the accident which killed Huskisson, the circumstances of which are well known. Huskisson, who had been on terms of disagreement with the Duke of Wellington, went up to speak politely to the Duke at Manchester when they met at the opening of the railway. Afterwards, when an engine was coming up, he tried to get into a carriage, but clumsily fell back. Sir Robert Peel said he never should forget Huskisson's shriek when he was crushed.

CHAPTER VII

1837

ANECDOTES OF SIR ROBERT PEEL

I HAD a great advantage in living not far from Drayton, where Sir Robert Peel [then Prime Minister] lived during the recess, and received all the statesmen of his party. He was kindness itself to me, and gave me constant and general invitation to Drayton. There I met the proudest of the old style, the Duke of Newcastle, and heard Croker ask him why he had bought Hafod—in Wales—which, he replied, was a retreat necessary to a man in his position. [This was Henry Pelham, fourth Duke of Newcastle (1785—1851), the most uncompromising of Tories of the old school. So unpopular was he with the mob that they destroyed Nottingham Castle in 1831, and his house in Portman Square was broken into by the rabble. He fortified Clumber, and his purchase of Hafod, "as a retreat" from the populace, led to much discussion in Parliament.]

A quiet evening at Drayton, with only Sidney Herbert and Cardwell there, gave me interesting knowledge. Once, returning late in the evening from London to Hams, I found a note asking me to meet the Duke of Wellington. I rode over next morning to express my regret, and found the Duke had just gone; and Sir Robert told me I had missed the only evening he had heard him tell anecdotes of his campaigns.

Sir Robert urged me to get into Parliament, and one evening talked about my property, and said Saltley ought to be worth all the rest so near a town [Birmingham], most certain of sustained prosperity as central, and depending on a variety of trades. He wrote to Lord Lincoln,[1] who was Commissioner of Woods and Forests under his Premiership, to send the best men down to lay out Saltley for building, whose plans I have followed since.

All his life nothing gave Lord Norton greater pleasure than to drive over to Drayton, where every room, every window, almost every table, as he said, recalled memories of his early days with the illustrious statesman. The following anecdote was told by Lord Norton[2] on one of these occasions, and, if trivial, it gives so amiable a portrait of the great man, who had the reputation of being somewhat frigid and buttoned-up in his dealings with the outside world, that it seems appropriate to record it here. " I remember," said Lord Norton, some sixty years after the incident, " being in this room with Peel one morning after breakfast—it was when he was Prime Minister. It was a beautiful summer morning, and the window (which opens to the ground) was open. He said to me, ' Would you like to see my partridges?' He took a handful of corn from a basket in the corner of the room, and went to the window—' Chuck! Chuck! Chuck!'— holding out his hand. In a minute or two a part-

[1] Eldest son of the Duke of Newcastle, succeeded as fifth Duke in 1851, and died in 1864 ; an eminent statesman.
[2] Told to Sir Arthur Godley, K.C.B., in 1903, in whose words, and by whose permission, the anecdote is here related. See page 306.

ridge appeared, then one or two more; and in a very short time he had a whole covey of partridges feeding in the room!"

Lord Norton used to tell a story illustrative of the wonderfully orderly methods of Sir Robert Peel. One day Lord John Russell was making a furious attack on him in the House of Commons. Sir Robert turned to Lord Lincoln, who was sitting beside him, and said, "I have a letter at Drayton which, if I could produce it, would utterly confute all he is saying. If the debate is adjourned will you go and fetch it?" Lord Lincoln said, "Yes, but how am I to find it?" "No difficulty about that," replied Sir Robert, and, giving him the key of a cupboard in a corridor lined with cupboards, he said, "In the cupboard marked with that year you will find all the letters arranged alphabetically. Look under R and you will find it."

The debate was adjourned. Lord Lincoln went down to Drayton and found the letter exactly as Sir Robert had described, and it was triumphantly produced next day.[1]

Other anecdotes of Lord Norton's early days at Drayton have been related by Sir M. Grant Duff in his Diaries. "There was a shooting party collected in the house, and the hour for the start had just been arranged when Sir Robert Peel said to his eldest son, 'You had better go and improve your mind till it is time to go out. Croker is in the library; go and talk to him.' Norton [or rather young Adderley] followed to the library, and heard the following conversation. 'Which do you think, Mr. Croker, was the greater general of the two, Hannibal or the Duke of Wellington?' 'Oh,' replied Mr. Croker, 'certainly the Duke of Wellington.' 'But there is a good deal, is there not,' replied young Peel, 'to be said against the Duke of Wellington? Did he not behave very badly in connection with the death of the Duc d'Enghien?' 'Good God! my boy,' was the rejoinder, 'what can

[1] This anecdote Lord Norton related to Lady Knightley, of Fawsley, one day at Drayton, in the corridor where Peel's cupboards formerly stood.

you be thinking of? I suppose you mean the execution of Marshal Ney!'"[1]

Further reminiscences of Croker at Drayton were: Once Adderley happened to be there with a large party composed principally of Tory Ministers, when the news came that Talleyrand's Memoirs were not to be published for thirty years. "How shall we be able," said one of them, "to restrain our impatience for thirty years?" "I," said Croker, "shall have no difficulty in restraining mine, for if they came out now I should not believe a word of them."

When Croker, in old posting days, was travelling with the Duke of Wellington, the two whiled away the time betting as to what might be beyond the hill before them. The Duke said, "That's what I've been doing all my life—guessing *from what I know* as to what I don't yet see, the other side of the hill"![2]

Nothing contributed so much to the strengthening of my mind and the formation of my character at this time as my friendship with John Robert Godley, the influence of whose strong mind and sense was the making of my career. For over twenty years, till his death in 1861, we constantly corresponded. When he died I had a volume of extracts from his letters to me privately printed, for circulation among his inmost and very distinguished friends. Gladstone called this "the best of monuments." Some of his letters on political purity, philosophy, Church principles, literature, and American affairs—on which the American Minister thought him our best English writer[3]—have been

[1] Grant Duff Diaries, Feb. 27, 1901.
[2] Lord Norton's MSS., 1892.
[3] "'Letters from America,' published by Murray in 1844, dedicated to myself, which the American minister (Mr. Everett) recommended as the soundest and most original English work on America, to the Select Committee to which Parliament referred the Inquiry about Irish Emigration."—Dedication by Lord Norton of J. R. Godley's letters, printed for private circulation, 1863.

highly praised, and have all the interest of deep and commanding thought.

Lord Norton, forty years after the death of Godley, wrote, à propos of the statement that a man is to be judged less by the letters he writes himself than by those which he causes others to write: "*I* would wish to be judged by *Godley's* letters"—and this after his own life-long correspondence with the most eminent statesmen.

In 1840 I travelled through Ireland with him, and spent a night with the "Liberator," Dan O'Connell, at his house, Derrynane.

Lord Norton used to relate how his horse fell just at the gate, and that knowing the Liberator kept open house he presented himself, and was welcomed with the words, " I am very much obliged to your horse for falling just where he did." The great man was treated as Royalty, and sat at dinner with a *cap of maintenance on his head.* When dinner was over he retired to bed, and a wild Irish revel began and lasted till morning.

I went with Evelyn Shirley[1] to his place in Monaghan, where his father and he were making a magnificent house, and were in the midst of earnest plans for civilising the people. I saw with him some two Sessions' work, and a raving mad magistrate kept in order by my firm, quaint friend as chairman.

[1] Evelyn Shirley, M.P., of Ettington Park (Stratford-on-Avon), and Lough Fea (Monaghan), author of " The Noble and Gentle Men of England."

CHAPTER VIII

1841

PARLIAMENTARY PROSPECTS

THE year 1841 was a turning-point in my life through two events—the death of my sister, Mrs. McGeachey, and my entrance into the House of Commons.

It was during my sister's last illness that I was asked to come forward for North Staffordshire. A little before Christmas, through the instrumentality of my Uncle Ralph Adderley, who had hitherto taken no part in my introduction into life, I had been invited by Lord Sandon to his aged father's, Lord Harrowby's [Pitt's friend and colleague], and went there with McGeachey, and accepted the offer of the North Staffordshire Conservative Party for me to stand for a vacancy about to be made by Bingham Baring's resignation. Sandon was my head-quarters, where the accomplished host and his friends Sir Charles Bagot and Ralph Sneyd [Sneyd of Keele Hall, Staffordshire], often guests there, formed a trio of most highly cultivated and refined companions, and made a society of the highest instruction and interest to me as modest listener

This was in the time of the first Earl of Harrowby, who was born in 1762, and died at Sandon in 1847,

35

a very able statesman of the intellectual, critical type. He was for many years in the Cabinet, and filled various high posts—Lord President of the Council, etc.—was twice offered the Premiership, but refused on account of delicate health, suffering constantly from headaches, the result of a serious fall on the staircase of the Foreign Office. In politics, he is said to have seen so keenly two sides of a question that he had often difficulty in making up his mind. He was very hospitable, fond of travelling, and liked foreigners. Highly accomplished and cultivated, he was an excellent linguist, wrote verses in several languages, and painted with much skill in water-colours. In 1805 he was accredited to the Emperors of Austria and Russia to effect a coalition against Napoleon, but retired on account of ill health, and returned to find his friend Pitt dead. He married, in 1795, Lady Susan Leveson-Gower, daughter of the first Marquis of Stafford, a leading lady in the world of fashion and politics, who died suddenly in 1838. By her he had a son, the above-mentioned Lord Sandon, who, at the time when Mr. Adderley was brought forward as a candidate for Parliament, was M.P. for Liverpool, and highly distinguished in the Tory ranks, virtually turning out Lord John Russell and Lord Melbourne's Whig Ministry in June 1841. He succeeded his father in 1847, as second Earl of Harrowby, and remained Mr. Adderley's warm friend and political supporter till his death in 1882. It was remarked of him that he inherited from his father the Ryder intellect, and from his mother the Leveson-Gower charm and brightness; he took a double-first at Christ Church. He used to relate the story of the Thistlewood Conspiracy which was planned to take effect at his father's, Lord Harrowby's, house in Grosvenor Square (then No. 39, but now changed to 44), and how great was his astonishment when on returning home from the Opera on that memorable evening to find his father and mother sitting alone tête-à-tête—the great dinner to Cabinet Ministers which was due to take place having been countermanded unknown to himself. On the conspiracy being discovered the Ministers had been privately warned not to come, *though the preparations for the dinner went on.* The plot (as is well known) was to knock at the door of the house in the middle of the dinner and when the servants were busy, to shoot the porter, to rush into the dining-room, which then had only one door, and to kill all the Ministers. It ended by Lord and Lady Harrowby dining alone, while soldiers arrested Thistlewood and his associates in a loft.

I soon had to make my maiden speech at Stone[1] to the county I was to represent for nearly forty years. It was the occasion when Bingham Baring had to announce his retirement, and I to offer myself for the vacancy. It was a successful start; but a speech in the Town Hall at Birmingham, when I had to propose the health of Sir Eardley Wilmot and Mr. Dugdale, M.P. for Warwickshire, gave me more advantage as an opening to public life.

On the eve of all this my sister fell into a rapid decline at McGeachey's mother's house at Clifton. She was now my chief relation and devoted sister, rich in mind and taste, authoress, musician, deeply religious and sensible. She recently had had her only child, which died soon and was buried at Hams. Her last visit was at Killerton,[2] where Sir Thomas Acland's eldest daughter Lydia was long an invalid—the cause of the yacht voyage to Rome— and their deep colloquies made the preparation for my sister's calm and thoughtful end which deeply impressed me. I then first *realised* the nearness of the future state, and I had ideas

[1] Stone is near Sandon Hall.
[2] The home of the Aclands in Devonshire.

of my own liability to early decline. [Lord Norton told his eldest son that he said to his sister on her death-bed he should soon follow her, but that she replied, "No, for you are destined to live to an old age, and do great good."] Among my scraps is a very full diary of my last days with my sister. From school my holidays were always with her, from college my vacations. Abroad I was her guest, at Hams she was mine, and I was planning a house for her at Curdworth. Nothing ever separated us long till her death. I find among my papers discussions with myself, what to do on my sister's death. I was anxious to take a becoming share and position in public life, and thought the greatest safeguard was continual work, and wished for a scheme of life by which to train myself to give a good account in the end of everything connected with my property and position. I note for the rest, my aim at home to be "hospitality without vying with others."

I complain of irritable temper bred of natural indolence, and express a hope that a little knowledge of the world and business and reading were wearing off shyness and giving me zest to life and self-command. I recollect my neighbour, Sir Francis Lawley,[1] a thorough popular man of the world, telling me afterwards that when he first called at Hams he thought little of me, but that I improved on acquaintance. . . .

My reflections turn on the immediate prospect of public life in Parliament, of action succeeding education, yet distinctly taking the whole of life

[1] Seventh Baronet, died suddenly, January 7, 1851 ; succeeded by his younger brother, who had been created Lord Wenlock in 1839.

as an education for permanent life beyond. *"Nunc est vivendum"* is the idea : and so I threw myself into Parliamentary life, which I have never left.

In this completely unexpected and unsought turn in my life, which now drew me into a fixed routine of business in Parliament, and in its having been brought about by a series of unlooked-for circumstances, I traced one of the many instances of the guiding care of the higher guardianship in answer to my mother's dying prayer.

I note my finding my career and circumstances thus settling themselves in the best possible way, in spite of my total inexperience of men and affairs. I note also, what all through life has struck me— the mind's constant adaptation to each phase of circumstances, each stage opening out a prospect of the next, and naturally lending itself to the pursuit of duties appropriate to each.

The Election in June 1841, which threw out Lord Melbourne's Ministry and brought in Sir Robert Peel, was my introduction to the representation of North Staffordshire, which I retained till I became not far short of " Father of the House."

I recollect Lord Elgin's—then Bruce, fresh from Christ Church—famous first speech moving the Amendment to the Address.

I recall, by way of associations characteristic of the times, Sir Francis Burdett, in breeches and top-boots, kindly inviting me to dinner. I had a friendly eye on me from Sir Robert Peel and Sir Thomas Fremantle [afterwards Lord Cottesloe], our Conservative whip, as well as Grenville

Berkeley,[1] the Whig whip, both friends of the Leighs [his future wife's family]. Young England came out thus : Disraeli, Angerstein Stafford, G. Smythe [Lord John Manners]. I did little but sit and listen this year in the House.

[1] Mr. Grenville Berkeley was married to a sister of the first Lord Leigh. He died 1896, aged 90.

By Hayter.

MARGARETTE LADY LEIGH, WIFE OF FIRST LORD LEIGH, HON. JULIA LEIGH,
LADY NORTON (RIGHT), AND HON. EMMA LEIGH (LEFT).

p. 41]

CHAPTER IX

1842

COURTSHIP AND MARRIAGE

I NATURALLY thought much about marriage, both for a home and domestic life, and because with my sister died the only woman I cared for—that is, intimately—for I had then fixed my desire on the one who soon was to make my happiness for life.

The late Sir Thomas Acland, my father's chief friend, in cherishing his memory taking deep and kindest interest in me, became my introducer to Stoneleigh, first at a cricket match on my future brother-in-law's [afterwards Lord Leigh] birthday. This was in 1841, and in the spring of 1842 I recollect on my way to the House of Commons one fine morning posting the letter which led to my good fortune for life. . . . I argued against my want of courage : " He that feareth is not made perfect in love." But the Guidance ever over me brought this crisis right, allowed the want of courage often to keep me from harm, but not in this crucial case from good.

He now became engaged to the Honourable Julia Leigh, daughter of Chandos, first Lord Leigh of Stoneleigh.[1] For a short period after the betrothal the course of this "true love" did not run smooth owing to a report which reached Lord and Lady Leigh that Mr. Adderley had inherited the seeds of the disease which had proved fatal to his parents. This report, spread by busy-bodies who professed to have received it from the Hartopps, harassed for a time the family at Stoneleigh, and caused cruel distress to Miss Leigh. Happily it proved to be unfounded, and the passing cloud was succeeded by sunshine.

J. R. Godley wrote, on hearing of his friend's engagement :

"It is certainly very disinterested in me to rejoice so much in your marriage, for I must necessarily be the sufferer by it, not (God forbid) that there should be less cordiality or friendship or affection between us, but that we must necessarily live much less together from the difference in habits and life of a married man and a bachelor.[2] No more *tête-à-tête* dinners, no more tours on cars, etc. But I will not go on to enumerate the *désagrémens* of a change for which I have been long most anxiously wishing, for I really did not think it possible for you adequately to perform your duty in the line of life marked out for you till it took place. Do you remember how you once, in the romantic mood engendered by that magnificent sunset which we witnessed on the Kenmare Road, vowed that you would spend your honeymoon at Killarney ?"

Later: "I will not forget the 28th [July]; I hope it may for many a year be still in our flowing cups freshly remembered—Vive, valeque ; et me, ut facis, ama."

Letters written by Mr. Adderley to his *fiancée*

[1] So created in 1839. A former Barony of Leigh of Stoneleigh in this family had become extinct. Lord Leigh (1791–1850) gained a favourable reputation as a poet.

[2] Mr. John Robert Godley married, in 1846, Charlotte, daughter of Charles Wynne, Esq., of Voelas, Denbighshire, and sister of Charles Wynne-Finch, M.P. Sir Arthur Godley, K.C.B., Permanent Under-Secretary for India, is their eldest son.

between their engagement in May 1842 to the time of their marriage having been preserved, it is thought that extracts may be here appropriately introduced.

C. B. ADDERLEY TO HONOURABLE JULIA LEIGH

35, ST. JAMES'S PLACE,
May 27, 1842.

MY VERY DEAR JULIA,

I confess a little disappointment at not having seen your handwriting to-day. However, it will be so much the dearer to-morrow. You have been studying Adam Smith [" Wealth of Nations "], that the scarcer things are the dearer they become. But, now that we are all but husband and wife, we must not let any days pass without hearing or seeing one another. When will you believe that everything that happens to you or, in the least, interests you, happens to me and interests me as well. Every lesson you give your sisters, every box you give their ears, almost every mistake they make, or, at least, the scolding you give in return, would interest me ; but a thousand times more every beauty that strikes your fancy in Dante, and every anecdote or point in Coxe or Sismondi, as you wade through the sixteen volumes knee-deep in Guelphs and Ghibellines, Bianchi and Neri ; all the occurrences of to-day and all your anticipations of the future. . . . Now, for my own part : as I said I would, I write to you about all that affects your new property and home—I always dwell on its being *yours*—I loved it before, but now ten times over and over as *yours*—I am in a great perplexity about the new Staffordshire church. . . . The subscription I have promised for myself—i.e. *ourselves*—is £500—as much as I could spare, as a County Member is expected to give to everything, and, I suppose, our expenses will not diminish by marriage. . . . We might perhaps add an annual stipend. We must begin reading together, and when we travel together I hope you will teach me Italian. There's one passage in " Woman's Mission " marked by you, or Lady Leigh, I liked very much : on the folly of breaking off one's education on settling in life—it should be carried on *through life*, for all life is a progress to a more perfect state. At the same time mere book-knowledge is useless without a little knowledge of mankind and its use and practice ; and all knowledge to be useful must bear on one's own life. . . . I have to read through 140 folio pages of evidence before four o'clock, in order to make my motion for a new writ for Newcastle (Staffordshire) if I am allowed time from graver subjects to-night [in the House of Commons]. The borough is rather a corrupt one, and the Whigs are very savage at this moment, so I expect opposition, and must get up the subject ; but I shall not venture above a few words myself, and leave others to discuss the merits of the case. I'm far from being at my ease in that awful assembly yet! . . .

Ever your most affectionate,
CHARLES.

OXFORD AND CAMBRIDGE CLUB,
May 28, 1842.

MY DEAREST JULIA,

I must begin the day by replying to your note, as I cannot set to any work till I have a little unburdened my mind of its twenty-four hours of accumulations of love to you. . . . I am in high delight at your loyalty to Victoria, and shall certainly go to the same Drawing-room to have a peep at you. I pity the dear old goodies at Stoneleigh when they lose their guardian angel. But you will soon be where you are still more wanted, among my thousand half-formed floating ideas of our future occupations. I fancy the cottages of Lea daily getting neater and happier-looking, and their gardens as well as their faces smiling under the influence of their new guardian. Though there must be no distinction between what is mine and what is yours, and yours mine—yourself in the bargain—yet I think it will be an admirable plan that you should have the entire care and management of the villages—the schools and clubs and cottages. What say you ? I think it would be a good thing for you to feel that the entire responsibility

of the interests of the poor around Hams rested in
your hands. You should have the cottage rents
separately paid to an account of your own, and
laid out by you on the cottages and poor. It would
be a noble occupation, and all the good done
amongst the villagers should be identified with
your name, which shall rest for ever in their
memory as not only the channel of God's earthly
blessings all around, but the gratitude and love of
many shall follow you into another world. . . .
I quite agree with you as to our soon settling at
Hams. Tell me every plan that you would like,
that I may arrange it. I am sure we shall hit upon
the same ideas in every plan, for I see that in all
things we think alike. I do not send messages to
all your party, as I might stereotype them for every
day. Only all love to yourself from
Your most affectionate
CHARLES.

33, ST. JAMES'S PLACE,
May 31, 1842.

As soon as your letters arrive, I find myself
scribbling, almost unconsciously, a reciprocation of
every idea contained in them, and I can generally
not even wait till I get through them before I
scratch off a thought or two which seems to come
in pairs with yours. Every word of this morning's
note I love with all my heart. So, you see, my
moment of breaking silence [in the House of
Commons] is again deferred, as Sir Robert Peel
requested to have last night to himself. Imagine
his rage when, having got the course clear for
himself, the news of the Queen being shot at forced
him to adjourn the House. I think it will go hard
with the Queen Shooter for this!
  We were talking of Winnington's marriage. The
two *fiancées* are here, and I cannot help contrasting
his proceedings with my own. I believe Miss D——
will make him a good wife, as she is neither so gay
nor so vulgar as her mother, but quiet and sensible,
and apparently attached to him. But the mother
is bent on a flare-up wedding. A series of dinners

and balls are now putting the hero and heroine to nightly suffering, both being sufficiently shy to feel all the pain and embarrassment that the most affectionate mother could desire. The whole seems like a very judicious arrangement for two rather commonplace people to keep house together *à la mode*. The world will be none the wiser, nor they much the better for the affair. . . . I am getting a close carriage and my little phaeton ready for us, and there will be room for all your paraphernalia, which I have a righteous dread of and respect for, scarcely knowing what amount or what kind of wardrobe generally follows a lady, but having an indefinite idea of an *olla podrida* in which gowns and scarfs and flowers and bonnets and shawls mingle together in a sort of bottomless chaos. Winnington's friend, Lord Falmouth, has lent him a house for the honeymoon. Can you imagine a more disagreeable plan?

June 7, 1842.

I have just feasted on your affectionate letter, but, before I answer it, I must tell you that I was kept so long waiting in the House before my writ came on that the post had gone by the time I was at liberty. Congratulate me that the dreaded ice-breaking is over, and the sea clear for the future. I had only to state my case, which did not occupy more than ten minutes. However, I gained my point, and am congratulated by all my friends, so that I am tolerably well satisfied with my evening's amusement. There never was so much bribery as at the last election, and all parties wish to put an end to it; but the Radicals are violent upon the subject in hopes of raising a hubbub and getting the ballot-box into play. So they move for suspending all writs for new elections. The borough Newcastle was not so bad as the rest. Individual cases of bribery were proved, and a system of each candidate giving a pound apiece to his supporters. My point to argue was that individual cases were not sufficient grounds for a general punishment by disfranchisement, and the system of treating was not bribery, as, when all received alike there was no inducement to a voter to prefer one candidate to another! In the division on my motion I had to tell off with O'Connell, so finding myself *tête-à-tête* with the agitator I began to conciliate, and said I had little expected when I was his guest in Ireland a few months ago, that I should so soon confront him in the House. He said my visit had only one fault—being too short. I said it had left exactly the same impression on me. In a few minutes we were the best of friends. I did not ask him to Hams, so don't be frightened!

By the bye, instead of reading the debate on Newcastle bribery, you would be much more interested in Lord Ashley's [1] speech last night on the horrors going on in the mines. You and I have mines in Staffordshire, but I'm happy to see that there is a more favourable report of that county; no women or very young children are worked in them. But the horrors of other mines are scarcely to be conceived, except that one may imagine what human nature, unchecked and uncontrolled down in the underground story of the kingdom, where no law and no inspection can get at them, would gradually arrive at. Lord Ashley spoke with all the feeling of a man accessible to the influence of religion and kindness of heart, and for my part I felt even foolishly affected by the touching pathos of his appeal. It was so unusual a strain for that cold and business-like assembly, and the sympathy it drew even from cast-iron hearts gave it a double interest.

3, PRINCES BUILDINGS (CLIFTON, BRISTOL),
July 12, 1842.

I have been breakfasting at Blaise Castle [2] this morning. Sir Thomas Acland, Dr. Buckland, and the American Minister were there, and they [the Harfords] were expecting an importation of Prussian diplomats from Bunsen. We stood out about two

[1] Afterwards seventh Earl of Shaftesbury, the great philanthropist and statesman.
[2] Belonging to the Harford family.

hours seeing ploughing matches in the rain, and to-morrow we are to see the Exhibition [at Bristol].

AT OUR OWN HOME (HAMS),
July 19.

I have just had a solemn dinner by myself in the room where I hope in nine days to be *tête-à-tête* with Mrs. Adderley. As soon as I had finished I sent for Mrs. Scott and gave her your gown, which, with many fine speeches and touching smiles, she finally bundled under her arm. I quote very badly all the thanks and messages to Miss Leigh. But she so soon passed to a subsequent era when you figured as Mrs. Adderley that I have forgotten the maiden speeches. I believe you will find the commissariat sadly deficient; for, to tell the truth, I have thought of little else but yourself for some months back, and all other subjects have been neglected. I had a shower of complaints which referred to as many heads as Sir Robert Peel's tariff. It began with lamp-oil and spices and preserves, and I forget where it ended. I cut it rather short, as I thought you would manage such things better than I, and I should be sorry to deprive you of the amusement. We must have a grand Cabinet Council some day after we have got here. But poor Mrs. Scott was most horrified when I candidly confessed I had not got a butler. "What *will* you do? I'm sure you won't be able to get one when you come here! and then as soon as you return the house will be full of company." "I hope not," I interrupted, so *con amore* that she really doubted the possibility of her pre- diction. However she soon returned to the charge. "It must be so, sir!" All the neighbourhood will be here, sir! It can't be otherwise!" My head is finally so full of a jumble of butlers and spices that I hardly know what arrangement at length wound up my evening's colloquy. The people about here are so anxious to show their goodwill, that if it once got abroad that we were coming here we should scarcely arrive by Thursday night. They expect us in a month, and talk of taking the horses off and drawing the carriage in triumph, and the Yeomanry want to escort us. I doubt if we shall escape all on our return from the Lakes. But for next week I have enjoined silence on our change of plan, so that I think we may escape.

Nine days later the wedding took place from Stoneleigh Abbey. The memoranda continue :

On July 28 I married. I will simply say that all my happiness and good in life was thus secured. All that firm and sound judgment, highest sense of right, warm affection and high breeding, could make a wife, I have had for my portion. . . . From a girl she was the health and sunshine of her home.

CHAPTER X

1843

EARLY MARRIED LIFE

WE at once began home duties to our neighbours in the happiest way. Ever since, our plan of life, varied by excursions, has been half the year in London and half in the country. My unbroken Parliamentary occupation has given simplicity to this plan, by which duties private and public naturally have become the constant pursuit, and the only drawback has been the consequent rapidity with which time has seemed to pass.

The first part of 1843 I worked in the House of Conmons without much footing gained, yet training slowly on, and I recollect Sir T. Acland encouraging me as "making way." I was dissatisfied with myself, I distinctly recollect, and that in itself was some indication of progress.

At the end of the Session we bought a little pony-carriage and drove down to the Isle of Wight, starting from our hired house at the upper end of Charles Street, Berkeley Square, one fine evening, half-ashamed at meeting all the gay world returning from a "Breakfast" on our way to Bushey. Man and maid took luggage by coach—railway not opened yet. The fourth day we crossed, and in two or three days drove round the island, stopping at Bonchurch for me to revive associations of infancy, which I clearly could, though only three when my father was dying there; and resting at other places, and at Cowes, where my father died.

On returning to Hams he devoted himself to the duties of a country gentleman. "I am very glad," wrote his friend Godley, "you are going to remain a farmer. It is part of your vocation, and country gentlemen in these days should be cautious of divesting themselves of their characteristic employment and duties more than is unavoidable."

1844

November 25, 1843, at 37, Portman Square, our first child, Annie, added greatly to our happiness. The year 1844 opened with the baptism at Hams, in a crowded village church; my guardian Uncle Sir Edmund Hartopp, lately become a widower, was Godfather, with Lady Leigh and Mrs. Ralph Adderley, Godmothers.

The winter passed in home, village, and neighbourhood relations.

As illustrating the interest which he habitually took in "village" life and occupations it seems appropriate to insert here some lines found in his handwriting among rough notes:

No yachts nor four-in-hands
Such joys can find
As smallest village doth
For cheerful mind!

Some thoughts at this time I transcribe with reference to Society. First, what is the best? for the best of everything in one's way is desirable, and the extent and mode of one's exertion to arrive at it are the only subjects for question. Indolence speciously replies, " Be satisfied where you are. Pride only is dissatisfied with the neighbourhood and associates which birth or education or your lot in life has given." But a worse pride resents the effort and humbling process of getting into good society, and is ready to be great among inferiors.

If a man on first becoming his own master finds himself already in a certain set and line in life, there may be obligation and duties fixing him down at once to a routine which leaves him neither time nor choice in making his society. He must get with the best men he can in his line of work, and not let the season pass unimproved, nor allow himself to fancy other plans or follow impulses till he gets unfitted for any regular occupation at all. But the man who enters life free to choose his set, has a more difficult beginning, but an easier course if well begun. By advice of older men and observation, and gradual experience, and most of all by committing himself truly to higher Guidance in constant prayer and self-discipline, he may surely find the clue to his right direction. The best society should surely be that of those most forward and leading in the same line. Are the " leading " synonymous with " of highest rank " ? They are the independent of men, and most distinguished and important. There is a great difference between toadying rank—aping it, seeking to shine by its borrowed light—and allying with its worth and use. The one takes the glitter for gold, the other finds the gold through the glitter. Now my matured conviction is, that the slavish desire and intense labour to be known and recognised in the world, is the lowest form of that mere ambition of notoriety which runs through all the forms of selfish egotism in fallen human nature.

I find in my "locked book" [January 1844] self-accusation of too much luxury in my double Paradise at Hams and Stoneleigh [his father-in-law's], and a fear of forgetting the object and discipline of life. Plans of fasting occupied me, which the Church-move then brought into prominence and discussion. . . . I have since expressed in a pamphlet my views on fasting, to which I adhere; also my views on Sunday.

A well-known Lenten preacher, with whom Lord Norton corresponded later in life on the subject of fasting, maintained that Lenten fasting was intended to lower a man's body beneath his usual standard of health and strength in order to render him the more susceptible of the influences of the spirit. Lord Norton, temperate in all things, combated this argument, and, while habitually practising *self-denial*, gave up "fasting" (in its strict sense) because he found that it reduced his powers of working. Neither did he sympathise with teetotalism, though he was surrounded by ardent teetotalers among those whom he loved most. He often said in public that he was not to be denied his glass of wine because some chose to get drunk, and he used to quote a remark of his friend Lord Bramwell, the eminent judge, who compared the phrase "Intoxicating liquor" applied to wine and beer as much the same as speaking of water as a "drowning fluid." Lord Norton always strongly maintained that reform in Licensing Laws should aim rather at punishing drunkenness and correcting the abuse of drink than at restricting the legitimate use of it.[1]

[1] A clergyman of his acquaintance, being accused by a busy-body of being too fond of "the *bottle*," Lord Norton—no friend of tale-bearers—humorously remarked, he hoped he would be better from the *wood* (the pulpit).

A story is told of him in his old age at a parochial luncheon given by his son, Father Adderley, then Vicar of St. Mark's, Marylebone, on the festival of St. Mark. All the drinks were teetotal. Lord Norton produced a flask with which he had provided himself, and turning with affability to his neighbour, Canon ——, a strong advocate of total abstinence, remarked: "I regret to say that my son gives heed unto 'doctrines of devils, commanding to abstain from meats'—and *drinks*," he added with emphasis—"'which the Lord hath created to be received with thanksgiving'": thus interpolating, in accordance with his own views, an addition to St. Paul's injunction which the Apostle himself has omitted to give!

As to his views on Sunday: twice to Church on Sunday was his fixed principle—often he went thrice—and, like Gladstone, he rigidly did no business on a Sunday. He once told his eldest son that if he (himself) failed not all his life to go through the church gate on Sunday, it would be for him, when carried through it after life, like a gate to heaven.

Great pains getting a clergyman for Lea [parish of Hams], which was only served once a Sunday from a distance till then. Presented it to Mr. —— ; Low Church, to the delight of my neighbour, old Lord Lifford, who was, however, scandalised at my servants' dance on the christening evening.

June, 1844 [Chesham Place].—I recorded feelings of satisfaction with work to do and interest in it, but of disappointment at not having the courage to speak [in Parliament] when once or twice prepared.

This autumn I worked steadily with my land-agents, and out with my Yeomanry; political meetings; shooting actively—up at 6 a.m. on September 1.

One memorable visit we paid this autumn was

to Alton Towers, in the Roman Catholic Lord Shrewsbury's[1] time: Duke and Duchess of Cambridge, Grand Duke and Grand Duchess of Mecklenburg Strelitz, Prince and Princess Doria, Duc de Bracciano, and the Duchess of Sutherland. All in stately formality and foreign manner of life.

1845

We had a house in Lowndes Square for the Session. I spoke for the first time in general debate in the House of Commons, and got more into Committee work, and spoke three or four times. I spoke against Game Law; against Irish colleges. I took at this time much to improving prison discipline and schools. I incurred an unfortunate ill-feeling from my Uncle William Hartopp [afterwards Sir William], having been employed to break off his daughter's match; but got over it well by calling and having it out with him.[2]

[1] John, sixteenth Earl of Shrewsbury—last but one of the head line of Roman Catholic Earls of Shrewsbury.
[2] How completely this temporary breach with his Uncle (afterwards Sir) William Hartopp was healed is shown by the fact that Sir William by his will appointed Mr. Adderley as guardian of his younger son.

CHAPTER XI

1846

REPEAL OF THE CORN LAWS

This was the year of the Repeal of the Corn Laws. No one had more often than Adderley, from his youth up, heard his illustrious neighbour, Sir Robert Peel, in private conversation and public utterance, descant on the necessity of maintaining the existing Corn Laws. Peel's complete recantation of his former principles and pledges seemed to Adderley little short of dishonest, and inspired him at this time with distrust of his former chief. It was this feeling, and the sense of personal responsibility to his own supporters 'who had returned him to Parliament and whose interests it was his duty to represent, rather than any enthusiasm on his own part for Protection, that made him at this time unwilling to abandon Lord Stanley's policy. It should be said, however, that Adderley's personal respect for Sir Robert Peel remained undiminished.

The feelings of the Tory party and of the country gentlemen at the time of the Corn Laws Repeal, were amusingly expressed in the following verses— a parody upon a popular " Ethiopian melody " called " Lucy Neal." They were sung by a guest at Strathfieldsaye to the Duke of Wellington, who, it may be added, was especially amused by the reference to his influence with "the Peers." [1]

[1] These verses are here introduced by the kind permission of the Hon. Mrs. James Swinton. Born the Hon. Blanche FitzGerald de Ros, daughter of the twenty-third Lord de Ros, her mother, Lady de Ros, was daughter of the fourth Duke of Richmond and of the Duchess of Richmond who gave the historic ball at Brussels on the eve of the Battle of Waterloo, or rather of Quatre-Bras.

I.

I came in for a county—how proud it made me feel!
We used to own a leader bold—his name was
    Robert Peel;
We made his name our watchword, drank his health
    at every meal—
We were not half acquainted, as it proved, with
    Robert Peel.

CHORUS

Oh, Sir Robert Peel!
False Sir Robert Peel!
If you had not left our side, how happy
    we might feel!

2.

At length we made him Premier, then he shuffled
    every deal;
Instead of staunch Protection, we heard rumours
    of Repeal.
He caught the Whigs a-bathing, and away their
    clothes did steal—
Which caused a separation between us and Robert
    Peel.

CHORUS

Oh, Sir Robert Peel! etc.

3

Lord George [1] had shut his betting-book, his
    country's wounds to heal;
D'Israeli at "Peel-ipics" is a perfect non-pareil;
But neither Jew nor jockey can our fallen state
    conceal—
Our party's broken by the League of Cobden,
    Bright, and Peel.

CHORUS

Oh, Sir Robert Peel! etc.

[1] Lord George Bentinck.

4.

There's Stanley in the House of Lords well argued
   our appeal;
But the Duke, he twists the Peers about like any
   cotton reel;
Of fallen rents and prices dark visions round us
   steal,
And the deadly sound that haunts us is the name
   of Robert Peel.

CHORUS

Oh, Sir Robert Peel!
False Sir Robert Peel!
If you had not left our side, how happy
   we might feel!

The course of Adderley's opinions and reflections
during this crisis may be traced in extracts from
a succession of admirable letters from his friend,
J. R. Godley, the " master mind " and " king of men,"
as Gladstone called him in Homeric phrase.

LETTERS FROM JOHN ROBERT GODLEY TO
C. B. ADDERLEY

January 22, 1846.

I quite agree with you about the Jacobinical tone
of the Anti-Corn Law League, but I think the way
to meet it is not by maintaining that which is in
the abstract indefensible, and thus giving them an
opportunity of attacking, under cover of sound
principles of Political Economy, the aristocratic
influence of which they are the enemies. By
abolishing the Corn Laws at once, you put an end
to the Anti-Corn Law League, just as by conceding
reform you put an end to the combinations of the
working men called Trades Unions, which presented
a yet more offensive and formidable appearance. . . .
I cannot admit the wisdom of defending a bad cause
lest concession should be misinterpreted as weakness. . . . Just ask yourself whether you consider
that there is the smallest shadow of possibility that

against the present weight of opposition (composed of all the talent and statesmanship and the greater part of the active wealth of the country), the Corn Laws in any shape can stand longer than a certain limited time.   As a permanent arrangement, I suppose no Hampshire farmer even hopes for them. If so, I cannot see the advantage, in any point of view, of a protracted defence which you know beforehand will ultimately be unsuccessful.

March 13, 1846.

Peel acts, as I firmly believe, for what he is convinced is the good of the country, and in so doing deliberately faces the almost certain loss of place. Peel was to blame *before*, but I am sure he is *now* acting on his convictions.   The great evil of the course which he has pursued, and which his supporters have imitated, is that it shows how very weak and ill-grounded, however conscientious, men's convictions are, and consequently throws one into a state of uncertainty as to what will come next.   For my own part I am very hopeful, and have no fears about the ultimate effects of the shock. I am sure the measure itself is a good one, and that when people find that out they will forget their present mutual animosities, which must, I fear, *for some time* prevent any cordial co-operation between the sections of the Conservative party.

March 28, 1846.

While I sympathise with and admire the spirit which your letter expresses, and join fully in your vituperation of Peel, whom I hardly know whether to consider disingenuous or unstable and absolutely destitute of fixed principles, yet still I cannot help warning you to reflect more calmly than you have perhaps done on the grounds of your opposition to this measure.   Burke says: "Legislation and government are matters for reason and judgment, not passion and feeling," and it certainly behoves you, before you commit yourself, to reflect on the alternative consequent on Peel's defeat.   If the measure be good for the interests of the country at large (which I think you will hardly deny), don't reject *it* because Peel brings it in.   Pass it, and then vote want of confidence in him if you like— which would far more effectually mark your indignation at his proceeding—but do not engage in a hopeless struggle for an unsound principle.   The question of resigning is a very difficult one, and unless the circumstances were very peculiar indeed I should not do so, for I maintain that you are sent to maintain a free and unbiassed judgment for seven years upon every question according to the circumstances of the matter and the period, and that you are not delegates bound to obey the dictates of your constituents. . . . You yourself, as you once told me, would repudiate "Protection abstractedly from inequality of taxation"; and that *must* be the cry if there is a dissolution.   It will not be enough to say: "I dislike Peel though I like Free Trade; and I will vote against him though I cannot maintain the existing Corn Laws."   I mean, this will not do for an election cry *now*.   After the Corn Laws go (as go they must), you may say: "Out with the Jonah."

Mr. Adderley's notes for 1846 record:

Thoughts of retiring from Parliament.   But why throw away a position which came unsought to me?

Son and heir born March 10.   A ball to the county and other festivities were given in honour of the event.

CHAPTER XII

1847

RE-ELECTED

THE year opened busily about schools at Kingsbury with Sir Robert Peel, and Girls' Industrial Home at Stoneleigh. Building churches at Saltley, Milton, and Smallthorn. Friendly Societies of Warwickshire and North Staffordshire founded. Warwick Gaol on new Separate system. I took much part in it.

In July Parliament dissolved, and elections came. I was on circuit, thanking every one for a walk-over in North Staffordshire, when Lord Brackley,[1] failing to get in for Newcastle, started at the last moment for North Staffordshire [as a second Tory candidate], involving me in great expense. [Lord Brackley was defeated ; while Adderley and Buller, the Whip candidate, were returned.]

On the occasion of this election Sir Robert Peel wrote to Adderley (August 9) giving his reasons for " plumping " for Adderley :

I had great satisfaction in giving my vote for you at Burton this day. All my previous feelings

[1] His father, Lord Francis Egerton, second son of the first Duke of Sutherland, had been created Earl of Ellesmere and Viscount Brackley in the previous year.

and inclinations were in favour of Lord Brackley as well as of yourself; but having read what passed at Stafford, and having no other means of forming a judgment than from that which did pass there, I own to you I cannot reconcile Lord Brackley's address to the constituent body of South Lancashire, or his admission to Brookes's Club, with a coalition with you for the purpose of defeating Mr. Buller. So far as local considerations are concerned Lord Brackley's claim on the northern division of this county [Staffordshire] must mainly rest on his connection with Trentham [the Duke of Sutherland was his uncle]; but I find it equally difficult to reconcile that claim with a letter which professed to have been written by the Duke of Sutherland so recently as the 19th July last, conveying a violent assurance of support to Mr. Buller. I have so much confidence in Lord Ellesmere [Lord Brackley's father] that I dare say there is a satisfactory solution of my doubts, but with those doubts I reluctantly gave a single vote in your favour.

Very truly yours,

ROBERT PEEL.[1]

I spoke more often in the House this year, supporting Godley's Irish Colony scheme as corollary to Government Poor Law.

In favour of Pakington's Juvenile Offenders Bill; the Maynooth Grant,[2] urged by Bateman, etc.

October 7.—I began farming with long pedigree

---

[1] A postscript to Sir Robert Peel's letter alludes to local politics in North Warwickshire : "I saw Mr. Leigh yesterday [late Lord Leigh] and recommended to him immediate communication with Mr. Bracebridge [later noted for his philanthropy in the Crimean War], who has declared himself a candidate for North Warwickshire. If Mr. Leigh resolves on standing, I shall feel strongly disposed to give him my vote. I certainly shall not vote in any event either for Mr. Newdegate or Mr. Spooner. I think the county has a great right to complain of the concealment of the intention to oppose Dugdale."

[2] The "Young England Party" was broken up by the Maynooth Grant, in which Disraeli opposed and Lord John Manners supported the Government.

Herefords under Sir Francis Lawley's auspices. Planted a good deal in the Park. Training College at Saltley founded on my land.

1848

Year of Revolutions all over Europe—Governments falling on all sides.

April 10.—Great preparations of Duke of Wellington against Chartists' invasion from Kensington Corner. Special constables sworn. I was ordered out with my Yeomanry Troop in aid of civil power.

Pottery schemes, School of Design, Emigration to Pottersville, Mendicity, Friendly Society. Seeing all this quarter in worse state, and being connected with it myself, gave me much to know and feel. Some years afterwards I told Gladstone, when splendidly laying the foundation of Wedgwood Institute, that he threw a halo of poetry over a dark spot, which I had looked on only as a duty and discipline. To Julia [his wife] I gave over all the cottages, she spending the rents on clubs, etc., with the cottage agent.

The " Battle of Bodymoor Heath " was fought by my clergyman (Thompson), a young neighbouring farmer, and myself, against a Birmingham prize fight. The farmer afterwards emigrating to our Canterbury Colony in New Zealand sent me a chief's cloak and assegais in memory. I had put down a fight last year, and this finally drove the nuisance off.

The incident of the fight is still remembered. News having leaked out that a fight had been arranged to take place at Bodymoor Heath (some distance from Hams) and that many people were assembling to witness it, Mr. Adderley, being informed of this, decided to prevent the fight if possible. He collected some of his tenants, and, with the parish constable and the Vicar of Lea Marston, proceeded to the scene of action. There he found several hundreds of people, many of whom had come from Wolverhampton and the "Black Country," and the combatants had just arrived in a furniture van from Birmingham. Mr. Adderley seized the horses' heads and turned the van into the roadway, being immediately assailed by a volley of stones. For a while there was a general scrimmage, stones and brickends flying in all directions, and the farmer who came to Mr. Adderley's assistance was injured. It was found impossible to effect any arrests, but the proposed prize-fight was prevented, and the van with its occupants were escorted part way back to Birmingham by Mr. Adderley on the one side and by the parson on the other. When later Mr. Adderley rejoined his wife and little girl, who, in great alarm, had taken refuge in a cottage, he appeared triumphant but bruised and battered from the fray, his clothes torn and his hat smashed in—a sight never to be forgotten by those who witnessed it.

Lord Norton used to say that Lord Dartmouth made a race-course at Birmingham on condition that the people gave up prize-fighting, bull-baiting, cock-fighting, etc., and said he would take it away instantly if they renewed these sports. Lord Norton's horror of betting caused him to have misgivings as to the moral dangers of races. Once he gave some umbrage to a friend well known and esteemed for his honourable connection with the turf. The two were walking together, and, as their road lay between the Birmingham sewage farm and the race-course, Lord Norton epigrammatically remarked : "Material corruption on the one hand, moral corruption on the other ! "

Canterbury Colony in New Zealand was now set on foot by Godley, Gibbon Wakefield, Gladstone,

Lord Lyttelton, Sewell, several others, and my-self.

Among marriages of relations this year, Matilda Grove[1] [his first cousin] married Eliot Warburton, author of "Crescent and Cross";[2] Henry Leigh [brother-in-law, afterwards 2nd Lord Leigh] married Lady Caroline Amelia Grosvenor.

The first great domestic calamity in our married life—little Julia's death [second daughter, aged two]. Driving with us the day before, and quite well and bright—in a moment gone, stillness and silence in the house, the little spirit fled.

With a view to clearing my mind and for accuracy of thought, I wrote articles in *Spectator* and *Morning Chronicle*, and an essay " On Human Happiness," which I felt a relief from sense of worthless con-versation, and a check on my own conduct as well ; and I expected scorn from the world, who would probably ridicule it. " Your essay makes me *un-*happy," said Sir Edmund Hartopp. " Is this your idea of happiness ? " said Milner, one dull night in the House of Commons. " You're like the rest, all

[1] Daughter of Edward Grove of Shenstone Park, Staffordshire. Her mother was Mr. Adderley's aunt.
[2] The celebrated Lady Morgan boasted that this marriage was "made up on my little balcony." The following year, 1849, this entry in Lord Norton's memorandum occurs : "*December* 23.— Returning one dark night in a covered brake, without lights, from hunting at Gopsall [Lord Howe's] in frost with Eliot Warburton, author of ' Crescent and Cross,' Edmund Adderley [his brother], John Hartopp, and W. Spooner, the coachman fell off the box turning sharp round a corner, and the horses went on driverless. Warburton jumped out and was hurt—soon afterwards to perish in the *Amazon* on fire at sea." Just as he was starting on his fatal voyage Warburton published in " Darien " a description of the horrors of a ship on fire, to make which accurate he had spent much time in investigating the history of the buccaneers, his imagination constantly picturing the fearful scene which was soon to be for him a reality.

5

for progress," said Urquhart. The Societies liked it and re-published it in a smart little volume.[1]

When this essay was re-published in 1861, Dr. Temple, afterwards Bishop of London and Archbishop of Canterbury, wrote : " I like it much, but somehow I wish there were (since it is an essay on Human Happiness) more of a perpetual acknowledgment that happiness is not the highest of all things. I know that you feel what I do on that matter ; but I want more of it in the book : more of a sort of Christian stoicism. Do you think this hypercriticism ? " Gladstone, in after-years, said to Adderley : " It was your book on Human Happiness that first gave me regard for you " ; and thus began a friendship which lasted through life. " Its tone of vigorous moral health is truly refreshing," he wrote, " and I hope sincerely that many may read it and profit by it."

I wrote at this time many letters and articles in *The Morning Chronicle*, which was the rival of *The Times*, and not long before headed it. I recollect S. Knight's anecdote of *The Morning Chronicle* getting the news of the capitulation of Ulm[2] before *The Times*, whose editor complained to Pitt, who answered that he had heard of it first from *The Morning Chronicle*. Yet this is the only paper I ever knew to die out altogether. In my time Cook was the editor, who had been second in *The Times*. [Sidney Herbert and the Duke of Newcastle were both interested in *The Morning Chronicle*, and both lost heavily by it.]

[1] The essay began with a definition of human happiness as a " state of constant adaptation of action to right intention." The headings of some of the aspects treated in it are : " Every man has some occupation befitting him " ; " The condition of wealth gives a man a choice of occupations, but on that very account a greater obligation to industry " ; " Proper employment of men of wealth and leisure is in the nature of superintendence, etc."

[2] In 1805.

The following is an extract from a letter from Mr. Adderley to his wife :

CARLTON CLUB,
April 5, 1848.

I spoke in the House last Monday after my arrival, being got up by a vile speech of the Leicester member against the Church.   Both *Times* and *Morning Chronicle* to-day take notice of my denouncement, which seems to have made the wretch a little sore.   I have sent a report of what I said to *The North Staffordshire*.

CHAPTER XIII

1849

HE REPRESENTS COLONIAL INTERESTS

I began the Session actively on colonial subjects, attacked Lord Grey and Lord Torrington,[1] and so was put on the Ceylon Committee with Sir Robert Peel, Gladstone, Sir W. Molesworth, etc.

The year 1849 was a memorable one in Mr. Adderley's political career, when he suddenly came into prominence in the House of Commons.

In order to explain the circumstances which led to the prominent position occupied by Mr. Adderley in 1849 in regard to colonial affairs, it is necessary to describe the circle of his friends who each influenced one another in this direction.

To the "master mind" of John Robert Godley was now added the fine intellect and high character of George, fourth Lord Lyttelton ; and these two friends with Mr. Adderley formed a trio bound together if not by unity of thought, at least by common aspirations. Lord Lyttelton and Mr. Adderley were already intimately associated in county affairs, and in educational and philanthropic enterprises. Both were zealous Churchmen, and they were, moreover, warm friends.

[1] George, seventh Viscount Torrington, Governor and Commander-in-Chief in Ceylon 1847-50.

The energies of Mr. Godley had, since 1847, been turned more especially toward colonial emigration, and he began at that time to inspire his friends with a like enthusiasm on the subject. He had himself fallen under the influence of that remarkable originator Edward Gibbon Wakefield, who, by the power of his genius, founded the whole machinery of our colonial system. "The strangest genius I ever met," Mr. Adderley calls him, "though intriguing and without scruple in carrying out his designs." Some twenty years before his acquaintance with Mr. Adderley, he had become notorious by the abduction of a wealthy young lady, daughter of the High Sheriff of Cheshire, for which breach of the law he was sentenced to three years' imprisonment, while the marriage was annulled by Act of Parliament. By his ability and indomitable persistency, however, he overcame the stigma of this episode, and turning his abilities to colonial matters, published, in 1833, his great work, "A View of the Art of Colonisation," in which he broached his new theories on the principles of which the Colonies of Australia and New Zealand were subsequently founded. His main idea was the sale of the public lands and the devotion of the proceeds to the promotion of industrial immigration. He had been instrumental in establishing self-government in Canada, where he was adviser to the Governor, Lord Durham, who used to declare that he himself never erred except when he rejected Gibbon Wakefield's advice. It was later, while immersed in the affairs. of New Zealand,[1] that Gibbon Wakefield came across Godley in England, and the two collaborated the idea of forming a Church of England province in that Colony, English of a good class being induced to settle in it on Wakefield's system— the object which more especially appealed to Godley, Adderley, and Lyttelton being to establish a footing for the Church of England in New

[1] His brother, Colonel William Wakefield, may be said to have been the real founder of New Zealand under his brother Gibbon's plan. Colonel Wakefield died in 1848, having married, in 1826, a sister of the first Lord de Lisle and Dudley.

Zealand, where hitherto Presbyterians and Dissenters had reigned supreme among the settlers.
Thus originated the important Colony of Canterbury, of which Lyttelton and Adderley became the
principal supporters at home.

Godley, whose burning energy was undermining
and consuming his bodily strength, necessitating
his absence from an English winter, went out to the
salubrious climate of Canterbury, and there guided
on the spot the "infant fortunes" of the Colony.
In the meantime Lyttelton was Chairman of the
Canterbury Association in London, and Adderley
its chief representative in the House of Commons;
while Wakefield, as a number of letters from
Adderley to Lyttelton, preserved among the Lyttelton papers at Hagley, attest, was in turns "machia-
velian," "satanic," "sulky," sometimes merely
"Wakefieldian," but nevertheless always indispen-
sable.[1]

Adderley's interest in New Zealand led him to
widen the field of his colonial outlook, and to
identify himself with the cause of self-government
for all the British Colonies, most of which, as
Gladstone remarked in a letter to Adderley,
were at this time "simmering with discontent"
and demanding the management of their own
affairs.

Henry George, third Earl Grey, was Secretary of
State for the Colonies in the Administration of Lord
John Russell from 1846 to 1852. All who knew
Lord Grey were aware that a man more high-
minded and conscientious did not exist; but his
contempt for the opinion of those who differed from
himself, and the tenacity with which he clung to
his own, rendered the Government of the Mother-
country distasteful to the Colonies; and it has been
said of him, with good reason, that he was singularly
unfortunate in his treatment of enemies.

It is true that, as early as 1846, he had pro-
pounded an elaborate scheme for the Government

[1] All letters from Mr. Adderley to Lord Lyttelton are in the
possession of his son, Viscount Cobham.

of New Zealand ;[1] but, as Mr. Adderley said, it had been "hanging over the Colonists' heads" ever since, and "they would rather have anything else than accept it." The fact was Lord Grey was possessed with the idea that it was practicable to give representative institutions, and *then stop without giving responsible government.*[2]

The giving of representative institutions, while responsibility was withheld, Gibbon Wakefield compared to "lighting a fire in a room with the chimney closed." The question was "how long a

---

[1] Sir George Grey, Governor of New Zealand, who has been called the "Prince of Governors," had refused to put this constitution into effect when sent out to him in 1848, his reason for doing so being certain difficulties with the Maori natives. Sir George Grey, although *in theory* in favour of liberal institutions, *in fact* preferred to govern solely through the power of his personal magnetism, and posing—in no invidious sense—as the champion and protector of the interesting and picturesque Maori, managed to get Lord Grey's promised constitution suspended for five years. In spite of Sir George Grey's personal fascination this caused the greatest discontent among the colonists. Not that Lord Grey's constitution was by any means ideal, or that it would have satisfied the colonial leaders, among whom, it must be remembered, were men of conspicuous ability and enlightenment.

[2] These are the words of that eminent authority on colonial government, Lord Blachford (Sir F. Rogers). He describes Lord Grey's notion of Colonial Constitutions as "something like the English Constitution under Elizabeth and the Stuarts. He did not understand either the vigorous independence of an Anglo-Saxon community or the weakness of an executive which represents a democracy." With regard to responsible government, Lord Blachford says (writing about 1885): "Fifty years ago the Colonies were divided in general into two classes : Crown Colonies, in which the Crown was almost absolute, and Colonies having representative institutions—that is to say, Colonies in which money could not be granted or laws passed without the consent of an elective assembly. The executive government was, in all cases alike, composed of permanent officers appointed by the Crown. To this limitation of the colonists' power the Canadians first objected, and it was determined in Canada, and in the North America Colonies, to establish what is called responsible government, under which the executive government is composed of persons who command the confidence of the local legislature. This is, of course, the English Constitution—the Governor, like the Queen, being obliged, except in a few matters of Imperial interest, to endorse the action of his Ministry, and being unable to exercise authority without them."—"Letters of Lord Blachford," edited by his nephew, G. E. Marindin, p. 295.

fire in a room without a chimney may be tolerable ; and that," he added, "partly depended upon the strength of the fire."

Lord Grey's plan was to *prepare and educate* colonists for the management of their own affairs during a long stage of control from Downing Street, but his process of preparation and education was so prolonged, his schemes and promises were so long delayed, and the distance from the Home Government was so vast, that confusion and discontent had everywhere increased rather than lessened under his well-intentioned rule. So great, indeed, was the irritation which he caused, that he was called the " Blister " of the Colonies ; and, moreover, while refusing or postponing responsible government, he at the same time wished to limit the dimensions of our Colonies as much as possible, and announced that it would be far better for Great Britain if her territory in South Africa were confined to Cape Town and Simon's Bay—this would be convenient as a settlement for convicts ; and by his endeavouring to force "ticket-of-leave " convicts on Cape Colony, he added still further to his unpopularity.

His name had thus come to be associated with much that was objectionable in the system of Home Government, and, although Adderley " will not have all Wakefield's anti-Greyism," throughout the private correspondence and public utterances of the little band of colonial reformers at this time, attack on Lord Grey means, really, attack on the system which he personified ; and in this sense, while the new cause is fought step by step, the last enemy to be destroyed is Lord Grey !

Thus Adderley, warming to the fray, early in 1849 delivered himself of a dashing speech in what appears a strain of sarcasm quite foreign to his nature, but which, in reality, was prompted by firm conviction, and was not the less effective on that account. " For myself," he said, " so far from being inclined to pass a vote of censure upon the noble lord, I am more disposed to propose him a vote of thanks, for if ever there was a man raised by Providence to damn the system he supports, that noble lord is the man who, by his very character and temper, has brought to a crisis the difficulties and dangers with which we have been so long struggling. I do not look upon this as a vote of censure, but rather as an attack upon the system than on any person."

The occasion was the "Ceylon Commission" debate on February 20. "The hon. member," as *The Times* of the next day reports, " then criticised Lord Torrington's administration of Ceylon, and admired (!) the attempt of Mr. Hawes (Under Colonial Secretary) to separate the causes of the rebellion from the taxes imposed by that noble lord."

Adderley was now called to a more prominent responsibility than any he had hitherto undertaken, namely to resist Lord Grey's determination to transport British convicts to the Cape. This high-handed proceeding had raised a feeling of bitter indignation among the colonists, who, finding that their Governor Sir Harry Smith's remonstrances with the Home Government on their behalf met with little or no attention, sent over agents to England, and entrusted their cause to Adderley as their representative and mouthpiece in the House of Commons.

The Times, according to Mr. Godley, upheld Lord Grey's views at this time, and did not scruple to ask, in so many words, " If we are not to use our Colonies for Convict Settlements, what is the good of a Colony ? "

While both the Manchester party of reformers and the Peelites were in sympathy with the cause of the Cape Colonists, few of the leaders in any party were willing to come forward and identify themselves with it, and the chief responsibility of preventing the Cape from becoming a penal settlement rested in Mr. Adderley's hands. He, however, secured the open support of Disraeli, who welcomed any means of discrediting Lord John Russell's Administration.

On March 27, 1849, Disraeli opened fire on Lord Grey's scheme, and Adderley followed with a vigorous attack.

"Our connection with the subject of colonial administration," said he, " has never been a reputable one. We began by making Colonies to send convicts to, and we now send convicts to maintain those Colonies. . . . To New South Wales," he continued, "we spread selected convicts under ticket-of-leave over the largest possible range of the dependencies of this country. The consent of the Legislative Council of New South Wales had only been obtained by the promises of the Government that, for every convict sent out to the Colony, there should also be a free emigrant sent out. The latter part of the contract was never carried out for want of funds—the Colony had the convicts without the free emigrants; and I must say," added Adderley, "they deserved the treatment they received for accepting the proposition of the Government upon such disreputable conditions. . . . If, however, the present plan is persisted in for the Cape, it will be without the consent of the in- habitants, who protest that it will lead to a state of things inexpressibly dangerous to life and property." He moved that "out of consideration for the honourable pride and moral welfare of the Cape Colony" Her Majesty would be pleased to order that the Cape should cease to be a receptacle for convicts. This motion was carried, and the agitation was so far successful that Lord Grey conceded that no more convicts should be sent to the Cape. Those only who had already started in the *Neptune*, which was awaiting orders, were to proceed to Cape Town. He reckoned, however, without the Cape colonists, who had determined that the convicts should never be landed at the Cape. The sequel is well known. On the arrival of the *Neptune* on September 20 the tolling of bells and the sounding of the fire-alarm gong announced the unwelcome news. Shops were closed and business was suspended. Sir Harry Smith, the Governor, would not allow the convicts to be landed. No other course was open to him. The *Neptune* could get no provisions from shore. Men, women, and children were leagued together to " boycott " her crew,[1] and she ultimately had to sail away with her cargo of convicts.

The gratitude of the colonists to Mr. Adderley for his advocacy of their cause is shown by the following letter addressed by the Chairman representing the principal inhabitants of Cape Town :

To C. B. ADDERLEY ESQ., M.P.

TOWN HALL, CITY OF CAPE TOWN,
CAPE OF GOOD HOPE.
December 13, 1849.

SIR,
I have the honour to convey to you the thanks of the municipality of the city of Cape Town for the very handsome manner in which you have accepted the advocacy of the cause of this Colony until it is fully and fairly vindicated.

Your communication and the fact you mention that strong and hearty sympathy is now felt with the Colonies by a large party whose wish it is that all the Colonies should enjoy the same freedom and scope for their energies and happiness as is enjoyed by their fellow subjects at home, have been received with feelings of no ordinary satisfaction, considering the anxiety and pain which this convict question has already occasioned and the severe disappointments which the people had from time to time to experience ; and although no doubt was ever entertained of the existence of such principles among an influential portion of British statesmen, it did create surprise that so little notice was taken of the grievances of the inhabitants of this Colony arising out of certain proceedings of the Home Government totally at variance with those principles. Feeling, however, that much of the apathy must be ascribed to the want of a competent person to represent their interest, and satisfied that in this they have at last succeeded, and that the colonists are already under lasting obligations to you for the eminent

[1] The only man who refused to boycott the convict ships, and supplied them with food, was knighted by the Home Government for his " patriotism," an act which was characteristic of official opinion in Downing Street.

services you have rendered to them, they confidently entrust the further management of their case to your charge, well knowing that no effort will be wanting on your part to prevent this much-neglected but hitherto unpolluted Colony from being converted into a den of robbers and thieves.

I have the honour to be, Sir,

Your most obedient servant,

HERCULES JARVIS, *Chairman.*

Gladstone wrote to Adderley (Dec. 6, 1849) :

" In my judgment the authority of the Crown has received this year in the Colonies two blows heavier than anything since the tea-riots in Boston—in Canada by the Rebellion-Losses Act, and at the Cape by the Convict Scheme and its failure."

The memoranda continue :

My speech against convicts being sent to the Cape led me into converse with leading men and gave me a parliamentary position, as it enlisted colonial connections, and it brought me endless presents from the Cape [among the most valued of these was the beautifully carved chair now at Hams presented by Cape Colony ;as a testimonial of gratitude [1]]; and my name was given to the principal street in Cape Town [Adderley Street]. . . . I had constant misgivings as to the moral effect on me of all this prominence. . . .

Lord Norton used to tell a story illustrative of the appreciation of the Cape Colonists :

One day he was travelling from London by the L. & N.W.R. train to hunt in Warwickshire when a man in the carriage asked a great many questions about passing objects. At last Mr. Adderley

---

[1] "The Adderley chair" was designed and carved by Hart of Grahamstown, and was exhibited in the Great Exhibition of 1851. A picture of it is in *The Illustrated London News* for that year.

(as he then was) said to him, "Excuse my asking where you come from, but you speak English as well as I do, and yet you appear to be a stranger in this country." "I come from Cape Town," was the reply, "and my name is —— ; and now, in return, will you tell me your name?" "My name is Adderley." Whereupon the stranger, overcome by emotion, threw his arms round Adderley's neck, and could not sufficiently express his gratitude.

"I cherish still," wrote Lord Norton in his nine-tieth year, "the happy recollection of having got the House of Commons to support [the Colonists'] in-dignant refusal to let the convicts land. To this hour (1903) I receive continual records of their high appreciation of this assertion of their superiority to any such demand of home service; and only free men can enter Cape Town by the main thoroughfare of 'Adderley Street.'" [1]

[1] Lord Norton's "Imperial Fellowship," p. 44.

CHAPTER XIV

1849 (*continued*)

FORMS COLONIAL REFORM SOCIETY

THE formation of the Colonial Reform Society,[1] which promoted an entire change of policy in colonial affairs, was now planned and set on foot, Adderley being among its most active founders and representatives in the House of Commons. " I keep the records of this Society, of which I was Secretary," he wrote sixty-four years later. " Between the years 1850–53 it perfectly achieved its work." [2]

Gibbon Wakefield was, more suo, wherever his commanding genius presided, the corner-stone of the Society's foundation, the laying of which is sketched in the letters of Godley written in the months preceding his departure to the Canterbury Colony. Writing to Adderley, August 8, 1849, Godley remarks : " What a battle we shall make next session for colonial self-government if we are alive ! Canada and the West Indies must bring things to a crisis and force us to decide finally according to what views our Colonies are henceforward to be governed "; and on the eve of departing for the Canterbury Colony in November he writes : " Wakefield is full of a plan of seeing me off at Plymouth and then adjourning *with you* and Rintoul,[3] and any-

[1] Society for Reform of Colonial Government.
[2] Lord Norton's " Imperial Fellowship of Self-governed Colonies," p. 33.
[3] John Stephen Rintoul, sole proprietor and editor of *The Spectator*, who opened the columns of that newspaper to Wakefield's views.

one else you can think of, to Molesworth's [Pencarrow] near Bodmin to concert a colonial campaign for next session." Before starting Godley sent a letter publicly addressed to Gladstone to be published in *The Morning Chronicle*, in which he aired the views of the " reformers "—first submitting the MS. to Adderley's supervision.

" I should be very glad," he says in this letter to Gladstone, " to be as sure that the flag of my country will not be hauled down in my lifetime, in any part of the Queen's dominions, as I am that the hours of Mr. Mother-Country's [1] reign are numbered. The point therefore which I am most anxious to urge upon you as upon all colonial reformers is, that whereas they have hitherto pleaded in the interests, as they thought, of suffering Colonies alone, they must now plead in the interests of British honour and British supremacy. . . . Many causes contributed to this change in the aspect of the question ; but the chief of them are these : firstly the increased consciousness of strength ; and secondly the growth in England of a political school holding the doctrine that the Colonies ought to be abandoned."

" Responsible government of the Colonies by themselves under the banner of imperial unity and fellowship," may be said to have been the ideal of the first organisers of the new society, and, as it was that of Mr. Adderley in 1849, so it remained, to the day of his death, that of Lord Norton in 1905. The following words, written by Adderley at this time,[2] are remarkable not only as expressing views so in advance of those then almost universally

[1] Twenty years later Gladstone said : " In the days when I was accustomed to wear with my footsteps the stairs of the Colonial Office, that office was haunted by a disembodied spirit that received a painful distinction under the title of ' Mr. Mother-Country.' " (Speech at the Colonial Society meeting, reported in *The Times*, March 11, 1869). Sir James Stephen, Permanent Under-Secretary for the Colonies, received a painful distinction under the title of " Mr. Mother-Country," being presumably the embodied representative of the spiritual essence alluded to by Gladstone.

[2] Introduction to a speech of J. R. Godley's in New Zealand.

held by his contemporaries, but as being prophetic of a state of things which he happily lived to see realised ; and they prove how firm and unaltered his opinions remained during a period of over fifty years. " The vitality of English Colonies," he wrote, " is truly astonishing, and, if emancipated from the Downing Street incubus, they would no doubt encircle England with a brotherhood of first-rate cognate nations faithful to the same Crown, carrying the same flag, and co-operating with similar institutions, identical interests, and joint enterprises throughout the world."

The imperial fellowship part of the scheme however did not appeal to some of the Radical elements in the new Reform Society, who said little about it, but were strongly in favour of emancipating the Colonies from the Home Government, chiefly with a view to economy for the British taxpayer.[1] Amongst the Radicals, however, was the highly distinguished Sir William Molesworth, whose speeches frequently breathed the spirit of Imperialism at the same time that he was a most ardent advocate of responsible government. He was in consequence much *lié* with Adderley in this cause, though there was little in common between them as to general views. "I had seen much of him," relates Adderley in a note, "in my colonial work. He affected the sceptical philosopher—edited Hobbes's works, of which he gave me a copy. He made his speeches by first dictating them to his secretary while lounging in a gorgeous dressing-gown, with two macaws screeching in cages, so that he might learn to exercise abstraction in the similar noise of the House of Commons ! The dictated essays were lithographed, and he learnt them by heart. He once gave me a copy of one a month before it was

[1] " Lord Wodehouse, afterwards Earl of Kimberley, was another associate in favour of the reform advocated ; while such eminent men as Roebuck, Joseph Hume, Cobden, and Milner Gibson joined in the association seeking for reform in a very different sense—that is, the commercial. Robert Lowe brought Australian experience, with his great ability, to the discussion, taking Wakefield's view."—" Imperial Fellowship," p. 33.

delivered as a speech, verbatim, in the House from memory—'spoken pamphlets,' Godley called them. His Scotch mother, in his early days, lamented his perpetual practice of speaking in a room over her head. 'It's just William speaking and Mr. Leader saying, "Hear, hear!" and then Mr. Leader speaking and William saying, "Hear, hear!"'" . . .

How keen an organiser of the Colonial Reform Association Adderley was, and how forward a part he played in its promotion, appears in a letter addressed (November 12, 1849) to his friend Lord Lyttelton, who was, of course, among the first members enrolled. "F. Baring [afterwards first Lord Ashburton], you, and Wakefield are in fact the only persons as yet consulted [as to the Chairmanship]. I think Molesworth should be a member, but I should be sorry to see *so powerful an engine in his hands.* It ought to be under Gladstone [1]—the fittest man. I should be sorry if all the energy and dash got into the Radicals' hands. Why should he leave us, who need him, inevitably to fall into their leadership? I know the party must be a mixed one both in and out of Parliament. . . . The Bishop of Norwich and Archbishop Whateley should be of our number."

Gladstone, however, did not join the Colonial Reform Association. The friendly and lengthy letters which he wrote to Adderley at this time show the extreme caution with which he tempered the sympathy he felt with the general objects of Colonial Reform. While entering into minute details in reference to a vote of censure on the Government, which the reformers were preparing for the coming Session, on the Australian Constitution, he writes: "I can well understand the anxiety for a Colonial Amendment to the Address; but I cannot say that as yet my mind is made up either to having one or to its form or aim. I do not think a merely abstract communication of political doctrine about Colonies would be in place as an amendment on the first night

[1] At this time a Peelite.

6

of the Session. It must bear upon recent or current events; and this in the way of blame, or at the least of warning akin to blame. This of itself is not a bar to me, because, since what I said about Canada, I can have no confidence in Lord Grey's colonial administration. . . .

"There are many things I wish to alter in the Australian scheme, but none of them would, I think, warrant the degree of censure probably to be implied in an Amendment to the Address. . . . I have, and I always have had, a thorough Sir Robert Peelian horror of *abstract* resolutions, and I fear you could not frame any more *general* engagement to improve Colonial Government and Constitutions for which I could with a safe conscience vote. I have never avoided, and never will avoid, giving a judgment upon any practical question, but I will condemn nothing before I am prepared with the means of mending it. . . . I like very much your succinct sketch of your New South Wales Bill, but I am rather alarmed. . . ." etc.

One point is especially characteristic of Gladstone in this correspondence, as showing how Church interests were uppermost in his mind. "There is one object of great importance in connection with colonial freedom which I think might be most advantageously considered in your Committee, and on which I know not why there should be any difference of opinion. It is this: On what footing is the Church to stand? As matters now go it appears to me the tendency is this: to deprive her of the advantages of civil establishment but to leave her under its disqualification. I think this much is plain, *where colonial freedom exists,*— (1) that the Colonial Church (i.e. the Church held by law to correspond with the Church at home) should be bound in substance at least to the Articles and Liturgy; (2) that it should stand in the same relation as other bodies in the Colony to her Colonial Legislature; (3) that unless as to some intervention of the Crown in the appointment of bishops—which exception, however, I would leave dependent on the will of the people there—it should enjoy self-government; (4) that this self-government must be started by some at least enabling procedure from hence; and (5) must *widen the basis* of her old Convocation instrument. I do very earnestly hope you will have this matter looked to. There can be no thoroughly good Australian Bill which does not settle this part of the question. At present, both the citizen and the Churchman are fettered, you are going to knock the bonds off the hands of the first; do the same for the second. . . ."

He concludes the correspondence by saying: "One cause, and one only, namely private and family affairs, prevent me from commanding my time and consequently my mind in such a degree as to write about Colonial Government. . . . I yet cling to the hope, however, of doing so, and your kind encouragement will give me a powerful stimulus when I can find or make opportunity."

Two illustrious statesmen, in opposite camps, both wrote at this time to Adderley declining his request that they should respectively join the Colonial Reform Association: Sir Robert Peel, the ex-Prime Minister, whose career was a few months later to be cut short by death, and Disraeli, the Tory leader, formerly of "Young England" fame. The letter of Sir Robert is docketed by Lord Norton "Peel's doubts about the Colonial Reform Society (which John Bright said I should go down to posterity for as hastening Constitutional Government in the Colonies)." It runs:

DRAYTON MANOR,
December 13 (1849).

MY DEAR SIR,
I am very much obliged to you not only for your attention in giving me information on the subject of your letter, but for the consideration which has induced you to select a mode of communication least likely to submit me to any embarrassment in respect to the acknowledgment of it. I will not conceal from you my opinion that the experiment you are about to make is a hazardous one. I think you run the risk of disunion among the leading members of your society, and I am not sure that,

even in the event of union, measures submitted to the consideration of Parliament at the instance of a *Colonial Government Society* will be likely to meet with greater acceptance on that account. I think, too, that the relations of such a society with discontented Colonies *may* assume a character of great delicacy. I give you credit for the best intentions, and it is because I give you that credit that I venture to trouble you with unpalatable but sincere opinions. With these opinions, and considering the relations in which I have stood to the Crown at various periods of my life, I could not feel justified in taking any part in your prospective association.

Believe me, my dear Sir,
Very faithfully yours,
ROBERT PEEL.

Disraeli wrote:

HUGHENDEN MANOR, HIGH WYCOMBE,
December 14, 1849.

DEAR ADDERLEY,

. . . I am very sensible of the honour of your wishing me to become a member of the council of the new society, but I could not perform the duties of the post in a manner satisfactory to myself. . . . [The letter concludes] I write more hurriedly than I could wish, but clear enough, I hope, to convey my general impressions and also my cordial wish at all times to co-operate with you in your public labours.

Yours very faithfully,
D.

Again:

HUGHENDEN MANOR,
December 23, 1849.

DEAR ADDERLEY,

It is no thought of the future that prevents my being a member of your council, but of the present. I can by no means give an unqualified adhesion to the programme you have enclosed me. Let there be no mistake between us about my readiness to support Molesworth in order to prevent the appearance of a mere party move from our benches. I meant to say, and hope I did say, though I wrote hurriedly, that if we agreed upon the language of a motion to be brought forward by Sir William, I was prepared to recommend my friends to support it ; but of course I assumed that on the language of this motion I should be consulted. My object is to obtain, without any compromise of his principles, the greatest possible assistance to the common end, which is a change in our existing colonial system.

As to the mode of attack on the coming season Disraeli gives the following advice :

"An Amendment on the Address is a very hazardous move, and rarely a successful one. The attendance on the Opposition side is seldom good at the beginning of the Session. The Address is so worded that lukewarm men are easily persuaded that they are not pledged to anything by assenting to it. . . . Under any circumstances an Amendment to the Address on general policy could not be decided on until the meeting of Parliament were much nearer. As to an Amendment on a branch of policy, all these objections, I think, apply with increased force. . . . It would be much better to prepare some substantive and well-concerted motion, and bring it forward with all the strength of the Opposition in addition to that of the independent colonial party. I should be prepared myself to support Molesworth under such circumstances."

AUTOBIOGRAPHY (*continued*). DOMESTIC EVENTS DURING 1849

In April [1849] died my uncle, Sir Edmund Cradock Hartopp, who had been my guardian and brought me out into the world. The suddenness of his death at Knighton [Leicestershire],—his second wedding just expected—with Lord Wrottesleys, sister,—distressed me. . . . His wife had been a more leading influence—an Eden [Lord Henley's daughter]. With him died all my associations with the opening of my life at Four Oaks, etc. Four Oaks now passed to his brother, Sir William— agreeable himself—who let the place be given over to his Irish wife, a very different Lady Hartopp from her predecessor, and to his pretty daughters and racketing. It was her boast that with her cook and her daughters she could always attract the most matrimonially eligible men to her house. It proved no idle one. But the eldest son, afterwards highly distinguished in the Crimean campaign . . . did not ever come to Four Oaks, and on succeeding to the property which he had never known or cared for sold it, and my old home, with all its beauty and neighbouring forests, became a Birmingham race-course. Said I, " Sic transit ! " But it impressed me with a useful lesson—nothing in this world lasts ; and as I look back on those scenes, I feel that nothing is left but the character formed with them.

The Leicestershire property, Knighton Lodge, where I was born, was left by Sir Edmund to Grove Cradock [Principal of Brazenose] for life, and then to my brother Edmund, with the injunction to take the name of Cradock instead of Adderley.

Both Saltley and Smallthorn churches were con- secrated this year. [Newly built on his property.]

CHAPTER XV

1850

AUSTRALIAN CONSTITUTION

THIS year opened on me very full of colonial politics and undertakings. Julia thought me getting undomestic, and thinking more of the Colonies than of the children. I had to say to her, " A shopman must attend to his shop, and you married him when he had already put up his sign." Godley having gone out to found our Canterbury Colony in New Zealand, I felt myself without the " master mind," and yet, *lié* with one very powerful, though intriguing and unscrupulous, in Gibbon Wakefield ; and with many prominent men in Parliament, Gladstone chiefly, and G. Home, Sir William Molesworth, Roebuck, etc. Our Canterbury Colony had great trouble with the old New Zealand Commission, and nearly got involved in serious litigation and personal liability.

The following letters to Lord Lyttelton show how immersed Mr. Adderley and his circle of friends were in colonial schemes :

January 12, 1850.

Fitzgerald and Walpole are concocting the Bill [the Australian Constitution Bill]. Gladstone has also concocted a Church clause which is to give the colonial bishops freedom to constitute their own

Church, i.e. have their Convocation, etc., free of State. Roebuck accepts a post in our Colonial Council. We must not have all Wakefield's *anti-Greyism* gratified.   Lord Grey wrote a most civil letter.

January 21, 1850.

I find all our colonial friends mortified at *The Times* report of our Birmingham meeting, disparaging it as a failure, etc., and they all attribute it to your attack on the *reporters making nonsense of everything.* They want you to write to Walter of *The Times* to neutralise the anger of the reporters, and to put a better notice, which he would be ready enough to do at your suggestion. The Government fix next Monday for Australia, etc., and we show fight also.   On the 12th Molesworth speaks.

We drew the Australian Constitution Bill, and successfully formed the Colonial Reform Association, which led to entire change of colonial policy. I had thus to take much more part in debates, and in writing both articles and pamphlets—my pamphlet on " Transportation " was the best thing I ever wrote. [Lord Robert Cecil[1] wrote to Mr. Adderley saying he envied his publishing pamphlets—an expense, he said, he himself could not afford.] I moved that Penal Settlements should never be made by mere Orders in Council, but always require an Act of Parliament. This was *à propos* to my great success in saving the Cape from Lord Grey's convicts. I served also on both the Ceylon Committee and on that for the Australian Constitution. I worked also at a Friendly Societies Bill.

The following letter from Gladstone to Adderley has some personal touches, and follows up the fortunes of the Australian Constitution Bill.

[1] Afterwards Marquis of Salisbury, Prime Minister.

6, CARLTON GARDENS,
July 30, 1850.

MY DEAR MR. ADDERLEY,
I am obliged to abandon the hope of visiting you as I am detained here by Baron Rothschild until Friday, and it would be contrary to nature were I not to join my wife and children, the rather as I must leave them again very soon for Scotland. Besides, I am this moment so laden with a violent cough and its accompaniments that the only kind of hospitality for which I am qualified is a hospital. Neither shall I, it appears, be in a condition to make a protest against the Australian Bill as it stands, unless by coughing when the Lord's Amendments are read; but perhaps I may be able to invite my voice into a capacity of speaking some few sentences, in which case I mean to spend them in the manner you would wish.

With many thanks for your kindness, by which perhaps you will allow us to profit at some future time,
I remain,
Very sincerely yours,
W. E. GLADSTONE.

Cobden writes to Adderley on the subject of the Colonial Reform Society, from his own point of view.

LONDON,
November 29, 1850.

DEAR SIR,
What I meant was, that in order to secure support out-of-doors, we, *the Society*, ought to avow some principles the advocacy of which would imply a reduction of the burdens of the people of *this* country. The notice of motion does not commit us or the House to more than inquiry. *It is good in itself* and would no doubt be ably handled by Mr. Gladstone, but it still strikes me that to excite any enthusiasm for the Colonial Reform Society we must avow ourselves the advocates of views which favour the general wish for a reduction of expenditure.
I remain, dear Sir,
Faithfully yours,
RICD. COBDEN.

Gladstone, who was now occupied with Italian affairs and with the release of the Neapolitan prisoners, writes :

5, CHIATAMARE, NAPLES.
December 20, 1850.

MY DEAR MR. ADDERLEY,

You know my vicious habit of saying No to requests which tend to make me assume a kind of leadership of your society, and therefore you will not be surprised at my returning that unpleasing answer in reply to your kind letter of the 23rd Nov. But you know also that notwithstanding differences in the *modus operandi* referable chiefly to our respective antecedents, we are cordially at one in desiring the full and final establishment of real local freedom in every Colony of which the state is normal ; and I hope that during the next Session we shall be found co-operating for the purpose you name, as we did, and as satisfactorily as we did, during the last.

Unfortunately I have not been able to see here the particulars of the Cape news, which I should have read with great interest.

As to particulars, I could not, I fear, so completely detach myself from family affairs as with a safe conscience to give the notice you desire, and undertake the study it might need at the beginning of the Session. I should not like to have the notice in my name dancing from week to week : it would disparage your cause and might wear the appearance of insincerity.

Nor do I much like the idea of a *Committee*, after the scandalous experience of the Ceylon case. I liked better Molesworth's old notion of a legal Commission ; and though most keenly anxious to find the system workable, I should like a strict examination of it by enlightened lawyers before finally and unconditionally asserting it.

But I assure you I am so very anxious as to the main object, that no difficulty of a secondary kind will prevent my fighting in your ranks.

I remain, very sincerely yours,
W. E. GLADSTONE.

THE TERRACE AT HAMS, WHERE THE CONSTITUTION OF NEW ZEALAND
WAS PLANNED.

SOME OTHER EVENTS CHRONICLED IN THE AUTO-BIOGRAPHICAL NOTES FOR 1850

A riot at a Stafford election meeting ended in trial and acquittal. Old Lord St. Vincent, passed eighty, and the sailor, Lord Shrewsbury, brazened it out amid showers of stones. One stone through the Shire Hall window hit *The Morning Post* reporter. "Good shot!" said *The Daily News*.

The great political event of the year was the death of Sir Robert Peel through an accident the day after Lord Palmerston's triumph in debate. My feelings on his death are recorded in my "locked book," see July 6th. Frederick [Peel] was to have dined with us on the Saturday. [The locked books for the early years cannot be found, but doubtless they contain expressions of admiration for the character and genius of the great Minister with whom Adderley had been intimately associated in his early manhood.]

The death of my father-in-law, Lord Leigh, occurred at Bonn, in October. Before this, among events of domestic interest, we had the visit to us of Prescott, the American historian, who ever afterwards continued in friendship and ordered his publishers to send all his works always to me; the visit also of Gibbon Wakefield—the strangest genius I ever knew—which was marked by our walks up and down the terrace at Hams concocting the New Zealand Constitution. This historic event, he said, should be recorded on one of its plinths.

Christmas, 1851 at Hams was as full of colonial business as had been the same season the year before. Since his successful advocacy of Cape interests in March 1849, Adderley had become the principal representative in England of the views of certain leaders among the Cape Colonists, chief of whom was Sir A. Hockenstrom, who sent Mr. Fairbairn as their delegate to England, where he arrived in December 1850.

Adderley writes to Lord Lyttelton :

HAMS, *December* 21.

MY DEAR LYTTELTON,

Fairbairn is to come here next Tuesday, and then I am to go to London to talk matters over with him and Wakefield, after which the Society must be convened. You have no doubt seen how the Government have got up a counter popular move in Cape Town, and have started the *Cape Monitor* versus the popular newspaper. Hockenstrom is kept away by ill-health, and Fairbairn is represented to me as an inferior sort of man [to Hockenstrom]. All this is bad, but Wakefield thinks we can put things straight through Fairbairn, i.e. *coach* the Cape Town folks to our own views through him, and get them in good order by the meeting of Parliament. This is very Wakefieldian, but I wish to let you know all.

Ever sincerely,
C. B. ADDERLEY.

The names of Sir A. Hockenstrom and Mr. Fairbairn occur frequently in a correspondence between Lord John Russell and Adderley. The following June 29, 1851, Lord John writes : " I think it right to inform you that since the reception of Sir A. Hockenstrom and Mr. Fairbairn's letter, I have thought it necessary to place my correspondence with these gentlemen in the hands of Lord Grey, with a view of having it officially transmitted to Sir H. Smith, Governor in British Caffraria." The Cape Colonists represented by these gentlemen desired " immediate relief from their present critical position."

CHAPTER XVI

1851

TRANSPORTATION NOT NECESSARY

THE pamphlet, "Transportation not necessary," published in 1851, to which Adderley alludes as "the best thing I ever wrote," was widely read in Parliamentary circles, and did much to influence the subsequent abolition of the Transportation of convicts. "That Transportation from England to her Colonies," says Adderley, "should, in the present conditions of the country, be employed as any portion of a penal system, is perhaps the most astounding piece of folly any nation has ever been guilty of; and when we are informed by our law reformers that 'Transportation must be considered the highest secondary punishment,' though we may concede the necessity for such an axiom for the foundation of their proposed code, we cannot but consider it as the readiest condition for the real subversion of all punishment whatever. . . . The conclusion to which an able discussion brought the Archbishop [Whateley] in 1832 was that 'Transportation may be said to unite in itself all the attributes of a bad punishment—to furnish a model for a penal system which should be imitated by contraries.'

"The proudest reflection I have is, that I believe I was the humble instrument of a death-blow to the system in the share I took in the gallant resistance made to its infliction on South Africa. It had indeed previously become so confused and shaken

93

that Sir George Grey[1] had ceased to defend it, except as a tentative system of punishment. I now believe that the *coup de grâce* has been practically given to the experiment. Nevertheless it has still its defenders, and more last attempts may aggravate the mischiefs it has already heaped upon this Empire.

"But it is said we have no choice—the modes of punishment in this country are exhausted . . . our prisons are choked up, and such is the crowded state of our population that our liberated prisoners are not only dangerous, but a necessarily recurrent burden on our hands. Transportation, if not required as a punishment, is supposed to be 'absolutely necessary for the disposal of our convicts.'"

This last argument in favour of Transportation was held by Lord Shaftesbury to be unanswerable.

He wrote, *November* 14, 1851 :

"DEAR MR. ADDERLEY,

"It would give me pleasure, I assure you, to aid in obtaining for the Colonies as much relief as is possible from the convict system, but I really do not see how we shall deal with the other question of Transportation. The thoughts of retaining all our convicts in England, and thus bringing ourselves to the condition of France is perfectly terrible. We shall very soon have twenty thousand *forçats* in this country, in addition to the floating mass of thieves and burglars which is already formidable enough."

It is unnecessary to trace the various arguments with which Adderley combated this view, as they have long since been accepted and acted upon. One sentence in his speech in Parliament on the Prison Discipline Motion (June 27, 1849), summarised his whole contention, when he expressed the hope that England "would not settle down under the practice that that which was vicious in principle must nevertheless be submitted to "; and declared that

[1] Home Secretary, to be distinguished from Sir George Grey, Governor of New Zealand.

he " never could be brought to believe that God rendered anything necessary which was in principle vicious."

That crime was in great measure reducible by stopping its causes he was never weary of urging at a time when some of the institutions of the country were more calculated to foster and spread crime than to suppress it. "If our national institutions were fairly considered," he thought, "if crime were fairly classified, it would be found that one half of those who were called criminals ought really to be otherwise described, and much that was called crime ought to be characterised as misfortune." As things were, there was no essential difference, so far as education was concerned, " between a national school, a national workhouse, and a national gaol—the lack of education, crime, misfortune, punishment, all mixed up together : virtue degraded, crime dignified, misfortune, by a false classification, mingled with the grossest offences."

The cause of the "juvenile delinquent" had no more earnest pleader than Adderley. An experienced official in the Home Office declared that "the gaols would have been full if it had not been for the efforts of Mr. Adderley in Reformatory work."

"I myself recollect," Mr. Adderley tells us in his pamphlet, "soon after Parkhurst prison was opened, the Home Secretary visiting it, and the governor and chaplain praying hard for the pardon of a child of eight years old, who had just come there, the offspring of two thieves, born and bred in theft as the natural mode of livelihood. The chaplain said that in all his life he had never met with a child of better natural disposition, so gentle and affectionate, so grateful for care and teaching, so ready to follow proper leading. 'Must this little boy,' said he, 'whose only mode of keeping the fifth commandment was by breaking the eighth, and whose opening mind had never even heard the eighth commandment hinted at, must he be treated with punishment for example's sake ? ' I heard the Home Secretary himself lament that he did not dare to obtain a pardon in this case.

Such was the suspicion in the public mind of the first advances at Parkhurst towards a better treatment of the young outcasts of society. Since then a great progress has been made. Still, however, many young children continue (1851) to have their early training of neglect and destitution consummated in the corruption of our gaols, which all opinion, and all evidence, unanimously declare to be the unfittest of places for any children, however vicious they may be ; and still more grossly inappropriate for the innocent little victims of their evil surroundings."

More will be said in a future chapter of how Adderley did not confine his theories to speeches and writings, but gave practical effect to them, and became himself a pioneer of reformatories in forming the reformatory at Saltley, Birmingham.

CHAPTER XVII

1851

NEW ZEALAND AND THE CAPE

THROUGHOUT 1851 Godley wrote, at frequent intervals, from the Canterbury Colony, urging Adderley that the Canterbury Association in London, which he himself had been instrumental in founding, should cease to interfere with the affairs of the Settlement; as he now found, exemplified in it, the evils of government from a distance, and felt "the impossibility of making a decent stand against the Colonial Office till we have purged the beam from our own eye."

"It is time," he writes, "to get rid of the Canterbury Association, which attempts too much to meddle with details best left to the Colony itself." In May and June he urges the immediate transfer of the whole legislative and administrative powers of the Association to the Colony. "Wakefield and Sewell," he says, "both of whom I suspect are fond of power, will doubtless abuse me heartily, but I trust to Lyttelton and you and Simeon to take the matter up and carry it through."

Adderley's comment, in forwarding this letter to Lord Lyttelton (August 22, 1851), is: "Am delighted at this early scream for Home Government. They say it is lucky for an infant to squall as soon as it's born!"

Godley continues, August 29: "The people come out from England in nowise radical or bitter against authority. After a short apprenticeship of colonial agitation, however, they get bitter, abusive, disloyal, democratic—in short, colonial.   This process has made the Wellington and Nelson people Chartists in about eight years ; how long will it take to chartise Canterbury ?   It makes me mad to see this deteriorating machinery [Colonial Office government] at work before my eyes, to see what the end must be, if it be suffered to go on working ; to see also, so plainly and clearly, the remedy [self-government], without being able to get it applied. . . . I trust Sir George Grey's [1] bitter and wanton attack on us may do him harm at home.   That depends upon your relations with the Colonial Office when the news of it arrives."

AUTOBIOGRAPHICAL NOTES (*continued*)

I sent out several labourers' families from near Hams in our four ships from Plymouth to Canterbury, our Settlement in New Zealand.   Flourishing despatches from Godley on their arrival there.   [In his dedication to Lord Lyttelton of Godley's letters Adderley says, in allusion to the Province of Canterbury : " Its chief port bears your name, its seaward headlands bearing mine and Godley's."]

The uncertainty of the Ministry, and Julia's expected confinement [before ·the birth of the sixth child] led us to take 4, Lowndes Street for only four months—less than our usual *séjour* in London.   We gave large dinners in our small house to prominent politicians.   Our circle, if small, was a good one.

Writing to Lord Lyttelton, February 18, 1851, he says : " Our Transportation move is very important. I have given up the motion to Molesworth *quo ad* Van Diemen's Land, for which Wakefield says I'm a fool."   The motion was for the discontinuance of Transportation to Van Diemen's Land, which Sir

[1] Governor of New Zealand.

William Molesworth moved on May 20, 1851, but the House was counted out.

I moved in the House of Commons for Commission on the Kaffir question [May, 1851]; Lord John Russell's Amendment; Select Committee. [Adderley blamed Lord Grey for the Kaffir War, and said the Cape, which was not consulted, should not be expected to pay a farthing towards the expenses of the war.]

I had conferences with old Lord Lyndhurst on Cape Town Bill and Commission. [Gladstone writes: "July 2, 1851.—I hope Lord Lyndhurst will act according to your wishes, and that this may lead to some solution. . . . Am not free to go deeply into the subject myself, as I expect to set to work on behalf of the poor Neapolitan prisoners, whom I have long ago, and very solemnly, promised not to forget—promised to themselves and within their prison walls.]

I got on with the New Zealand Bill and Constitution, which had been drafted on the terrace at Hams with Gibbon Wakefield. . . . Fox, Sewell, and Lord Lyttelton assisting.

I worked with them in Parliament for revived free colonial policy.

Writing to Lord Lyttelton (July 23, 1851), Adderley says: "I look gloomily on the evident recklessness and hostility of Downing Street. I found Sewell and Wakefield at the last gasp of rage, *ready to eat Hawes*" [Under-Secretary for the Colonies, who endorsed his chief's, Lord Grey, views].

Thomas Gisborne [who was formerly Member for Stafford] proposed my health at a Staffordshire Conservative dinner as having identified myself "with a great Imperial question"; and, about the same time, John Bright spoke approvingly of my colonial work.

I was now for the first time talked of for office, which gave me a new interest, yet my "locked book" shows me to have been full of thoughts of retiring from Parliament, my party not liking my colonial work with Gibbon Wakefield's influence. Yet the views I advocated eventually prevailed.

I was dissatisfied also with the general religious state, from the opposing Church views then striving and dividing, and also with myself inwardly as to sincerity and truth. I wanted more practical work amongst the poor and distressed, as proof, practice, and probation for self. I offered Liddell[1] my services at St. Paul's [Knightsbridge].

Two sermons struck me, and I resolved neither to seek nor to shun any offer of work or office, as also neither to add to property nor diminish it needlessly, but make the most of whatever came to hand.

This was the year of the Great Exhibition in Hyde Park. I took up my tenants from Hams to see it.

We made acquaintance at Stoneleigh with Fanny Kemble—her Shakespeare readings there. [Her daughter, Miss Butler, afterwards married Lord Norton's brother-in-law, the Hon. and Rev. James Leigh, now Dean of Hereford.]

A dull political year ended eventfully with the *coup d'état* of Louis Napoleon in Paris on December 2, and Lord Palmerston, Minister of Foreign

[1] Rev. the Hon. Robert Liddell, Vicar of St. Paul's, Knightsbridge.

Affairs, having been privy to it without the knowledge of the Queen and the Cabinet, led to his dismissal from office.

Adderley wrote to his wife:

CANTERBURY ASSOCIATION,
9, ADELPHI TERRACE,
December 29, 1851.

It seems Lord P. was actually intriguing with foreign politics at his own discretion, and had been consulted by Louis Napoleon before the *coup d'état,* through Count Walewski, the French Ambassador! It is clear the Government will patch up their vacancies with Peelites. . . . *All the talents* in office, they will be very strong, and we shall have to reside under their shadow a long time to come . . . [A premature prognostication.]

CHAPTER XVIII

1852

ADDERLEY'S CAPE MOTION

THE year began with great excitement in Paris over the new Constitution, and with parties at home unhinged. Parliament opened in the new Houses of Parliament. Fortune soon turned, after the dismissal of Lord Palmerston, against Lord John Russell who advised it; and also against the Peelites who supported him.

Adderley wrote to his wife :

February 3, 1852.

To you I write my first letter in the new library of the new House—a long and gorgeous suite of rooms fitted to contain thirty thousand volumes, with Russia-leather bindings—looking out on to a broad terrace along the river. Between this and the House is an equally splendid dining suite of rooms. The day is glorious—May sunshine— and I am provoked now to think how very soon a *mauvaise élection* may oust me from so tip-top a club. The general impression is that the dissolution will be in a fortnight. I went to breakfast in Port- man Square with Henry [Lord Leigh] and Caroline [*née* Lady Caroline Grosvenor], and I think he has prepared well for a short speech to-night [in the House of Lords], and is not nervous. He dined with the Ministerial dinner of course, last night [being a supporter of Lord John Russell], and went to Lady Grey's party afterwards.   The Palmerston and Grey parties being so near each other was great fun, and the gossips went from one to the other. The pageant of the opening of Parliament to-day was very fine, and the Queen read her speech in a clear, loud voice, the old Duke [of Wellington] listening over her shoulder, and the Duchess [of Kent] beaming with radiant smiles and diamonds. The House was full of ladies.   The speech is highly colonial.   Cape and New Zealand occupy two paragraphs.   The Reform Bill comes limping in a post-script.   They say Lord Derby would send me to the Cape if he came in !   Lord Ward [afterwards Earl of Dudley] flirting in the House as fresh as a bachelor.   [His first wife had recently died.]

February 9.

Lord John's speech is just over, proposing his very moderate Reform Bill, which will satisfy none, and attempts to include the Jew question in it. . . . Disraeli has just asked me to go to him at 1.30 to-morrow to arrange my motion, so I shall have hard work now on my hands.

To indicate what that motion was and the importance that was attached to it, it must be prefaced that an " assegai thrust " at Lord Grey, early in the Session, in regard to the Kaffir war and the conduct of it, had for some time been determined on by Adderley.   To ensure the support of the " Peelites," he consulted Gladstone in January, a few weeks before the meeting of Parliament.   Gladstone wrote from Cuddesdon Palace, January 21, 1852 :   " I should say that we can hardly go wrong in believing that the Kaffir war and Lord Grey's relation to it deserve notice on the Address, whatever the number, interest, and importance of competing subjects.   In what form that notice should be taken, whether it should be in discussion only, or whether it might with propriety form the subject of a motion, is a question of delicacy and moment. Why this new delay in bringing the Constitution to

bear ? Is Lord Grey fairly answerable for it or
not ? I do not like to rely simply on the strength
of what I have read in the newspapers, but I think
it probable that you who follow the question with
closer and more sagacious scent are in a condition
to gauge such a reply. If so, I should like much to
have it from you, whether in writing or *vivâ voce*,
before the 3rd [when Parliament would meet]. Most
sincerely yours, W. E. GLADSTONE."

During the month which elapsed after the writing
of this letter the prospective Cape motion had
grown greatly in importance, Disraeli, as we have
seen, making arrangements in regard to it on
February 10, and the Peelites having at their
meeting agreed to support Adderley.

How keen became the excitement in political
circles as to what, it was expected, would be a
death-blow to the Government, is shown in a letter
from Adderley to his wife written on the eve of the
intended " thrust."

February 19 *and* 20, 1852.

This Cape motion grows in intensity of interest.
Mind—I never forced myself into the way of it. I
was drawn into Parliament unexpectedly—I did not
seek it—it came to me unsought—and I then was
drawn into having all this great imperial question
placed in my hands. I could leave it all to-morrow
with pleasure, except for sacrificing great interests
I have taken up. . . . . I should immensely prefer
direct attention to the poverty and distress of the
lower classes than this political strife and jobbing.
. . . . Nevertheless, I incline to remain where I am
at this post as long as it retains me, and shall be
very glad to leave it as soon as it deserts me. As
to my present work it grows so big and important
. . . at Lady Granville's last night all the world
was talking of it. I overheard Thiers [1] asking

[1] " Thiers was at Lady Granville's last night, and was enchanted
with the spectacle of the Opening. He said, though he did not
understand a word of English, he could have cried at the Queen's
voice in reading the speech."—Lord Normanby to Colonel Phipps,
" Queen Victoria's Letters," vol. ii. p. 441.

questions about it, and all conjecturing the downfall of the Ministry on it. . . . Frederick Peel [Colonial Under-Secretary] will be drawn out for a first and last grand effort. My case is excellent, but I shrink from the stir made about it. The House is crammed full already for it. Ladies, foreigners, and strangers of all sorts. It is enough to make me nervous to extinction. . . . If the Government weather my attack, you may safely come up immediately."

But a totally unlooked-for event at this juncture occurred, and as by the magic touch of Harlequin's wand the whole aspect of St. Stephen's was suddenly changed. An unforeseen move on the part of the Government prevented the completion of the schemes of the Opposition, and before Adderley's motion was reached, Lord John Russell, anticipating a vote of censure on the colonial policy of Lord Grey, took the occasion of being beaten on Lord Palmerston's Amendment on the Militia Bill to announce the resignation of the Ministry (February 20).[1]

The leading article of *The Times* next day throws light on this dexterous ruse: " Possibly," comments *The Times* (Saturday, February 21, 1852), " as has frequently happened before, the Ministry has stooped to avoid a fatal blow. The little cloud that was ultimately to blacken the heavens has long been over the horizon. Need we mention the Kaffir war to be brought home at last by Mr. Adderley's motion on Tuesday next ? On Thursday [the day before the resignation] we observed ' the day will come soon enough when the present Government will stand on its trial and probably be condemned.' In this we alluded to the debate which was then expected to occupy the greatest part of next week, and to terminate in the

[1] " Lord John Russell presents his humble duty to your Majesty, and has the honour to report that Lord Palmerston has just carried his motion for leaving out the word ' local ' in the Bill for the Militia. Lord Palmerston said he was astonished at the Government for giving up for so slight a cause. 20th February 1852."— " Queen Victoria's Letters," vol. ii. p. 444.

censure of the Colonial Secretary [Earl Grey] and
the resignation of the Ministry.   If that expectation
were well founded, Lord John has certainly selected
a much softer place to fall upon than fate seemed to
threaten.   He has made his own bed with considerable judgment."   It is amusing to pursue the article
a little farther: "Were the resignation doubtful,
that very matter-of-fact man, Sir Benjamin Hall
[afterwards Lord Llanover] took care to clinch it
by expressing a hope that Lord John was resigning in earnest, and not merely to take office again.
Sir Benjamin likes to make safe.   No African sports-
man ever watched the lion pierced by his rifle
with more anxiety to see if it were really dead ; no
undertaker could be more shocked to see the revival
of the body already laid out. . . . 'But are you really
dead, and may we trample on you?' was the substance of the worthy baronet's question ; and the
reply was of the most reassuring nature.   Lord
John Russell's Administration is actually no more."

Speculation was now rife as to whether Lord
Palmerston would or could form a composite
Ministry, or whether it would devolve upon the
great Protectionist chief, Lord Derby, to form a
Tory Administration.   The latter was the course
actually pursued ; an express was despatched to
Lord Derby at Badminton (where he was on a visit
to the Duke of Beaufort), and Lord Derby's short-
lived Ministry came into being.
The Autobiographical Notes continue :

I had some share in Lord John's defeat.   *The
Times* gave my Cape motion "assegai thrust" at
Lord Grey a part with Lord Palmerston's Militia
Amendment in forcing Lord John's resignation.
All said, I should have won by forty—Disraeli
arranging and the Peelites promising me support.

Although Adderley's motion and the intended
censure on the Ministry were now consigned to
the limbo of half-forgotten "might-have-beens," the

Kaffir war was still to form the subject of acrimonious debate on a future opportunity. Mr. Henry Drummond, indeed, was determined that interest in it, with a view more especially to the defence of Sir Harry Smith,[1] whom Lord Grey was about to recall from the Governorship of Cape Colony, should not for one moment be allowed to flag. We find Mr. Drummond actually writing on the very next day after the Ministry's resignation, and before the new Ministry had been formed, to urge Adderley to proceed with his motion without delay!—in common parlance, to strike while the iron was still hot:

32, ALBEMARLE STREET,
February 21, 1852.

I cannot resist the temptation of troubling you with this note to urge you not to be persuaded to postpone your motion on the Kaffir war, as you certainly will be. Every unexpected occurrence places people off their balance, and whatever merits certain of our friends possess, that of knowing how to make the best use of popular assemblies is not one. The feeling now is strong on every side in favour of Sir H. Smith, and this is that which will operate most favourably for you; but if you let it cool down by time, you never can revive it; soon

[1] General Sir Harry Smith, the gallant victor of Aliwal, and celebrated as having given his name to Harrysmith, and his wife's to Ladysmith, had annexed British Kaffraria in 1847, and established the Orange River Sovereignty, in which Lord Grey had unwillingly acquiesced. Lord Grey thought that Sir Harry had acted without proper consideration in regard to the war, and recalled him on April 7, 1852, in favour of General Cathcart. This raised a storm of indignation among Sir Harry's friends and Lord Grey's enemies, the Duke of Wellington warmly eulogising Sir Harry's conduct as a soldier. According to Mr. Herbert Paul ("Modern England," vol. i. p. 14): "Sir Harry Smith was a gallant and pious officer, a man of the Bible and of the sword. Trusting in his own personal influence he thought he could reconcile the Dutch farmers with the British and with the natives by attending at Boer prayer-meetings and by ostentatious patronage of native chiefs. His eccentric enthusiasm got him into trouble, and Lord Grey was justified in removing him from his post." It was this leaven of piety with gallantry which especially attracted Mr. Henry Drummond—himself the most religious of men—to Sir Harry Smith.

the House gets disgusted with works and subjects which are continually repeated in its ears. It is fear of your motion which made the Ministers resign last night; but you should not let them choose their own line, or the Radicals will soon bring them out of their difficulties. I am certain that nothing which has occurred ought to influence your motion.

Ever yours very truly,
HENRY DRUMMOND.[1]

Presumably this letter was written on the supposition that although the Ministry had resigned it would be succeeded by another Whig Ministry under Lord Palmerston, which would contain many of the same elements as the outgoing one. Mr. Drummond could not have realised that the Tory Ministry of Lord Derby would be formed in a few days. It was too late for Lord John to be prevented from "choosing his own line," and as *The Times* said two days afterwards (Monday, February 23), "Kaffirs will go on fighting and we shall go on paying, and Lord Grey can no longer be called to account for the mischief." It was as vain to strike at the late Colonial Secretary as at a phantom—he could no more be caught hold of than could the 'Vanishing Lady.' But though extinct as Colonial Secretary, Lord Grey was free to give his own version of affairs (which he doubtless implicitly believed), and he did not fail to do so to the Queen and Prince Albert on the first opportunity vouchsafed to him. The Prince's memorandum noted that " Lord Grey said he was

[1] Henry Drummond, M.P., born 1786, died 1860; politician and philanthropist. A banker of noble descent, his high character and his wealth made him a powerful friend or opponent; by traditions a Tory, he was perfectly independent, attacking all parties in turns. He was especially noted for his religious fervour as a follower of Irving, being himself one of the founders of the sect called the "Holy Apostolic Church." Carlyle, *more suo*, said of him he was a "singular mixture of all things—of the saint, the wit, the philosopher—swimming, if I mistake not, in an element of dandyism." His daughter married the sixth Duke of Northumberland, and was mother of the present Duke.

sorry that the resignation had taken place before the Kaffir debate, in which he had hoped to make a triumphant defence," while he blamed Lord John for the way he had managed matters and declared he could never have the same confidence in Lord John as before.[1]

Lord Palmerston, however—than whom no one was more surprised at the result of his " tit for tat " on John Russell, as he termed his Militia Amendment—was himself well aware of the real reason of Lord John's manœuvre in resigning on so slight a pretext. Writing to his brother he assigned one special reason for it, namely " the fear of being defeated on the vote of censure about the Cape Affairs which was to have been moved to-day " (Tuesday, February 24).

[1] " Queen Victoria's Letters," vol. ii. p. 554.

CHAPTER XIX

1852 (*continued*)

AUTOBIOGRAPHICAL NOTES

February 23.—Lord Derby [becoming Tory Prime Minister] sent for me to St. James's Square and offered me the *Secretaryship of Board of Control.* I declined, saying the only post that would tempt me was an Under-Secretaryship in Colonial Office, which Lord Derby said I should be dangerous in. Many years afterwards it was my second appointment, my " dangerous views " having been adopted, and found *not* dangerous.

Another diary states :

Any other Office [than the Colonial Office] would only tongue-tie me without escape ; and Gladstone will soon be in, and I with him. [This shows Adderley's leaning towards the Peelites, among whom Gladstone was prominent, Adderley being now on terms of growing intimacy with him.]

Adderley's interview with Lord Derby is thus recorded in an undated letter to the Honourable Mrs. Adderley. " I have won your £1. Lord Derby offered me the first Secretaryship of the Board of Control, a vastly important office just as the Charter is immediately to be revived. I had made up my mind to accept nothing but the Under-Secretaryship of the Colonies, so I at once refused—I fear so precipitately as to offend.   However, it's done irrevocably, and you'll be delighted! Lord Derby had just returned from the Queen.   I drove up to the door with him.   He sent in for me, paid me some compliments and said he would not complete his Ministry without offering a place to me.   I said I wished to decline all office, but hoped to support him.   He thanked me and said he supposed I deliberately refused.   I said I was surprised he offered it to me as I had run wild on colonial matters.   He said, 'I don't pretend to agree with all your colonial views,' on which Baron Brunow interrupted, and off went I!"

Thus Adderley did not become a member of the Government which was facetiously described as the "Who? Who?" Government.[1]   Hardly any member of it, saving Disraeli, who became Chancellor of the Exchequer and Leader of the House of Commons, was known to fame; and each addition to it of an unknown name was greeted with the question "Who?" and again, "Who?"   The post of Colonial Secretary was filled by Sir John Pakington, of whom the Duke of Wellington did not remember ever to have heard, and asked, "Who is Sir John Pakington?"   *The Times* knew him as a "worthy Worcestershire magistrate," and opined that he would "enter office with one great advantage over his predecessor [Lord Grey]—a thorough consciousness of his own ignorance."   "If he be wise," continued *The Times* mentor, "he will make this consciousness his guiding principle, and seek information not from the subordinates of his office but from the data which will be furnished by the numerous remonstrances and addresses of the colonists themselves.   If Sir John Pakington adopt this course, his very ignorance will have made him

---

[1] Lord Lyndhurst said that, though the materials were there for Lord Derby's Administration, they were very bad ones, and it was a question whether they would stand long.   He himself would keep out of place.

a valuable servant for his country. If not . . . his subordinate officials will lead him to conclusions injurious to the welfare of the Colonies and the stability of the Empire." [1]

Whether or not Sir John Pakington was guided by the advice so condescendingly offered him, he certainly acted in accordance with it in regard to the affairs of New Zealand. It devolved upon him to proceed with the new Constitution Bill for that Colony, and in adopting the " Hams draft," he frequently consulted with the authors of it as to details. Sir John was, in fact, a friend and country neighbour of Adderley; Westwood, Sir John's ancestral house in Worcestershire, was not remote from Hams; while Hagley, the home of Lord Lyttelton, that staunch New Zealand colonist, was in the same county.

AUTOBIOGRAPHICAL NOTES (continued)

March 1852.—I set to work with colonial schemes, e.g. the New Zealand Constitution, which I *forced* on Sir John Pakington, as he said, in the Colonial Office. I spoke much on it in the House, Sir W. Molesworth opposing, though generally I followed him in his colonial policy.

Sir John Pakington passed the Constitution Act, 15 & 16 Victoria, '86,[2] which finally enfranchised the local government in all respects except native control, which was still reserved to the Queen. " This measure," wrote Adderley years afterwards (in his review [3] of Lord Grey's " Colonial Policy of Lord J. Russell's Administration "), "with all its errors and complications, was a great step in *recovery of our old colonial policy.*" [Gladstone and Adderley

---

[1] *The Times*, Thursday, February 26, 1852.

[2] The islands were divided into seven provinces, of which Canterbury was one, each with a Legislature and with a Superintendent to be elected by the people, and *not*, as Lord Grey had first proposed, *appointed by the Governor*. The Colonial Legislature was to consist of two chambers.

[3] Published 1869.

always maintained that history proved that our earliest colonists were encouraged by the mother-country to act with entire freedom.] "But perhaps its chief contribution to the re-establishment of constitutional views was Mr. Gladstone's speech on its second reading (May 21, 1852).[1] . . . He said : 'We have not yet arrived in our legislation at a just and normal relation between a Colony and the mother-country—a relation which has been developed in former times. We think of a Colony as something which is to take effect by legislative enactments and by the funds of the people of England. This administrative establishment is the root and trunk around which by degrees a population is to grow, and, according to our modern unhappy phrase, *to be trained to freedom,* and to which in course of time some modicum of free institutions is to be granted. . . . The system which Burke studied when he warned Parliament against the destructive consequences of attempting to establish administrative power over distant dependencies —that sound colonial policy—reached its climax in what I may call Tory times. In 1662 the Charter of Rhode Island was granted, the most remarkable of all for its enlarged and liberal spirit. At this day it is considered monstrous that Colonies should have free local jurisdiction even for local purposes. . . .'" As to the detail of the New Zealand Constitution Act, "I cannot do better," continues Adderley, "than quote Mr. Gladstone's criticism, agreeing as I do with his general approval of the measure, which indeed was based on a draft I drew up under the guidance of Gibbon Wakefield. Condemning the Queen's reserve of native protection [i.e. by the Home Government], Mr. Gladstone said : ' Instead of telling the Colony to look for no help from us unless they maintained the principles of justice, we foolishly told them not to meddle with the relations

[1] In a diary for 1852 Mr. Adderley notes : "*May* 21.—New Zealand second reading. Molesworth opposed—I defended. Gladstone's great colonial speech at midnight. I too lazy and unprepared—might with a little preparation have spoken better and more effectually. *May* 22.—Molesworth promised me not to press opposition to New Zealand Bill in House."

8

between ourselves and the natives—that that was a matter for Parliament.'" To this clause of reservation Adderley in after-years attributed the disastrous disturbances which at a later date agitated New Zealand.

Godley, in New Zealand, received a copy of the New Constitution with mixed feelings. He wrote (September 1852): "On the whole it is workable, and, as coming from our friends, we will try to make the best of it thankfully and cheerfully." But he was dissatisfied with the clause of reservation which had been added to the "Hams draft" at Governor Sir George Grey's instigation, and contrary to the wishes of its originators. He wrote more graciously on November 11 : "You will see we have been meeting to thank you and others for your activity and zeal on our behalf. The Constitution Bill will do very well, and the people are as keen as possible about working it."

We promoters of Canterbury Colony in New Zealand being in money difficulties [afterwards escaped from] with the old Company—as to its claim and Crown-debts—and shipowners, we sent out Sewell[1] to settle things on the spot, and he took office there.

[1] Henry Sewell (1807-1879) came of a family remarkable for ability. Became first Premier of New Zealand on the introduction of responsible government, but resigned a week later because the Crown refused to allow the Ministry full responsibility.

CHAPTER XX

FEBRUARY 1852

CAPE SCHEMES

I HAD other colonial work—a Cape scheme—being kindly helped by the veteran Lord Lyndhurst.

Adderley was constantly interviewing Sir John Pakington at the Colonial Office about this Cape scheme.

February 28.—Told him of Sewell's scheme at his service if Lord Lyndhurst and D—— approved. Called on Lord Lyndhurst with Gladstone, and down to Pakington at Colonial Office.

Gladstone wrote :

6, CARLTON GARDENS,
February 23, 1852.

MY DEAR ADDERLEY,

I have seen Lord Lyndhurst and was delighted with my interview. A more lucid and sound exposition of principles of colonial policy I have never heard than came spontaneously from his lips. We went rapidly over most of the points of the subject, and I think he is much inclined, by way of commencement, to urge *emphatically* on the new Secretary of State the disallowance of the Ordinances, the giving an immediate start to the popular Legislature, and the reference of the frontier question to them, while looking forward hereafter to the interposition of Parliament, and contemplating, with much favour, Mr. Sewell's plan of an Union or Association of Colonial Settlements."

The Kaffir war delayed the introduction of self-government at the Cape, for which letters-patent had been issued by the Crown. Lord Lyndhurst said that a grant of this kind cannot be revoked. Nevertheless, while the Kaffir War was raging it was impossible to carry out constitutional reforms. Meanwhile, in the House of Commons, feeling ran high on the conduct of the war by the late Administration. Sir William Molesworth [1] reviewed the past frontier policy at the Cape, and maintained that, if the colonists were left to manage their own territory, our military expenditure for South Africa would be reduced to the cost of the garrison of Cape Town. Gladstone took a similar view—the matter of our relations between the colonists and the natives was not to be settled in Downing Street. It was not so with the first settlers in America, who had barbarous nations to deal with, and who saved this country from burdens while they regulated their relations better. Frontier policy should be a local question. Adderley observed that unless the instructions given to General Cathcart [who had been sent out by the late Government to supersede Sir Harry Smith] were qualified by the present Government England would have to bear the expense of another Kaffir war. He asserted that the Cape was ready to take the matter into their own hands, and to carry on all the wars which they undertake. The debate fell inevitably into abuse of Lord Grey, manfully defended by his quondam juvenile Under-Secretary, Mr. Frederick Peel. " There was nobody else who could defend Lord Grey," said Mr. Henry Drummond, that loyal friend and redoubtable opponent, who at last had the opportunity for which

[1] April 5, 1852.

he had so long thirsted of eulogising his gallant friend, Sir Harry Smith, and abusing the Government. They had the opinion of the Duke of Wellington, who was a competent judge, "*not a mere Downing Street man*"—the Duke of Wellington giving his testimony to the character of Sir Harry Smith, and censuring the despatch recalling him! Much of Mr. Drummond's "fierce onslaught" on Lord Grey was, perhaps fortunately, inaudible to the House owing to the hurried and inarticulate manner of speaking habitual to him; but, "Oh, it was a dirty business!" were words unpalatable to the Opposition.

Adderley wrote to *The Times*, April 15, 1852 : " I beg to add the testimony of leading colonists to your well-expressed imperial view of the future requirements of South African policy in your article of the 8th."

The Times article had said : " We can only take this fresh occasion to suggest that a 'policy' so fraught with certain loss and probable disaster should be exchanged without delay for such a positive course as the Legislature and country may determine on. . . . Lord John Russell has evidently a leaning to the 'claims of the aborigines,' to the extent, indeed, of providing one savage with protection from the onslaughts of another. We have no desire to quarrel with the promptings of abstract philanthropy, but we must earnestly recommend that, if the policy is to be confirmed, and if the Caffres are to have the preference over the colonists, the 'system' should be at once carried out by the bodily removal from South Africa of the settlers who have been encouraged to go there. If . . . British settlers are of less account than black bush-rangers—if an aboriginal or an actual possession is superior to that title by which old populations have hitherto colonised the world— then we have no business, and can certainly make no profit, in South Africa at all. And [satirical crescendo] as the feelings of the savages cannot possibly be more effectually gratified than by sweeping every white man from the land, why should we not indulge their fancies and terminate our own obligation at one and the same time by transferring the colonists elsewhere, especially since we could send out a 'carriage and four' for each European in these parts at less cost than that of a single 'war.' This would be fairly carrying out the Exeter Hall system without injury to the colonists, and with great saving to our-selves [!]. 'Africa for the African' would then be a realised vision, and Sandali might be crowned sovereign of a new black Empire, like Faustin at St. Domingo!"

Adderley continues in his letter to *The Times* in allusion to this article : " Lord John Russell's notion of ' defending' our colonists is met by caricatures on their part, which I receive by this mail, expressive of their utmost contempt, in return for our meddling and mischievous though costly defence of them from enemies, stirred up by our own egregious folly. Lord John's philanthropic anxiety, on the other hand, to keep native races safe from his cruel countrymen, settled in their neighbourhood, posi-tively disappears, buried in the absurdity of its present illustration (the seventh in half a century) of wholesale devastation, and a British army en-gaged for fifteen months in butchery and plunder. The colonists aloof, look on aghast at the disastrous results of English experiments in their affairs, fearing only lest their Colony may not hold out against such abuses, until the long-desired advent of self-government, when, these follies over, they will, like their neighbours the ' rebel' Boers, be allowed themselves to maintain their lands, without cost or bloodshed, as thriving and contented British subjects.

" France laughs at us now (see the *Revue des Deux Mondes*, last January) as wholly forfeiting all right to criticise their colonising blunders or their barbarous exploits on the same continent, yet fairly allowing that the art of colonising once was ours, when our colonies vigorously grew up into in-dustrious communities, able not only to defend themselves, but 'to furnish us alike with military as with commercial aid.

" The war indeed is not over, but may at any time be patched up as well as any former one, the last treaty of peace having been made *valde flagrante bello*; nor, as you say, is there any method or analogy to rules possible in the preposterous farce of our present dealings with these savages.

" The first thing needful is the completion of the Constitution. This, it seems, Mr. Montague is now desperately determined on preventing with all the energy of one who sees his death in the dreaded catastrophe. Petitions have come for his removal. Through his organ, *The Monitor*, he has not scrupled to sow jealousies between the Dutch and English, and to stir up strife, for his one great object, between the white and coloured races, but hitherto, I hope, without much effect. The draught Ordinances have been read a second time, and are now committed in the whole Council, which was so reconstructed by Mr. Montague as to put the Governor and his officials in a minority to his unofficial partisans.

" The Colony, in despair, petitions the Imperial Parliament to pass the Ordinances itself, as was recommended at first by high authorities both here and at the Cape. . . . Mr. Fairbairn and his colleagues have indeed received clearly enough, at length, that justification for their late proceedings which the ignorance and apathy of the English public on such subjects at first denied them.

" What makes immediate action on our part necessary now is the obvious wisdom of calling upon the Cape representatives to suggest, on behalf of the Colony, a present adjustment and future plans, on the conclusion of what is called the war. They should say what they are ready to do. The Imperial Power has only to sanction their proposal, and grant them requisite powers to carry it out. No doubt the Colony will occupy all the territory over which we have assumed powers. To discuss what frontier may seem best to philanthropists or political empirics at home, is as idle as it would have been eighty years ago to discuss the propriety of passing the Alleghany Mountains, or, of later years, to debate the 'mission' of the Mississippi as a national barrier.

"But we cannot afford to have another Lord Grey amusing himself in the name of the Queen and country with such questions as these. What the Colony is ready to occupy, let them ask Her Majesty to give them powers to take and defend in her name. The Boers have proved their ability, and the very first prospect of such sound self-acting policy being adopted, has already brought back those 'rebels' to Her Majesty's allegiance. What an epoch of revival in the success of British colonisation may not its entire realisation prove!

"But in writing the despatches of the 14th of this month, Sir J. Pakington has an awful responsibility on his hands—to choose between this and another chapter of English interference and colonial despair."

AUTOBIOGRAPHICAL NOTES (*continued*). 1852

My other public work related to criminals old and young; improved prisons; and Cobbler Ellis's Reformatory in Birmingham, who set up spectacle-making by criminal boys, and I offered ten acres at Saltley for a more regular institution. This Ellis, a shoemaker, was a most remarkable genius in his way. His influence over wild boys and his philosophy in dealing with them taught me many a deep lesson—simple as all truth, and of touching interest. [See chapter on Saltley.] I wrote a good deal in *The Morning Herald* about criminal and destitute children, and worked at getting a new county gaol on improved system at Warwick. I was in this year engaged in London, with Sidney Herbert, in most interesting work in St.-George's-in-the-East. My "locked book," however, is full of dissatisfaction with myself. I felt also a want of sympathy with my party, and preference for the Peelites.

CHAPTER XXI

1852 (*continued*)

ABANDONS PROTECTION

LORD DERBY's General Election came off in July. I had, in February, demurred to standing if *Protection* was not renounced, but Lords Talbot and Harrowby pressed me to say nothing and go on. In my address, however [to North Staffordshire constituents], I now abandoned Protection, and was threatened with opposition, besides Buller [Whig], of a Protectionist candidate against me. I got in after all without a contest.

Adderley's conversion to Free Trade, or rather, his surrender of a policy of Protection, was thus hailed by *The Times* in a jubilant leading article (April 15, 1852): "Here we have before us a surrender made by a distinguished man. Mr. Adderley, Member for North Staffordshire and a candidate for that constituency, repeats what he said at Burton early last recess, that 'Protection has become, whether rightly or wrongly, so odious in the eyes of the great body of the nation that it would be unwise to accept it any longer even if it could be obtained. . . . Some say it is necessary to postpone the decision of this opinion till the approaching appeal to the country has more clearly tested the national feeling. . . . For my own part I consider that the

national feeling is already amply tested. I believe the earlier the feeling is avowed the better, and I deprecate such a question being needlessly repeated on the part of the landed gentry, after the national feeling, be it right or wrong, is so fully known. . . . The landed gentry will provoke just as much animosity whether they ask little or much; they will get neither little nor much, but as long as they ask anything at all in the way of Protection, they will not obtain a hearing for other or more attainable demands, and they will lose the last chance of redress."
"It is important to add" (says *The Times*) "that Mr. Adderley supposes his views on the subject 'to coincide in the main with the opinions held by Lord Derby, and certainly prevalent among his party.' There is, however, a 'saving clause,' a 'lingering glance,' a hesitatory step, as the painful renunciation is delivered—slight though it be. Mr. Adderley still seems to think it possible that at some future day, under some new phase of British character, some change of circumstances, not to say some new conditions of existence, the industrial people of this country may spontaneously and imperiously demand a tax on all food and may tumultuously prevent the arrival of foreign supplies. Such a dream must certainly have flitted through the writer's imagination when he says: 'At all events, *until the nation changes its mind* on the subject and ceases to retain its present repugnance to Protective duties, I for one will not seek that kind of boon to a suffering class of the community which would only more deeply injure them. . . . Whatever other mode there may be for an adjustment of unequal taxation, it appears to me that those at least must be abandoned which have the tendency in any degree to raise the price of food.'"
Adderley's pronouncement was in accordance with that of his leaders. "Queen Victoria's Letters" tell us (March 30, 1852): "Lord Derby is quite prepared to drop Protection, as he knows the elections will bring a Free Trade though a Conservative majority." Moreover, it was well known that

Disraeli,[1] who had likened the agricultural interest to a cast-off mistress who makes herself troublesome to her late protector, had little scruple about abandoning her altogether. Adderley had a more tender conscience, and never ceased to hope some remedies might be found for the grievances of a class which were largely represented among his constituents. The Queen's Speech indeed, on the opening of Parliament in November, showed most uneasy qualms,[2] which were but decent in a Tory Ministry. It ran: "If you should be of opinion that recent legislation, in contributing to this happy result [namely, the generally improved condition of the industrial classes], has at the same time inflicted unavoidable injury on certain important interests, I recommend you dispassionately to consider how far it may be practical equably to mitigate that injury, and to enable the industry of the country to meet successfully that unrestrained competition to which Parliament in its wisdom has decided that it should be subjected."

The following extracts are given from letters addressed by Mr. Adderley to his wife at the time of the meeting of Parliament, and a few days before the funeral of the Duke of Wellington, whose death had occurred two months earlier. Political affairs were in a state of great confusion and uncertainty, which was to culminate at the end of the year in the resignation of the Derby Ministry, after their nine months' tenure of office. In this state of popular excitement even Nature seems to have added to the general sense of insecurity by a sharp shock of earthquake, felt all over England, which,

[1] "While his colleagues feel that in the giving up of Protection they break the last link which binds them to political life, Mr. Disraeli regards the emancipation from a desperate cause as the first condition to success in his future political career" (*Times*, November 10, 1852).

[2] "There is no question that a Protectionist Ministry has at this moment a bitter and distasteful draught to drink to the dregs, and drink it they must; the only question is whether they will prolong the nauseous sensation by repeated sips, or whether they will gulp down the whole decoction at once" (*Times*, November 10, 1852).

if it caused no serious damage, shook the nerves of the most apathetic.

HOUSE OF COMMONS,
Wednesday (about November 10, 1852).

What on earth the enemy will do to-morrow, *chi lo sa?* But Lord Hatherton, who was with me in the train and wound up by an affectionate invitation to you and me to Teddesley, told me he had seen the principal Whigs, and no attack was coming from them. Cobden will perhaps try to make her Majesty speak plainer against Protection, and cry Free Trade *for ever.* . . . The Ministers have asked me to speak for them to-morrow, and to go to the Treasury in the morning to take my part in the play. I suppose I must. . . . All sorts of rumours ; and poor Lord Normanby [Ambassador to France] *in extremis.*[1] *Earthquakes in divers places,* as you will see in the newspapers. Lewisham[2] says the earthquake shook fat Bagot out of bed at Patshull [Lord Dartmouth's]. It was felt all across the sea at Dublin. He gives a good account of his nursery. The Guernseys[3] came up in great force. I shall take my privilege of a ticket to see the [Duke's] lying-in-state privately on Friday. . . .

November 12.

I backed up Dizzy yesterday with, I think, the best attempt I ever made at speaking, and I have got proportionate thanks and praise since ; but I consider the evening fatal to the Government, and that they have not a month to live. What comes next, who can say ? The Duke of Newcastle is very bumptious and very angry—positively turns his back on me. We want stronger hands at the helm in these days. . . . This hostile move of Villiers, John [Russell] and Gladstone [against Disraeli, Chancellor of the Exchequer] will keep us busily employed ; I think till the second week in December. I have seen the lying-in-state. It was magnificent.

[1] He survived nine years.
[2] Afterwards fifth Earl of Dartmouth.
[3] Lord Guernsey, afterwards sixth Earl of Aylesford.

A few days later he writes to his wife :

November 15, 1852.

I hope to stay with you till Tuesday the 22nd, when Villiers' great attack comes on, but I will not desert you for the sake of the great pageant [Duke of Wellington's funeral], only for business, which threatens and gets most serious.   But I am glad Georgie [1] will see the greatest pageant of the age, and *well* from Northumberland House.[2]   Lord Derby's meeting went off well, but his Budget on the 26th will be most critical, being a very large and complicated measure, and with it he must break down.   Dizzy has just pronounced a grand flowing oration with some fine passages on the Duke.

On December 17 Lord Derby resigned.   Lord Aberdeen became Prime Minister at the head of a coalition Government, Whigs and Peelites uniting. Among them Sir James Graham, Gladstone, the Duke of Newcastle, Sidney Herbert, Lord Granville, and Sir William Molesworth were all in greater or less degree friends of Adderley.   He remained nominally a follower of Lord Derby; but, as Lord Aberdeen told the Queen, "The Derbyites would be very quiet, and many of them very friendly."

[1] His sister-in-law, afterwards the Honourable Mrs. Newdigate.
[2] Lord Norton told a story of Sergeant Mereweather (possibly he meant his son) laying a bet at the Carlton that he would be present in St. Paul's at the funeral of the Duke of Wellington, although the procession was on its way and he had no ticket.   He got on very well till he was close to the Cathedral, when he was stopped with the words, " No one can pass here except a general officer."   " And who, sir, told you I was not a general officer? " was the reply.   He passed the cordon and won his bet. See " Grant Duff Diaries," May 24, 1897, for a slightly different account of Lord Norton's conversation.

CHAPTER XXII

CREATION AND DEVELOPMENT OF SALTLEY

BEFORE proceeding further with these records in chronological order, it seems appropriate here to interpose a sketch of Mr. Adderley's great work at Saltley (in the suburbs of Birmingham, some ten miles from Hams), which, in his youth, had a population of 400 (chiefly railway carriage builders), and at his death a population of 27,000.

It has been well said that Saltley would have been a terrible place by this time if it had fallen into the hands of a mere money-maker. When, at the age of twenty-one, Mr. Adderley came into possession of his property at Saltley—then unbuilt on—he tells us: " I anticipated the coming population, and provided church, parsonage, and ground around as the centre of the place."

In the course of years he spent over £70,000 [1] in providing, endowing, and supporting places of worship in Saltley alone.[2] He began by choosing a site for the church on the top of a hill, long before there were any houses near. .He next laid out the plan of the streets, which are unusually wide throughout, without the possibility of their degenerating into slums. The plans were provided in 1837 at Sir Robert Peel's suggestion by Lord

[1] This he states in a draft letter to Mr. Joseph Chamberlain, found among Lord Norton's papers.
[2] Besides building and endowing the Vicarage of Saltley, he gave the site for St. Saviour's School, St. John's Mission Room, St. Luke's Mission Church, and the principal part of St. Mark's, Washwood Heath.

Lincoln, then Commissioner of Woods and Forests, afterwards Duke of Newcastle. Although the houses are in the unsightly Early Victorian architecture, and the idea of a garden city was of course then unknown, Saltley is a good example of what may be avoided by planning a town before beginning to build—the excellent German method which is now likely to be more adopted in this country. As a landlord he was ever ready to do much more than the law required in the way of making new roads, etc.

Among his benefactions was the gift to Birmingham of "Adderley Park." Though not large, it was the first park given to Birmingham, and the project was his own. Of the Adderley Park Museum and Reading-room, which he gave subsequently and which now belong to the Birmingham Corporation, mention will be made later. He was one of the original promoters of Saltley Training College in 1847, and with Lord Lyttelton (its first President) he was practically its joint founder, giving freely both in land and money for its establishment.

"It would be difficult to exaggerate the greatness of the debt which Saltley College owes to him," says one of the College reports, "for his earnest sympathy, unstinted generosity, and fostering care through a long series of years"; and under his Presidency[1] the College occupied the highest position among kindred establishments in this country.

He himself frequently declared that no other institution with which he was connected was closer to his heart; although, in another and very different direction, there was certainly one which occupied a large share of his affection and concern. This was the Saltley Reformatory, which may be said to have been among the first institutions of the kind in this country,[2] and of which he was himself the

[1] On the death of Lord Lyttelton, in 1876, Lord Norton became President, and during the following twenty-nine years of his life never failed to be present at the annual reunions of the College.

[2] Mr. J. Barwick Baker and Mr. Bengough had already opened the Children's Friend School at Hardwick, Gloucestershire, in March 1852. The original of the Saltley Reformatory began at Ryland Road a few months later.

principal benefactor. The small beginning of this enterprise opened in a little house in the Ryland Road, whither Mr. Sturge, a well-known philanthropist and member of the Society of Friends, induced Ellis, a shoemaker, to come from Westminster in the summer of 1852.

In December 1851 Adderley had been instrumental in forming a conference on juvenile crime, and in 1852 he introduced a Bill in Parliament to establish Reformatory Schools. In the meantime "Cobbler Ellis" began to receive young boys on the completion of their sentences of imprisonment in the Birmingham gaol, and "with his ready sagacity set them to work diligently at spectacle-making, shoemaking, carpentering, or other occupations for which they had a turn." In the spring of 1853 he removed with his pupils to a house at Saltley built by Mr. Adderley for the purpose, with workshops and dormitories, and with some acres of land attached for garden work. Such was the slender origin of a great undertaking. The institution was not to be in any sense a prison, and it was supported solely by voluntary subscriptions till the passing of Lord Palmerston's Act in 1854, when a valuable addition to the funds was secured by a grant from the Treasury. But it is still to a great extent " voluntary."

Mr. Adderley had a deep respect for " Cobbler Ellis," for the saintliness, simplicity, and originality of his character.

" I work upon their moral faculties through their affections," said Ellis of the Reformatory boys ; " I recognise them as my children, and they look upon me as their father ; and the latent power of their souls being brought into existence, there is every feeling that I can expect from a child towards me. I have seen that all that they did was to strive to know my will, and that will is their law." Again he would say : " I do not take them to make shoes and spectacles only. I take them to give them consciences."

Of late years Lord Norton used to relate a story of Ellis and the boys, in the early days of Saltley

Reformatory, which is thus recorded by the late Mr. Augustus Hare:[1]

Ellis said: "Many people say that the boys are fools, but they are philosophers. They reason at night. I overhear them; I hear them reasoning as to whether there is a God. There was one boy especially who denied this, who laughed at all who believed. One day this boy had a parcel to take to Sir Moses Montefiore. Now the boys may steal, but however much they do that, when they are entrusted with anything they are most tenacious to fulfil their trust. This boy only knew of Sir Moses by the popular name of the 'King of the Jews,' and all day long he asked his way to him in vain. He could not find him anywhere. Evening closed in, and he was faint with hunger and fatigue. He was quite sinking, but at the last gasp cried, 'O God, if there be a God, help me.' Immediately a policeman rushed at him. 'What have you got there, you young rascal? What's in that parcel?—something you've been stealing, I suppose.' 'No 'tain't, it's a parcel for the King of the Jews, and I can't find him.' 'Why, you young fool, it's Sir Moses Montefiore you mean; I can show you where to find him.' That night the boys were philosophising as usual, declaring that there was no God, there couldn't be, when the boy who had taken the parcel shouted, 'Stop that rubbish, you fellows; there *is* a God, and I know it; and as for you, you're just as much able to judge of God as a worm is of me.'"

The celebrated French Reformatory establishment of Monsieur de Metz[2] at Mettray, which had been founded nearly fifteen years earlier than any institution of the kind in England, Lord Norton, or rather Mr. Adderley, regarded with admiration as an exemplar of Reformatory schools in this country, and he studied the Mettray statistics and reports.[3] He sent them to Lord Robert Cecil (Lord Salisbury), who was characteristically critical, and wrote:

[1] "Story of My Life," vol. vi. p. 406.
[2] Formerly a judge at Paris.
[3] Mr. Adderley visited Mettray himself some years later.

9

" I return the Reformatory documents. . . . They are very interesting.   One only wishes one could see through a Frenchman's eternal *couleur de rose*. It's all too good to be quite true.   I cannot find out that Mettray pays any rates or taxes.   If so, what a delightful place France must be ! "   But Mettray was doing and had done a wonderful work.   Lord Norton used to relate that during the Revolution of 1848, when France was in a state of anarchy and all the Government schools were closed, at Mettray, without walls, without coercion, there was not a sign of insubordination—not a child attempted to run away.

Lord Norton was untiring in his exertions to get Reformatories put under Education Authority, and to minimise the penal character of such establishments.   His views are only now being carried into practical politics.   Among his principles in regard to the treatment of young criminals two were prominent, namely that education, not punishment, was the first consideration ; and that on no account were the boys ever to be reminded of their original fall into crime.   When a well-meaning bishop whom Lord Norton had brought to Saltley Reformatory began his speech, " Now, boys, you've all had a tumble," Lord Norton is described as having been wild with suppressed annoyance, which exploded later in private conversation with the bishop.

His own addresses to the boys were always striking and practical, and, as the boys' references to them in after-life indicated, made a deep impression.   On one occasion a batch of Reformatory boys were on the point of departure for Canada, and, as his invariable custom was, he had the boys brought before him in order to give them advice, and to exhort them to maintain their good character and keep up the credit of the school.   He had a profound admiration for the character of General Wolfe, and when he learned that the boys would land at Quebec, he questioned them about its history, and was particularly pleased when some of the boys answered intelligently.   He then graphically related to them the incident of the reading of Gray's Elegy by General Wolfe on the eve of the attack, and his remarkable aspiration in regard to its authorship. Many a time he invited the whole school over to Hams for an afternoon's recreation. He used to refer with pride to one old boy named Peach, who went out to South Africa and rose to be an influential man; and he deeply mourned when Mr. Peach, with twelve of his family, was drowned in the ill-fated *Drummond Castle*. Another who, Lord Norton used to relate, raised himself in South Africa to a position in which he was able to lend his carriage to one of our leading generals in the Zulu war, owed his early training to Saltley Reformatory.

Although desirous that the boys should receive an education such as should start them well in the world and make them good and useful citizens, he did not favour extras or accomplishments which, he said, were out of the reach of the children of honest working parents. For this reason he at first spoke contemptuously of a brass band of Reformatory boys, saying it would only "teach the boys to blow their guts out." But afterwards he used good-naturedly to ask for it to play to him, and on one occasion, when the boys played so vigorously that the noise was absolutely deafening and it seemed as if they would literally do as he expected, he merely remarked, " Well, boys, if your *pianissimo* is as good as your *fortissimo* you are the finest lot of players I ever heard."

To a system of cramming, in education, with a view to mere exhibition of knowledge, he had an especial dislike. To the education of the character accompanying the education of the mind he ever attached the highest importance—"the sum of the whole work," he called this; and it was with this feeling that when a certain peeress of the blue-stocking order had been for some time impressing upon him the necessity above all things of cultivating the intellect, he gave the following retort. Said the lady : " If we are really to progress, we must train the *intellect*! *intellect*!! *intellect*!!! " " Madam," replied Lord Norton, losing all patience, "a great intellectual force—the greatest I know of in this world—is the devil!"

These cursory remarks on Lord Norton's constant occupation and interest in the development of Saltley may appropriately be concluded by a quotation from a letter to the editor from Lord Norton's son, James, "Father" Adderley, the present Vicar of Saltley:

"My father," he says, "was very broadminded, and practically gave the first appointment to the living of Saltley into the hands of the Dissenters, who chose a very Low Churchman. He said he would otherwise have lost to the Church the whole of the railway-carriage builders who constituted the first importation to Saltley and whose manager was a very earnest and religious man, a Baptist. It was not till the last few months of his life that he had the appointment to the living again. Even then he would not give it to his son until the people of Saltley assured him that they wanted him. . . . My father was devoted to the spiritual work; I shall never forget his prayer over me when we started off to my institution: 'O God, bless what we are doing for Saltley.' . . . He was always sending cheques to the clergy for all sorts of little things. Bishop Gore said of him: 'He is the only rich man I know who does not wait to be asked, but *asks to be allowed to give.*' "

CHAPTER XXIII

1853

VISITS MANCHESTER

I BEGAN the year lionising Manchester with its first bishop, Prince Lee, of Birmingham and Rugby scholastic fame, and the warm-hearted, generous, puzzle-headed Bracebridge.[1] I recollect the remark of our lionising magnate. "We are all like fish here, the big ones swallowing up the smaller. Newly improved machinery supersedes old mills, and fortunes are made and unmade in a day." I had had a visit to Manchester before I got into Parliament, when Cobden good-naturedly showed me over his print mills at Chorley in the neighbourhood. Waiting at the station on my return he took me up the bank to look at some fields full of weeds and thistles, as is usual in land just about to be built on, and he said: " I have shown you my manufactures, *there is yours*; if we carried on ours as you landlords do yours, we should not expect a profit, nor dare to ask for Protection to get one." There was an old spinning-jenny in his mills which he kept for curiosity to show the

---

[1] The philanthropist who, in the Crimean War, took out Miss Nightingale and her nursing establishment.

advance in machinery invention "since Peel was a red-haired boy running about a cotton-mill."

Lord Norton used to relate of Cobden after his great exertions previous to 1846, how Cobden's doctor having ordered him to go abroad for a change, Cobden said to Adderley, "I have done with *corn*, and am going to *grass*."

After work in schools and gaols in Warwick and Staffordshire during January and February we took up our abode at the opening of the Session at 106, Eaton Square. The chief public interest to me this year was the national preparation against the possibility of foreign invasion, and the rousing of the *Volunteer spirit* for the enlargement of our forces and defence. The camp formed at Chobham gave me new ideas; and the Speaker, Shaw Lefevre [afterwards Lord Eversley]—keen about military matters as he showed himself galloping with his Hampshire Yeomanry in rank entire—introduced the practice of special accommodation for both Houses of Parliament to see the new Reviews.[1] With him and his quasi-staff of *militaires*, men and ladies, I rode along with the gathering host, some sunburnt with real service, and saw ten thousand men occupying a mile's length of the heath, and, at the sound of a gun, raise their tents simultaneously like a fairy town. I got with General Evans,[2] who commanded the left wing, and saw his A.D.C.'s tumbling in the hidden ruts

---

[1] "*June* 14, 1853. Off at 7. Breakfasted with Lord Hardinge (Lord Howe and two Ladies Curzon, Lord Worcester, Col. Colville, Wynne, Lord de Ros, and Lord C. Wellesley), rode on to Camp, Chobham Common; saw ten thousand march and pitch tents; stayed six hours inspecting" (Diary).
[2] Sir De Lacy Evans.

as they galloped on their errands. There was also a naval review at Spithead, where Queen, Lords, and Commons passed in successive ships between the contending fires, and the Speaker anticipated many writs for vacancies to be moved next day!

I spoke frequently in the House this year, chiefly on Colonial subjects; on the Canadian Clergy Reserves, which I agreed to leave to the Colonial Legislature; on the Cape Constitution; and on the India debates. I opposed the abandonment of the Orange River Sovereignty. Next year I tried again, taking Roundell Palmer's opinion [afterwards first Earl of Selborne] whether the Queen *could* absolve her subjects from allegiance.

In 1847 Sir Harry Smith had re-established British rule over all the country between the Rivers Kei and Keiskamma called British Kaffraria, and treated it as a sort of imperial advanced guard, sheltering the Cape Colony from Kaffir incursion. In 1850 he took upon himself to proclaim the Queen's Sovereignty over the Dutch settlers beyond the Orange. "It was resolved in 1853," wrote Sir Charles Adderley some years later, "to abandon the Orange River territory to the Dutch, a resolution which I stood up alone to resist in the House of Commons, and which is now regretted by both the parties concerned. . . . As to the general policy of abandonment, it was characteristically asserted to be simply a home affair, and thus the Cape need not even be consulted."[1] This abandonment of the Sovereignty has since been termed "one of the most imprudent acts ever committed"; and it was a matter of great interest to Lord Norton, after the lapse of half a century,

[1] "Sir Charles Adderley's Review of Lord Grey's Policy," etc., 1869.

when Great Britain once more resumed authority over the Orange River territory, to look back upon the part he had played in 1853 and 1854.

I took my own line on the Kaffir frontier war; I was against Australian Transportation; I was on the Slave Trade Select Committee.

But I took greatest interest in better treatment of young criminals, and introduced legislation on the subject, drafting the Bill which Lord Palmerston took up, and carried next year as the " Youthful Offenders Act." [1]

I went with Sir John Pakington and Colonel Jebb to inspect Parkhurst, the original attempt at Prison Reformatory, which naturally failed as uniting two ideas.

Lord Norton was from the first opposed to the combination of prisons and schools; up to the end of his life he was frequently speaking in the House of Lords in the direction of entire *separation of punishment and education.*

I took an active part in substituting for the old county gaol at Warwick a prison on the new panopticon plan, under great opposition; and attempted, though unsuccessfully, to get a district pauper school for Meriden Union, which, though it would have been a great improvement on the education of children in workhouses, is now much further improved by boarding out pauper children with foster parents at their homes.

[1] "*June* 2, 1853. All day concocting draft of Juvenile Criminals Bill; Lord Shaftesbury gave me his Bill, to make it agree with mine." "*June* 3. Finished off draft, and sent it, by Lord Palmerston's leave, to Foreign Office to print."

A letter from Gladstone to Adderley, dated July 14, 1853, bears on this subject. "I may say that I am sure that the object is one which the Government will view with favour, even apart from the special claims which your munificence, and that of others, established in the Warwickshire case. We shall have every motive for starting in concert with you, and letting yours serve as the model instance."

My paternal friend, Sir Thomas Acland, said, "You've talked less and done more this Session."

I wrote a good deal this year—*e.g.* a "Review of Lord Grey's Work on Colonial Policy" for *Fraser's Magazine*; I revived my "Essay on Human Happiness" for Blackader, who asked me to let him publish a new edition for a series of his own.

I began *poor* visitings in London this season, not very successfully. I took some pains in the establishment of Scripture-readers in Warwickshire. I attended a Reformatory Conference at Edinburgh in November; after which we went to Paris, and I carried on Reformatory studies there also, by a visit with Lord Ebrington [afterwards Earl Fortescue] and Bracebridge to Petit-Bourg, Monsieur Attier's imitation of Mettrai.[1]

My motto in London work was "Ad finem respice"—more constant aim at life's ultimate account. I thought of my Reformatory boys—"shall we meet in heaven?" Many of that strange natural genius, shoemaker Ellis' stories of his experiences with these little outcasts were striking and touching.

I think my feeling was one of safety and satis-

---

[1] "*June* 2, 1853.—Julia to Lady Cowley's box at the *Théâtre français* with Lord and Lady Ebrington."

faction in constant work such as fell in my way in Parliament or at home. This always seemed to me, if under a sense of duty and service and not for one's own distinction or display, the realisation of religious life to final account. To fill up the devil's opening for leading one wrong tests principle, and gives the best associations in life. . . .

My Parliamentary career now led to much society of the best kind. Both dinner-giving and receiving filled up our London season. Julia often took her sisters to balls.

In June Godley returned from New Zealand after three and a half years' absence—the founder of our Canterbury Church Colony, which has thriven and has collected many of the best ʼEnglish families amongst its settlers, more than any Colony since our old American States. We gave him a grand reception at Greenwich in August.

This year was plagued with storms and long rains, leading to a cold and failing harvest. The opening calamity at harvest was the loss of the largest oak [1] in the church avenue.

The oak avenue leading from Hams Hall to Lea Marston Church is the only one remaining of three avenues planted in the reign of Charles I. by Sir Charles Adderley, the King's Equerry.[1] A large and very beautifully proportioned cross standing near the churchyard at the end of this oak avenue, beyond which the avenue changes to one of Scotch firs (alluded to as "evergreen"), is the subject of some verses written by Mr. Adderley on a winter's day. The influence of Keble, who was a friend of

[1] Mentioned in Neal's "Views of County Seats." Mr. Augustus Hare erroneously supposed this avenue to be a remnant of the Forest of Arden ("Story of My Life").

THE OAK AVENUE AT HAMS LEADING TO THE CROSS.

p. 138]

THE CROSS AT HAMS AND LEA MARSTON CHURCH.

Adderley, and one for whose character and poetry
he had the highest admiration, is traceable in the
following lines :

    With withered leaves and wasted limbs
      The aged Oaken Way,
    So faintly cheered by sunset gleams,
      Speaks but of Earth's decay.

    But where, beyond, the CROSS is seen
      The hallowed dead we lay—
    The Way thenceforth in evergreen
      Smiles with eternal day.

    .   .   .   .   .   .

CHAPTER XXIV

1854

DOMESTIC EVENTS

THIS year began with heavy snow, drifting up traffic and ending in frozen floods. We dug our way through snow-drifts to Mildred Hartopp's [daughter of Sir William Hartopp, of Four Oaks] wedding with Sir Francis Scott [of Great Barr]. Arrived too late, but saw the handsome bride at *déjeuner* and the start afterwards.

Among domestic notes in Diary, March 29, 1854:

" John Hartopp [eldest son of Sir William] came over to Hams. He, under orders to start immediately for the war, asked me to act for him in negotiations regarding his engagement with Miss Howard—Heneage to act on her part." [Afterwards the late Sir John Cradock-Hartopp, Bart., 17th Lancers, who on his return in 1855 (after distinguishing himself in the Crimea) married Miss Howard, great-niece of Bernard Edward, twelfth Duke of Norfolk.]

We put up till after Easter at 9, Grosvenor Street, expecting an election; but then took 84, Eaton Square, for the rest of the Session. I introduced the Manchester and Salford Bill, the first for an education local rate. The second reading caused the longest debate ever known on a Private Bill [see Hansard, cxxx.]; Lord Palmerston· carried my "Juvenile Bill" of last Session as the "Youthful Offenders Act." I spoke in Poor Law debate, and Colonial Clergy Disabilities, and Middlesex Industrial School. In May I spoke and voted for the Government's Scotch Education Bill against my party, who defeated it on the second reading as secular and anti-Kirk connection. I also voted against my party, supporting Gladstone's Exchequer Bonds for the war, and I opposed Sir John Pakington on the Canadian Constitution, with nominated Legislative Council [Hansard, cxxxv.]. I thus took a line independent of my party, and unsympathetic with them. [His independence caused him to be called a "Liberal-Conservative" in the "Parliamentary Companion." It was probably the character he now began to acquire which made Disraeli unwilling in after-years to put him in the Cabinet.]

Ministers were in May defeated on the Oaths Bill, by which Lord John Russell meant to admit Jews, and they had other defeats, with which Disraeli taunted them ; but changes only took place in August within the Cabinet.

The great event of the year was the Crimean War, and Napier's fleet sailed for the Baltic in March. I saw [February 20] with Colonel Colville, his old regiment—the Scotch Fusiliers—march out of Birdcage Barracks at seven in the morning past the Queen, with the young Prince of Wales on the balcony at the Palace window [1]—they playing "The

[1] "Queen Victoria's Letters," vol. iii. p. 17 (to King of the Belgians): "The sun rising over the towers of old Westminster

Highland Laddie "—wives and sweethearts among their ranks; the men allowed to smoke, and they kissed feminine relatives as the railway gate shut them in. One third of the regiment fell at the first action, the passage of the Alma. Balaclava and Inkerman ended the year. At the last Heneage Wynne,[1] fell with Cathcart, his general—buried in the same grave. Parliament met in December for war measures.

The opening of the Crystal Palace was a significant event of a new era. It was the Prince Consort's Hyde Park Exhibition, moved and enlarged on a permanent site—Royalty, Ministers, Archbishops, and People inaugurating with prayer a palace for the people greater than the King's.

Our chief domestic event was the birth of my second son[2] [eighth child]. My " locked book " records my great joy and gratitude. I fully believe that the submission with which I thanked God for the last and finest of a succession of daughters was rewarded by the birth of this son, and of the five in all eventually granted.

My work at home this year was establishing a Girls' Reformatory in Birmingham, and proposing, though unsuccessfully for the time, a Boys' Reformatory for Staffordshire at Norton.

My writing work was chiefly for the Editor of *The Spectator* on colonial subjects.

I began my long Chancery suit against Birming-

Abbey—an immense crowd collected. . . . They formed line, presented arms, and then cheered us very heartily. It was a touching and beautiful sight ; many sorrowing friends were there, and one saw the shake of many a hand."

[1] Brother of Mrs. Godley and of Charles Wynne Finch, M.P., of Voelas.

[2] Honourable Arden Adderley, of Fillongley Hall.

ham for fouling the river Tame, which became famous as the precedent for all like restraint on towns.

The river Tame, which for three miles winds through the grounds of Hams and which had been noted for its crystal clearness and for the trout which abounded in it, was horribly polluted by the noxious fluids draining into it from Birmingham (ten miles away). The late Earl of Selborne (the Lord Chancellor) wrote some Latin verses in the visitors' book on this theme, together with the following translation :

In vain strives Vulcan with the Nymphs of Tame :
What though fish haunt no more this favourite
　　stream ?
What though, all envious, Birmingham invades
His still waves, gliding through Hams' ancient
　　stream ?
Yet Nature's charms and every virtue's grace
Cease not to guard the consecrated place.
While men tried worth and pure affections praise,
Fair Hams still lives in Friendship's grateful lays.

The lawsuits with the Birmingham Corporation, though often decided in Lord Norton's favour, did not terminate till nearly fifty years later. " Should the convenience of one man be considered before that of millions ? " exclaimed the Corporation's advocate at the first trial. " Yes," shouted the counsel for the opposition ; " for the grandeur of English law is, that millions may not interfere with the comfort and well-being of a single individual ! " The pollution was eventually partially diverted into a sewage farm five miles in extent.

" The view of the pretty windings of the Tame," says Mr. Augustus Hare ("Story of My Life," vol. vi. p. 406), " recalled [to Lord Norton] the exclamation of a famous landscape gardener when he saw it—' Clever ! ' ' It was not made, it is natural,' said Lord Norton. But no, his friend would not regard it except from a gardening point of view, and ' Clever ' was all he could say."

CHAPTER XXV

1855

ABERDEEN MINISTRY RESIGNS

PARLIAMENT met January 23, after a short recess from the December war meeting. The Aberdeen Ministry resigned on Mr. Roebuck's motion—censuring the Government on the mismanagement of the war, for which the Duke of Newcastle, as Minister for War, was held responsible. The resignation was brought about by the desertion of Lord John Russell, who sent in his resignation to the Queen with surprising suddenness, not wishing to be personally associated with the inadequate conduct of the war, having himself from the first counselled more vigorous measures. Lord Derby, being unable to form a Ministry, Lord John Russell also, Lord Palmerston became Prime Minister and Leader of the House of Commons, the " Peelites " (Sir John Graham, Sidney Herbert, and Gladstone) consenting to remain in his Ministry, on the understanding that Roebuck's motion for a Committee to inquire into the war was to be opposed. Palmerston, however, found he could not oppose it and gave way. The Peelites thereupon resigned (February 23). It was facetiously remarked that, like servants, they had not " served their month, and left their situations at great inconvenience to their mistress." Lord John Russell, who had meanwhile been sent as envoy to Vienna, now returned and became Secretary of State for the Colonies for a short time in Lord Palmerston's Administration. An undated letter from Adderley to his wife was evidently written on the resignation of the Peelites. He considered

Roebuck's attack on the Aberdeen Ministry unpatriotic, in exposing the weakness and disunion at home when the eyes of the whole world were fixed on England in her conduct of the war with Russia, and he feared that Palmerston, now unsupported by the Peelites, would be driven to resign, after his brief tenure of office, and confusion would again reign supreme. The tone of the letter is characteristic as showing the contempt he always had for mere place-seekers, even though they belonged to his own party.

EXTRACT FROM LETTER

" The new Ministry all tumbling to pieces already over this detestable Committee of Roebuck's. They talk of a dissolution and riots. It is a lamentable state of things, and much degrades us in the eyes of the world. Whether it will not break up our alliances, showing such weakness at home, is to be feared. I went to Lord Derby's meeting yesterday, and was disgusted at the chuckling blockheads who are only eager to get into Gladstone's shoes and ape wearing them. Cardwell made a very able speech last night. How much talent will now be stranded! It is their fault for holding aloof so much from their old Conservative party, when they ought to have rejoined. But Lord Derby [in the previous Administration] made hard times for them, insisting on Dizzy being Chancellor of the Exchequer."

At this crisis Lord Palmerston remained at the helm. The "chuckling" among certain of Lord Derby's supporters did not long continue, while Gladstone, who, as we have stated, had with the rest of the Peelites declined to remain in the Government, was succeeded as Chancellor of the Exchequer by Mr. George Cornewall Lewis, for whom Adderley always expressed the highest esteem.[1]

[1] Among Dean Leigh of Hereford's collection of autographs is a letter from Sir G. C. Lewis (August 2, 1856) : " My dear Adderley, I enclose you my autograph in the most authentic shape, and I hope that no member of the Birmingham School will pronounce it a forgery."

10

MEMORANDA (*continued*)

I took part in several debates this year. On the loan to Sardinia to enable her to assist in the war [Hansard, 138]; on Education Debate, Henley approving and seconding me; on Nuisance Removal; on my Juvenile Criminals Bills Amending; and Friendly Societies, serving on Committee; on several Colonial subjects—Newfoundland, New South Wales, and Victoria Government Bills, assisting, as Gladstone publicly acknowledged, the *development of responsible government.*

The New Zealand debt question between the old company and our Canterbury Colony was settled, I having, as Agent for New Zealand Legislature, to arrange with Lord John Russell, "splitting the difference as," said he, "most disputes are settled."

Friendly letters from Lord John Russell to Adderley refer to this subject.[1]

The Canterbury Colony undertook all the obligations of the "Canterbury Association" in London (which Adderley seven years earlier had been instrumental in founding, and which was now winding up its affairs) with regard to its difficulties with the original New Zealand Company, etc. How willingly the Colony, newly entering on its Parliamentary powers, did this, is told in a letter from Godley to Adderley, dated November 30 of this year (1855). "I have most satisfactory accounts from Canterbury. The Colonists accept every item of the 'Association's' debt without any cheese-paring—and with interest since it was incurred. . . . Nothing could be more creditable both to the Association and the colonists than the way in which it has been done; and, take it how you will, no verdict could be more complete on the merits of the Association's work. That a Colony four years old should be able

[1] Lord John resigned the Secretaryship of the Colonies in July, it appearing that he had made unauthorised admissions at Vienna compromising to the Government which he represented.

to adopt a liability of £30,000 without serious, indeed ruinous, inconvenience is a most remarkable proof of its material prosperity, and that they should be willing to do so is an equal proof of moral well-being. . . . There was not one single dissentient in the Council of twenty-four members elected by universal suffrage" ("Letters of J. R. Godley to C. B. Adderley," p. 248).

I spoke on the enlistment of criminals for servile works in the Crimean War—in trench-digging, etc. —like the French. I had interviews on this subject with Lord Hardinge, War Secretary, Sir John Burgoyne [Field-Marshal], who I believe agreed, Lord Panmore, Colonel Jebb, and Captain Crofton.

Lord Grey wrote to Adderley with reference to this subject (May 23, 1855) : " I have had the honour of receiving your letter of yesterday. It is quite true that I have expressed an opinion that a corps of prisoners might very usefully be formed from the best-conducted convicts. I made the suggestion to some members of the Government before Christmas, and I am not sure the subject was not mentioned in the House of Lords. The plan, however, is not approved by the Government, and there would be no advantage in trying to drive them into adopting it by a Parliamentary discussion, as it would have little chance of success if managed by those who did not enter heartily into it. I do not, therefore, con-template bringing the question before the House of Lords, and it is not necessary for me to avail myself of the information which I am obliged to you for offering to me."

All this year the war was dragging on, and there were endless motions for censuring the Government in consequence. There were many Conservative gatherings at Lord Derby's and Disraeli's.

The Emperor Napoleon III. and the Empress Eugénie visited the Queen. I saw, from the

Speaker's house, their entry into London [Monday, April 16] over Westminster Bridge, guarded by French detectives; and I was present at the Windsor review and stag-hunt in their honour.

Speaker Shaw Le Fevre was kept away from the Chair by an accident, *just after* a Deputy-Speaker had been for the first time appointed.

Lord Norton used to quote this as an instance of misfortune only befalling those who anticipated it! And he used to assert that nothing had ever ailed a Speaker before a Deputy was appointed.

Sunday, July 8.—The third Sunday riot since Lord Robert Grosvenor's Bill,[1] though it was withdrawn. Our windows were broken. . . . [The following Sunday] London completely occupied by police.

I was greatly interested going, in July, with Godley, now Permanent Under-Secretary for War, to inspect Dover and Shorncliffe, entirely manned by eight thousand German legions.[2] I remember the quiet and thrift of these compared with our own soldiers. They laid by their pay in the savings bank, supped at oyster stalls on the shore, and sang glees. They cost us largely, and we finally pensioned them off by grants of land in South Africa.

Adderley greatly disapproved of the proceedings of the Government in regard to the whole of this business. It may seem incredible that England, while employing foreign mercenaries to defend her

[1] "The rioters thought their liberty infringed by the Bill to prevent Sunday trading in the Metropolis. On July 8 the mob, not resting content with hooting and hustling the frequenters of the Park, broke many windows, and in one or two instances attempted to set fire to the houses" ("Annals of Our Time": Irving).

[2] For this the Duke of Newcastle and the Aberdeen Government were responsible; and later, Lord Palmerston actually attempted to raise a regiment from America.

shores, had actually refused the loyal support of her Canadian sons. Adderley strongly resented the neglect of this opportunity for colonial fellowship. A letter to his friend, Lord Lyttelton (October 24, 1855), expresses his opinion on the subject :

"You know how I urged the taking certain Canadian offers of volunteers for the Crimea, and the giving commissions—even Hincks[1] allowed that Government bungled this. They said, where wages are a dollar a day, troops could not be raised. Why! wages are a *dollar a day in Staffordshire*, and that county has made the largest contribution to our Volunteer forces, and thence to the Line—a double regiment of Yeomanry and three of Militia! It is military ardour or love of adventure, and, in the Colonies, the pride of *civis romanus*, that leads men to take a shilling instead of a dollar. But the Government were content to give five shillings a day in the Crimea to do work which convicts would have done better for nothing. Now it seems that, rejecting the Canadian offers,[2] they went to *recruit in the United States*, and forgoing the prestige of a force of young sons of farmers of British blood and allegiance (i.e. Canadians), they tried in preference to poach upon Jonathan, and so have roused his sensitive pride and half made a quarrel with America. A great opportunity of imperial action and extension has been lost, and a most perverse risk of foreign embroilment preferred. I wish you would send this to Gladstone."

Among notes :

Oratorios at Birmingham in August [Birmingham Festival]. Our party for it, Lady Denbigh and her daughters and Lord Robert Cecil [Lord Salisbury].

Mr. and Mrs. Bracebridge had a touching public

---

[1] The Hon. Francis Hincks, M.P.P., Canada.
[2] "Colonel Prince made the offer. He made it first to the Colonial Office, which red-tapishly referred him to the War Office; then to the War Office, which, on September 23, 1854, replied that His Grace of Newcastle did not think it expedient to make such a demand on the labour market of the province" (J. G. Godley to C. B. Adderley, February 24, 1855).

welcome home [September 3] from Skutari, on their
return from taking out Miss Nightingale and forty
nurses to the war; and the streets placarded, " Do
thou likewise."

My visit to Manchester with Monckton Milnes to
our Reformatories occupied the autumn. I visited
Gladstone at Hawarden Castle with Godley—
Gladstone giving a colonial lecture at Chester. Met
Archbishop Whateley, Martha Davenport Hill,
Fulford, and others on criminal treatment.

[Among deaths of friends this year.] The year
began with the sudden death of Sir Frankland
Lewis,[1] whom I had just met at Teddesley [Lord
Hatherton's] in perfect health; Sir R. Inglis [died
May 5] and Sir William Molesworth [died Oct. 26],
of different Parliamentary eminence. The death
of the latter shocked me—I had seen much of him
in my colonial work in Parliament. The last days
of his life he lay in bed in state for all the household to take formal leave. He left everything to
his widow, postponing for her life all his poor
relations.[2] I felt the death of Lord Jocelyn[3] from

[1] Right Hon. Sir Frankland Lewis, of Harpton Court; died
January 22, 1855. Father of Right Hon. Sir. G. Cornewall Lewis.
[2] This lady was the Lady Molesworth of Pencarrow, celebrated
in 'the world of fashion. Sir William Molesworth had reason to feel
profound gratitude to his wife. A widow, without parents to consult, she unhesitatingly accepted his proposal of marriage ; several
other ladies (or their parents) having in turn rejected his addresses
on account of his supposed " sceptical " and radical views, both
considered equally " dangerous." Mrs. Grote, his friend and con-
fidante, somewhat indiscreetly suggested that Mrs. West's social
position did not entitle her to aspire to become Lady Molesworth ;
Sir William, thereupon, broke off his friendship with the Grotes.
Gratitude in matrimonial relations was a sentiment he shared with
Disraeli, though for a different reason.
[3] Robert, Viscount Jocelyn, M.P., born 1816, eldest son of
Robert, third Earl of Roden, and father of the fourth Earl. His
wife, Lady Francis Cowper, was Lady Palmerston's daughter.

cholera—Dizzy's " Saracen's Head."   He would not leave his regiment quartered in the Tower.   I was reminded of what I knew of him with his cousin, Lord Powerscourt, at Spragg's School—"courageous and amiable."   The death of my old and valued friend, adviser, and neighbour at Astley Castle [James, third Viscount Lifford].

CHAPTER XXVI

1856

DISLOCATION OF PARTIES

THE year opened with a sense of check to the flow of domestic happiness which I had noted lately as being too smooth to be good to last. Scarlet fever attacked Annie first (we heard the news of it while on a visit to the Packes in Leicestershire), and slowly spread, scattering us all, and the more anxiously as Julia was nearing her [ninth] confinement. This ended happily in Arthur's birth—our third son.[1] Tait's (Dean of Carlisle) family was nearly destroyed by fever, the Queen showing great sympathy. We wandered with convalescents to Hastings, etc., and ended our season at 63, Lowndes Square. I had felt a slackening of interest at the opening of Parliament, but my reflections at the close of the Session attribute this feeling to the dislocation of parties, and suppression of opposition. Palmerston was omnipotent, and, while jauntily winding up the Crimean War, was making fresh business in America and Italy. Guns and bells on Sunday night, March 30, announced Peace. There was a great Naval Review on April 23, and the

[1] Mr. Adderley wrote to Lord Lyttelton, April, 1856: "Our earnest request that you will be Godley's colleague as godfather to our little mosquito."

152

Queen reviewed the Guards returned from the Crimea, in Hyde Park.

My own Parliamentary work was on the Transportation Committee, and on the Committee of the Cambridge University and Town Bill, on which I first acted as Chairman.

I attacked the Government on their wasteful disposal of the German legion, needlessly hired to garrison Dover, which was now to be pensioned off in South Africa.

Godley writes, August 29, 1856: "Very indignant about this monstrous proposal to found a German Military Colony at the Cape . . . the £40,000 voted by the Colony will go very little towards it." And again (Oct. 20.): "I did not overestimate the expense of settling the German legion at £20 a head" [referring to the debate raised by Adderley]. He adds that, although not more than 2,000 out of the 8,000 will go, he underestimated the cost per head. . . . (Later) "Nice fellows these Germans are! For two days they have been in open mutiny at Portsmouth, broken open the gaol at Gosport, and committed all manner of excesses. Fortunately, these loyal defenders of British Colonies had not been entrusted with ball cartridges."

I published a pamphlet this year entitled "Punishment is not Education." I did a good deal for Reformatories, getting larger aid from the Treasury. Saltley Reformatory was enlarged, and Humphreys formally installed as master, the doubly original author, Shoemaker Ellis, retiring to work near Norwich. We sent several older boys out to Natal, under a Mr. Corkindale, who became considerable landowners and magistrates.

A grand dinner at Greenwich of Canterbury

colonists [in July] ended in the second New Zealand bishop, Dr. Harper, going out in September —Bishop Selwyn divided his diocese and income with him.

April 14.—Breakfast at Monckton Milnes—Stanley [afterwards Dean], Bishops of Oxford and St. Davids, Froude.

This was one of many occasions when Adderley was a guest of Monckton Milnes, afterwards Lord Houghton, at his celebrated breakfasts. Monckton Milnes frequently visited at Hams. It is remembered that on one occasion in church in the middle of the sermon he emphatically exclaimed in clear tones, " I doubt it ! " Lord Norton himself was once heard to ejaculate audibly in church, when a curate announced the Epistle of *St. Paul* to the Hebrews, " So you've settled that in your own mind, have you ? " [1]

I had a Grand Bazaar in the Town Hall of Birmingham, August 30, for the opening of Adderley Park Institute at Saltley, and the beginning of its library and museum, for which Monckton Milnes composed an ode, and later there was a great meeting for a Discharged Prisoners' Aid Society, under the provision of an Act I had got through Parliament, which has lessened crime.

The " Inaugural Ode " composed at Hams by R. Monckton Milnes for the opening of Adderley Park Institute was as follows :

> Soldiers of Industry, come forth,
>   Knights of the Iron hand !
> Past is the menace of the North,
>   That frowned upon our land.

[1] This story has been also told of Dean Burgon.

They have no will to count the cost,
　No thought of what we bore,
Now the last warrior's gaze has lost
　The doomed Crimean shore.

That shore so precious in the graves
　Of those whose lustrous deeds
Consecrate Balaklava's waves
　And Alma's flowering reeds.

Where at some future festival
　Our Russian foe will tell
How British wrestlers, every fall,
　Rose stronger than they fell.

Now town and hamlet cheer to see
　Each bronzed and bearded man ;
Or murmur low, " 'Twas such as he
　Who died at the Redan ! "

Rest for his worn and crippled frame,
　Rest for his anxious eye,
Rest even from the noise of fame,
　A nation's welcome cry.

But ye, whose resolute intents
　And sturdy hands combine
To bend the obdurate elements
　Of earth to man's design.

It may not be the unpausing march
　Of toil must still be yours,
Conquest with no triumphant arch
　Unsung by Troubadours ;

Yet, as the fiercest knights of old
　To give " God's Truce " agreed,
Cry ye, who are as brave and bold,
　" God's Truce " in Labour's need.

" God's Truce " be their device who meet
　To work with generous zeal,
To work by many a graceful feat
　Their brethren's future weal.

From stifling street and populous mart
  To guard the ample room
For honest pleasures kept apart
  And decked with green and bloom.

Here let the eye to toil minute
  Condemned, with joy behold
The fresh enchantment of each suit
  That clothes the common mould.

Here let the arm whose skilful force
  Controls such mighty powers
Direct the infant's tottering course
  Amid the fragrant bowers.

Yet all in vain this happy hope,
  In vain this friendly care,
Unless of loftier life the scope
  In every mind be there.

In vain the fairest, brightest scene
  If passion's sensual haze
And clouded spirits lie between
  To mar the mortal gaze.

He only at the marriage feast
  Of Nature and of God
Sits worthily who sits released
  From sin's and sorrow's load.

And then on his poor window-sill
  One flower more pleasure brings,
Than all the gorgeous plants that fill
  The restless halls of kings.

All Nature answers in the tone
  In which she is addressed :—
Beneath Mont Blanc's illumined throne
  The peasant walks unblest ;—

The Italian[1] struggles in his bonds
  Beside his glorious sea ;—
For beauty from his sight absconds
  Who is not wisest free.

[1] A sympathetic allusion to the struggles of the Italian patriots
for freedom.

So, friends, while gentle arts are wed
  To frame your perfect plan,
Broadcast be Truth and Knowledge spread
  On this rich soil of man.

Ideal parks, ideal shade
  Lay out with liberal hand ;
But teach the souls you strive to aid
  To *feel* and *understand*.

We had many country visits this year, at Weston [Lord Bradford] ; Patshull [Lord Dartmouth] ; Arbury [Mr. Newdegate] ; and Doveridge [Lord Waterpark]. But the chief one was to Leigh Court [Sir William Miles] for Social Science at Bristol, whence we went to Pynes [Sir Stafford Northcote], and to Killerton, where Sir Thomas[1] was daily visiting Lady Acland's grave.

Many new home improvements date this year— Lea Bridge, and the new chancel.

[1] The Right Hon. Sir Thomas Dyke-Acland the elder (born 1787, died 1871), friend and contemporary of Lord Norton's father. His son (afterwards also the Right Hon. Sir Thomas Dyke-Acland), once wrote to him : " Adderley poured out his heart like a brother, as he feels to you like a son." (Life of Sir T. D. Acland.)

CHAPTER XXVII

1857

AN AMUSING LECTURE

THE year began with an extraordinary lecture at my Saltley Reading Room [at the Adderley Park Institute], which Sir Robert Peel [the third Baronet] gave [Jan. 5], satirising foreign diplomats!

The astonishment and dismay of the more sober-minded among the audience, and of Mr. Adderley, who had invited his friend and neighbour the brilliant member for Tamworth to lecture on the occasion, may be imagined when Sir Robert, instead of making a suitable speech, broke into a torrent of raillery at the expense of the Russian Court, to which he had been recently sent on a mission, and of the Court officials, totally irrelevant to the subject of the Adderley Institute. Not the less on that account, however, were the hearers literally convulsed with laughter at the witty stories and sallies of the lecturer, who was vociferously applauded.

As is well known, the untoward incident did not close here. It got reported in the local papers, the accounts were copied by the Russian and French press, with severe and indignant comments, and the affair eventually became the subject of a Parliamentary debate, causing the greatest annoyance to the Queen and the Government. Sir Robert, in the first instance, treated the matter with levity, and seems to have enjoyed the consternation he had

caused and the notoriety he had attracted.   He
wrote to Mr. Adderley :

· DRAYTON MANOR,
January 13 [1857].

MY DEAR ADDERLEY,
     You do well to offer me the comfort of your
congratulations, for in truth I have had to undergo
a perfect avalanche of comments for the last week,
and in addition to this you really would be amused
at the letters which from all parts of the country are
pouring in.   Twenty-three have already reached
me.   I yesterday received, or rather did not receive,
a deputation from Leicester ; and the tradesmen of
England are sending me samples of their tea, and
making inquiries as to the wonderful yellow tea
which, if the phrase had not been so commented on
of late, I might be allowed to say is called " Brick
tea."   Then, applications have reached me from two
eminent firms of publishers, and a naval man from
Cheltenham threatens me violence.   In fact I could
make your Saltley audience die with laughter with
a running commentary on what has been entailed
upon me from my first appearance before them.
But I am not disheartened nor likely to be brow-
beaten, and I have two or three more sketches
which, if ever the opportunity occurs, might be introduced with considerable effect ; and as I have not
been spared, I'll not spare any one else. . . . .
Yours very truly,
ROBERT PEEL.

     Sir Robert, however, finding later that matters
were serious, became furiously indignant, and re-
proached Adderley for not supporting him.   Finally
he challenged Adderley to a duel.   The latter replied
briefly : " Except from the language and tone of
your letter I should have expected the apology that
you claim from me."

CHAPTER XXVIII

1857 (*continued*)

WORK WITH COBDEN

EARLY in 1857 Adderley was associated with Cobden, in Reformatory work, and they together visited Stoke Reformatory, which Mr. Sturge had founded. Cobden was in low spirits, mourning for his only son, whom he had lost in the previous April—a sorrow which cast a lasting gloom over his home, for his heart-broken wife fell into a state of melancholy from which she never recovered during the rest of her life. He was further depressed by the ill-health of his friend John Bright, which he felt a personal affliction. Bright had for a year been suffering from nervous prostration, affecting his sight and hearing. To these private sorrows there was soon added the mortification of a great public repulse. Cobden's motion, censuring Sir John Bowring for having involved the country in a war with China, was carried by an extraordinary coalition, in which his party was joined not only by Peelites under Gladstone, and by Lord John Russell, but by Disraeli and the Conservatives, with whom was Adderley. Palmerston however at once dissolved Parliament and appealed to the country, which responded by returning an immense majority in his favour. Cobden, Bright, and nearly every member of the Peace party and the Manchester school, experienced disastrous defeat, the result being, as Adderley has it, that " Pam was set up again." The following letter, addressed to Adderley on the eve of the election by a well-known country gentleman of wide local influence, Sir Oswald Mosley of Rolleston Hall, Burton-on-Trent, aptly expresses the general tone of the country :

March 17, 1857.

I deeply regret the vote given by yourself and your colleagues upon the Chinese question. The mendacious eulogy of the Chinese by Lord Derby in the House of Lords, and the fulsome encomiums pronounced upon Yeh by Mr. Cobden in the House of Commons, are equally disgusting. When extremes meet there is ground for much suspicion, and I am surprised that your good sense and penetration did not detect therein a factious coalition, which the conduct of Mr. Gladstone also countenanced on his part. I am not about to defend Sir John Bowring, but a further explanation was necessary, and he ought to have been heard in his own defence before sentence of condemnation was pronounced upon him. Had Government countenanced such a vote of censure as Mr. Cobden's resolution contained, without further inquiry, they would have imperilled the position of every public functionary in the East. Bowring's recall may perhaps be necessary, but that was not the time for carrying it into effect. From information I have received from merchants and former residents in China that semi-barbarous people glory in acts of scorn and insult to European traders. Perhaps Mr. Cobden, had he been in Bowring's place, would have been equally provoked by them. Under these circumstances I do think Lord Palmerston has been shamefully treated by the House of Commons ; and after thus giving you a brief statement of my opinion on this momentous subject, you cannot be surprised at my declining to vote for any candidate who is not prepared to give his entire support to Lord Palmerston.

Nevertheless, while many of his party lost their seats, Adderley was returned for North Staffordshire (April 4) at the head of the poll, by a majority of

11

1,100 over the other Conservative candidate, both defeating their opponent, Sir E. Buller, and Adderley polling, as he tells us, "4,100 votes, and having to borrow as many pounds!"

John Bright, defeated at Manchester while residing in Italy for his health, bade farewell to Parliamentary life, but was elected, notwithstanding, for Birmingham in August, and consented to return to Parliament on condition of his remaining away from the House of Commons for another six months. Adderley, always a generous opponent, had sincerely regretted the illness and long-continued absence of so leading a statesman, with whom, on matters of colonial reform as well as on philanthropic enterprises, he had much in common. On Bright's return to his home, Rochdale, Adderley invited him to Hams, and thence to visit Birmingham; Bright, still an invalid, declined, writing (August 10, 1857), "I dare not go to Birmingham, and my friends there have been very moderate in their demands. I am not sure that I am right in accepting the seat so handsomely offered me; but I hope six months more of leisure will enable me again to undertake at least some part of my labours in the House of Commons. It would have been very pleasant to have spent a day with you, had circumstances permitted it."

Cobden also corresponded with Adderley during this year.

"My heart is thoroughly in the business," he wrote (Dec. 17, 1857), with regard to a Reformatory meeting at Birmingham, "and I entreat you to persevere in the good work. If my humble aid can at any time be of service, it shall be forthcoming, both within and out of the House. I am engaged to attend an educational conference in Manchester on January 18. They are kindred objects; for what better name could be given Free schools for the children of the whole people than 'Juvenile Reformatories'? I heard you offer some excellent remarks upon 'secular education' in the House. Are there not signs that the question can no longer be delayed with safety? Believe me, with sincere thanks for your kind offer of hospitality, Yours very truly,

R. COBDEN."

AUTOBIOGRAPHICAL NOTES (*continued*)

I undertook the Industrial Schools Bill, which was carried. I also took part in the Select Committee debate on Hudson's Bay; and in the New Zealand Bill. Parliament was prorogued August 28, and met again December 3–12.

In September the Leighs [Lord and Lady Leigh] lent us 30, Portman Square, where our fourth son, Reginald, was born. I spent the time with Godley, and in violincello lessons from Lucas, and in reading "Tom Brown."   .

The Duke of Cambridge [June 1] opened Calthorpe Park in Birmingham, given by Lord Calthorpe, and the Social Congress met there under Lord John Russell and Lord Brougham, whom I seconded in address and afterwards took to Saltley Reformatory.[1]

This year I became a member of "Grillion's Club."

From this time, both as Mr. Adderley and as Lord Norton, he habitually attended the breakfasts and dinners at Grillion's during the Session; and later, he was for many years its secretary, with the late Mr. Arthur Mills. Here he used to meet distinguished men of all politics, and took the greatest interest in their conversation. That his own conversation was appreciated there we gather from the pages of Sir M. Grant Duff's Diaries, where many of Lord Norton's anecdotes told at Grillion's are recorded. This very exclusive club was founded in

---

[1] Lord Brougham wrote : "The services in this great cause [Reformatories] of such men as Mr. Adderley are invaluable."

1813, the elder Sir Thomas Dyke Acland, then in early youth, being one of its chief promoters. It grew out of a meeting of Christ Church friends some years earlier, and was formed with a view to bring together, for social intercourse, leading politicians of opposite parties, and other distinguished persons. It first met at Grillion's Hotel, where a room was reserved for it. Afterwards it met at various places.

[Among domestic events :] Caroline Leigh [sister-in-law] married Saye and Sele [the sixteenth Baron, as his second wife].

CHAPTER XXIX

1858

ENTERS DERBY GOVERNMENT

WE bought 35, Eaton Place, [a corner house] after having for seventeen years hired houses every Session.

The division on the India Bill gave a great majority against Palmerston, with whom I voted against my party. Milner Gibson then beat Palmerston [February 19, 1858] on the Conspiracy to Murder Bill[1] [the outcome of Orsini's attempt to murder Louis Napoleon], and Palmerston resigned.

Lord Derby sent for me, and I was made Vice-President of the Education Committee of Council and President of the Board of Health, and, ex-officio, Charity Commissioner and a Privy Councillor, Lord Salisbury [James, second Marquis][2] was my chief

---

[1] The Conspiracy Bill aimed at making conspiracy to murder a felony instead of, as it had previously been, a misdemeanour, and leave had been given by a large majority to introduce it ; but when Count Walewski's despatch to Count de Persigny came to be published, the feeling gained ground that the Government had shown undue subservience in meeting the representatives of the French Ambassador. The opposition to the Bill was concerted by Lord John Russell, Sir James Graham, etc. The purport of the Amendment was to postpone any reform in the Criminal Law till the French despatch had been replied to ("Queen Victoria's Letters," vol. iii., note, p. 336).

[2] James Brownlow, 2nd Marquis of Salisbury, K.G., Lord President of the Council, 1858-9.

in the Council office; Cowper was my predecessor. I made McGeachey [brother-in-law] my Secretary, with £600 a year. I was re-elected for North Staffordshire without opposition.

My work this year was chiefly consolidating the accumulated Minutes of Council on Education, and, helped by Tom Taylor,[1] carrying a large Local Government Act, the title "Local Government" being my own invention.

Adderley corresponded much with Lord Lyttelton on educational matters, and wrote : "Am delighted you are satisfied with my exercise of that im-partiality which you so strongly recommended at the commencement of my official career."

I worked with Sir Roderick Murchison and Henry Cole at South Kensington Fine Art Department, and I was brought into most interesting contact with the Prince Consort over this work [founding the South Kensington Museum].

In connection with this the *Diary* has frequent allusions to "meetings with Lord Salisbury at Brompton." *April 8* : "Promised the Prince Consort I would try to get the £177,000 appropriated for Museum combined, etc."

I made the School Inspectors report *at once* in manuscript to the managers, and checked the little parliaments they used to hold in the office, dividing on questions. I had, of course, to move the educa-tion estimates in the House of Commons.

The Thames became this summer so full of sewage as to stink intolerably in Parliamentary nostrils.

[1] Tom Taylor (1817-80), the celebrated dramatist and editor of *Punch*, was at this time Secretary to the Board of Health.

GRAND HIGH ABBEY

" It was fortunate," says Justin McCarthy, " that
Parliament sat so near the miasmatic ditch of
sulphuretted hydrogen which the Thames had
become. If any obstruction had been offered to
the Bill the simplest remedy would have been to
open the windows." *The Times* said (June 26):
" It is difficult to say whether the stench is more
horrible under the sun of noon or amid the damps
of midnight, at high or low water. The fish are
dying. Do something, pray do something, is the
language on every side." [1]

The Queen and the Prince Consort visited Lord
and Lady Leigh at Stoneleigh Abbey [Monday,
June 14, 1858, till Wednesday, 16th], and we were of
the party to meet them—the Queen opening Aston
Park, Birmingham, etc.[2]

On this occasion the acquaintance which the
Prince Consort and Mr. Adderley had begun over
work at South Kensington was cemented, and grew
into a feeling of warm regard on either side.

It is remembered that on the first evening, a very

[1] Disraeli enabled the Board to raise a sewage rate at threepence
in the pound for forty years.
[2] The other guests were Lord and Lady Westminster (parents
of Lady Leigh), Lady Agnes Grosvenor, the Duchess of Suther-
land, Lord and Lady De La Warr, Lady Arabella West (afterwards
Lady Arabella Bannerman), Lord Dalkeith (present Duke of
Buccleuch), Lord and Lady Macclesfield (sister of Lady Leigh),
Lord and Lady Saye and Sele (sister of Lord Leigh), Lord and
Lady Wenlock (sister of Lady Leigh), and Sir Archibald Campbell.
With the Queen came the Duchess of Atholl (Lady-in-Waiting),
the Hon. Horatio Stopford (Maid of Honour-in-Waiting), Earl De
La Warr (Lord Chamberlain), Marquis of Abercorn (Groom of the
Stole to the Prince Consort), Colonel the Hon. Sir Charles Phipps
(Keeper of the Privy Purse), Major General Bouverie (Equerry
to the Queen), Colonel F. H. Seymour (Equerry to the Prince),
Right Hon. Spencer Walpole (Secretary to the Home Department).
The Queen and Prince Consort brought in their train eighteen
attendants besides their suite—Queen's dresser and a lady's
maid, two pages-in-ordinary, Prince's valets, eight men servants
in livery, a coiffeur, a clothes-brusher, an upholsterer (!), a
special messenger, and an inspector of police. A man came down
to inspect the roads before the Queen arrived.

beautiful one, about ten o'clock the Queen went out on the terrace in front of the house with Lord Leigh ; and, urged on by the Prince Consort, went right on to the end of the terrace overhanging the field below, where were assembled a vast concourse of people, who cheered and finally broke into "God save the Queen" as the Queen, after walking round twice, retired up the steps into the house again. The gardens and entrance gateway were brilliantly illuminated by myriads of coloured lamps. The police, who did not know the Queen was coming out of doors, were nowhere to be seen to keep the people back, and they came right up to the balustrade, almost within reach of her.

The Queen opened Aston Park, Birmingham, next day. The inhabitants of Birmingham and its neighbourhood resolved not to have a single fire lighted, in the factory chimneys or anywhere, in order that the city might not wear its usual black, smoky look. The Royal party returned to Stoneleigh, and in the evening the county people came and were presented ; the Queen went out into the garden again, but did not approach the people as before. The Queen sat out on the balcony and, placing her hand on Lord Leigh's arm, said : "You must be happy in such a lovely home as this." Next day the Queen, etc., went over to luncheon at Warwick Castle, after planting two trees in front of Stoneleigh Abbey and going all over the house ; and the Royal party left Warwick by train on the conclusion of their visit that afternoon.[1]

This year Edward Fitzgerald[2] went out to New Zealand to take part in the government of Canter-

[1] From information supplied by the present Lord Leigh.
[2] James Edward Fitzgerald (1818—1896) became Prime Minister of New Zealand. He sailed in one of the four ships which carried the pioneers of the Canterbury Settlement. A drinking song, written by him on the voyage—"The Night Watch of the *Charlotte Jane*"—expresses with some spirit the aims and feelings of the Canterbury pilgrims ("Dictionary of National Biography," Supplement).

bury Colony. [This distinguished and witty Irishman corresponded with Lord Norton at intervals during nearly forty years. A letter from him on which Gladstone based his arguments for Home Rule is given in these pages under date 1892.]

[Among domestic events :] *October 7.*—Wedding at Four Oaks—Annie Hartopp married Lord Walter Scott. Party : Duke and Duchess of Buccleuch, etc., Hartopps of Dalby, Cradocks, Custs, Coventry, Lady Bateman and Miss Hanbury. *October 27.*— With Lord Salisbury to Hatfield.

CHAPTER XXX

1859

VISIT TO WINDSOR CASTLE

THIS year began with a visit to Windsor Castle, where were the Clarendons and daughter, General Williams of Kars, Lords Exeter and Sheffield, and officials Colville and Ponsonby, and Colonel Seymour [afterwards Marquis of Hertford], Lady Jocelyn in waiting. The second day I shot with the Prince Consort at Bagshot. I had his company to myself driving there and back. He made the smokers go outside.

Mr. Adderley wrote to his wife from Windsor Castle (January 8): "I spent all the afternoon with Lord Exeter, an old Etonian, lionising every inch of Eton. Just after I had gone out at three o'clock with Lord Exeter, the Queen sent for all the visitors to see the children in the corridor, which we missed. I have been over the stables with Lord Colville this evening, and am to shoot with the Prince to-morrow." Next day he wrote: "I had a capital morning's shooting with the Prince, and a twelve miles' drive to Bagshot in the carriage with him—a long chat, very entertaining. He is by far the most agreeable and universally informed converser I ever heard." On the morning of this occasion, when Mr. Adderley appeared in velveteen and white cord breeches and leather gaiters, the Prince remarked: "We shan't shoot *you* to-day!"

The Grant Duff Diaries relate (March 17, 1894):
" Lord Norton told us [at Grillion's] that Prince Albert had mentioned to him that he had once been asked to accept the dedication of a book on Naval Architecture. He replied that he was unable to do so unless there was some reason. The author rejoined that the book was the *only one* on Naval Architecture. Much surprised, the Prince made inquiries at the British Museum, and found that the statement was not unimpeachably correct, but that the last person who had written in English on Naval Architecture was *Sir Walter Raleigh*."

Lord Norton used to relate that the Prince Consort, in conversation with him, said that German architects had to take a diploma in all sections bearing on their art—an advantage over English architects. Once when the Prince was talking to Mr. Adderley in the lobby of the House, Disraeli passed by, and afterwards asked Adderley, " What nonsense were the Prince and you talking ? " Disraeli was afraid of the great love the Prince had for Science and Art, and of his ambitious schemes in that direction.

NOTES (*continued*)

In the Reform Bill debate I ventured to follow Milner Gibson against my party. Lord Derby's Government was beaten [another instance of Adderley voting against his party and this time a serious one, he being Education Minister.]

Dissolution came in April, and I was returned again without opposition with Lord Ingestre. I brought out T. Acland [1] [as a Moderate Liberal candidate] against Bright at Birmingham, but in vain !

Lord Derby, defeated on the Address in the Commons, resigned—Lord Palmerston came in

[1] Eldest son of the Right Hon. Sir Thomas Dyke Acland, tenth Baronet, and himself becoming later the Right Hon. Sir Thomas Dyke Acland, eleventh Baronet (1871).

again. [Mr. Adderley was consequently out of office. Lord Palmerston's Government lasted till his death in 1865.]

During the Derby Administration Sir E. Bulwer Lytton [1] as Secretary of State for the Colonies, in which Adderley was as ever keenly interested, had become much *lié* with Adderley and Godley. On going out of office he corresponded with Adderley on colonial affairs. What manner of man he was is well described by Godley in a letter to Adderley in the previous year (August 21, 1858). "I had a most interesting and pleasant visit to Knebworth. Sir E. Lytton talked incessantly and charmingly, quite realising my idea of an illogical, eloquent man of genius. Sunday he spent entirely in the house, dressed in a black and red dressing-gown, and smoking the whole time a cherry-stick pipe. He is literally half mad about his responsibilities, and fancies he is going to reform the whole colonial empire.[2] He gets up in the middle of the night to write despatches, and is furious if they don't actually *go* in twelve hours."

The following letter from Bulwer Lytton to Adderley (dated October 21, 1859), written after Lytton had been succeeded at the Colonial Office by the Duke of Newcastle, has reference to Sir George Grey, Governor of Cape Colony. Sir George was personally extremely popular, but his rule at the Cape was as autocratic as it had been in New Zealand, and latterly his independent policy and disregard of orders had proved embarrassing to the Colonial Office.

MY DEAR ADDERLEY,
    It would be a false move to censure D[uke]

[1] Edward Bulwer Lytton (1803–1873), the celebrated *littérateur* and novelist, was Secretary for the Colonies 1858-1859. Created Baron Lytton of Knebworth in 1866.
[2] Lytton's principal measure was for the organisation of the New Colony of British Columbia, which had become necessary in consequence of the discovery of gold fields. Queensland was also separated from New South Wales during his tenure of office.

of N[ewcastle][1] for not recalling Grey. Perhaps the best plan will be to move for certain papers.

The fact is that on entering office I saw much in Grey that I admired, and he had no man more disposed to be indulgent to him. I pass over those faults for which, though grave, he was not recalled, though I felt he was a most troublesome public servant—the quarrels with —— were most unseemly, and his haughty self-opinion, and his way of dealing with public money, were like those of a Roman Proconsul. But after he had explained to me at length his views on the Federation with the Dutch policy, I was so impressed with their impolicy and peril—the general idea seemed to me so wild and so at variance with sound legislation and Colonial principles—that I bade him peremptorily take no step whatever towards the policy without my previous voucher ; in fact, his policy would have required the formal assent of Cabinet. Nevertheless he formally by speech declared in favour of his scheme, and for this disobedience of orders I recalled him in a detailed despatch, and with many civil expressions which I think just to his general ability. In this step the Office was unanimous in agreement with me. They all thought there was no option— Lord Derby the same.

But this was just before quitting office. I felt there must be a first-rate man to succeed him. I would not make a party job of his successor ; the only man I could think of was Sir John Lawrence, and he was nearly induced to go. Finally he decided against it, a day or two before we went out. I appointed no other ; and formally Grey was not therefore recalled—no successor being named. I wrote to the D. of N. a long letter on all great colonial points. I mentioned the one of Grey, and observed that, should he think proper, he could still retain Grey. The Duke, I was privately informed, wrote to Grey that he entirely approved all my views, but in consideration of his services would

[1] The Duke of Newcastle (1811–1864) was appointed Secretary of State for Colonies, 1859, in the Palmerston Government. Resigned 1865, and died October 18 of that year.

not recall him, but asked him to come to England for orders.[1] I don't see.that I could blame this resolve, though I think it an unwise one. Any attempt to press hard upon Grey would bring his friends round him, and no doubt he is very popular in the Colony. But it may be desirable to have the facts out ; we can judge better when Parliament meets. I warned the Duke of the American designs on St. Juan, and urged him to hasten the Foreign Office to complete the settlement of that controversy. I think I should have prevented all that mess had I remained in office. We can never give up that island—better give up the Colony.

I am coming to England. My direction—Kneb-worth.

Yours, E. B. LYTTON.

NOTE-BOOK (*continued*) 1859

I saw a pretty sight at Harrow—the Prince of Wales (aged 18) riding to Harrow Speeches through an avenue of boys. He knew exactly who to speak to in the room—his mother's Royal gift of knowing everybody.

Julia laid the Foundation Stone of the Stafford-shire wing of the Saltley Reformatory.

Mrs. Adderley's mother, the Dowager Lady Leigh, died early in this year, after being in failing health since the death of her husband. This bereavement placed Mr. and Mrs. Adderley in mourning for a year. The note-book has little to record beyond the outline of parliamentary work.

[1] Compare account in " Dictionary of National Biography Supple-ment," Sir George Grey, 1810-1898. " Grey always asserted that Queen Victoria protested against his dismissal, and approved of his South African policy. Much exasperated he returned to England after quitting Cape Town amid general expressions of esteem and regret. Before he reached home, however, the Derby Ministry had fallen, and the Duke of Newcastle, coming to the Colonial Office, reinstated Grey, albeit with instructions to abandon his federation policy." The statement that Sir George Grey had started for England on receipt of Lytton's despatch does not seem to tally with Lytton's statement that the Duke of Newcastle re-quested Grey to come to England " for orders."

CHAPTER XXXI

1860

NEW ZEALAND TROUBLES

THE affairs of New Zealand were clouded by the quarrels between the colonists and the Maori, and the situation had become one of great danger. The question as to how far the colonists had been to blame in their dealings with the natives, more especially with regard to the purchases of land, will always be matter of controversy, but the Maori's independence of local government and the well-intentioned interference of the Colonial Office on their behalf had not tended to decrease the friction. As Gladstone had said in 1852, condemning the Home Government's reserve of native protection in the New Zealand Constitution Grant, " Instead of telling the Colony to look for no help from us unless they maintained the principle of justice, we foolishly told them not to meddle with the relations between themselves and the natives, and that that was a matter for Parliament." " The sequel," wrote Adderley later,[1] " has shown how England's vicarious humanity and officious care end only in increasing warfare and confusion, for which the colonists ab-

[1] Sir Charles Adderley's " Colonial Policy," p. 138 (1869). See also the " Letters of Lord Blachford," p. 228 *et seq.*, who took a different view as to the origin of the conflict with the natives. It may be added that Blachford's ideals about the Colonies were totally different from those of Adderley, for he looked forward to a time when the Colonies, after a due season of education in government by the mother-country, should be released from all dependence on or obligations to her.

solve themselves of all responsibility; blaming us for all that goes wrong, and expecting us to pay for the blunders introduced into the management of their affairs." Godley writes to Adderley (October 1860): "We have encouraged, almost enforced, the absence of all military spirit and training among the colonists, and virtually adopted the whole responsibility of their defence. Of course they expect now we shall discharge it, and, as we can't or won't, consider themselves injured or deceived. . . ." Again (November 15, 1860): "The New Zealand Government seems to have plunged most unjustifiably into war, of course intending that we shall pay for it. Sidney Herbert writes to me in a tone of intense disgust at it, but says he has been obliged to send two regiments, etc. If we don't turn this affair to account in supporting our general views we shall throw away a good case. I quite despair of the present Colonial Office, and look now to your side."

Adderley was always urging that our troops should be withdrawn from New Zealand on the earliest opportunity, and that colonists should provide their own army. On this point Lord Blachford's words recording his own opinions at a somewhat later date may be quoted as expressing Adderley's also. He had "made up his mind that there could be no quiet for ourselves or safety for the natives until our troops were recalled, and the colonists forced to rely on their own resources, and to try mild and just methods rather than violence" ("Letters of Lord Blachford," p. 297). With Adderley this view followed as a corollary to his principle that the colonists should have undisturbed control of all their own local affairs. As regards *Imperial* interests, however, if Imperial interests were attacked in any part of the Empire "all the forces of the Empire," he says in a letter to Lord Lyttelton, "should rally round every part attacked—we round Canada and Canada round us; but Colonies are no more entitled to our protection than we are to theirs."

NOTE-BOOK FOR 1860

In April Lord Derby had a Party meeting on Reform.

The Paper Duties.[1]

My Education Bill [July 17].

I was recalled by a letter from R. Lowe from grouse shooting with Wynne of Voelas, for the New Zealand Government Bill, and found on my return it had been withdrawn.

My autumn was spent in visits to the Harfords at Blaise Castle—old friends who told me I knew not what I owed to my childhood amid such beauties as Clifton, and certainly much *in mente repostum.*

From Blaise Castle to Hagley —my best contemporary friend Lyttelton ; and thence to Westwood to help Sir John Pakington [afterwards Lord Hampton] at a public meeting.

1861

Adderley now employed his leisure in writing a pamphlet on " The present relations of England with the Colonies, with appendix of extracts from evidence taken before the Select Committee on colonial military expenditure." It was addressed by permission to Disraeli.

Towards the end of the year the proofs of the pamphlet were submitted to Lord Lyttelton, who made " many good corrections and suggestions "; and to Godley, who wrote (November 9, 1861—it was almost his last letter), " I return your proof. I cannot say how much pleased I am with it. You know how unpityingly I criticise when I think it necessary, and you will believe in the sincerity of this unqualified commendation."

" You have placed your views before the country," wrote Disraeli, " in a clear and complete light ; but what is taking place convinces me that the theme is beyond the domain of mere reasoning, however just and wise. The passions of the people are very high at the present moment, and if the Ministry chose to send fifty thousand men to Canada they would be supported. When our colonial system was reconstructed, either the Colonies should have had social representation, or the military prero-

[1] Sir E. Bulwer Lytton wrote (August 4, 1860) : " (Illness) will prevent my return for the Paper Duty debate, which, however, I regret the less because I have doubts whether a question so complicated by treaty obligations be a good fighting ground for the Conservative Party."

12

gatives of the Crown should have been so secured
that the faculty of self-defence in the Colonies should
always have been considerable."

Lord Robert Cecil (afterwards Marquis of Salisbury), who did not at that time endorse Adderley's
colonial views, wrote (November 15, 1861): "The
pitiful attitude that has been assumed by the Cape
and New Zealand gives no triumph to you and those
of your opinions. Whatever we may think of general
doctrines, something must be done to bring these
two to reason." Again (December 20, 1861): "I shall
like very much to receive your pamphlet, though
from what I know of your uncompromising doctrines
I cannot hope that I shall agree . . . I think the
present war, if it comes to that, will draw a good
deal of attention to the question of a colonial
empire, whether it be worth having, or at what
price. I am afraid it may possibly draw the attention of the Canadians to the question, too."

Robert Lowe (afterwards Lord Sherbrooke) took
a different view. He wrote (December 31, 1861):
" Many thanks for your excellent pamphlet, which I
have read with great pleasure, and I hope some
profit. A state of war is not a good time for raising
these questions ; but, as I have always maintained,
the Americans won't fight Canada. I do not despair of hearing more of it even in this Session. . . .
It seems to me that from a muddling tyrant the
Colonial Office has sunk into a parasite of the
Colonies, and that there is more danger of dis-
membering the Empire by over-indulgence than by
over-interference. I shall show your pamphlet to
Mr. Grote." [1]

[1] A month later Lowe wrote again : "You must count on no
success (as to colonial motion) while Palmerston is at the head of
affairs. As Goldwin Smith truly says, his mind is cast in an
antique mould, and is indeed full of the most vulgar fallacies,
which he would utter amid the cheers of both sides of the House ;
I could not, therefore, advise you to commit yourself to a motion
which would entail probably a positive rejection, and might
materially retard the growth of an opinion assuredly destined to
grow. I send you a letter by Goldwin Smith in *The Daily News*,
not as agreeing with all its contents, but as showing that the yeast
of last year's Committee begins to work. . . . Carlyle has carried
off *The Daily News* which contained Smith's letter."

Before the pamphlet was issued by the publishers a great bereavement had befallen Adderley in the death of his friend Godley, the originator of his colonial policy—the "master mind" and "ἄναξ ἀνδρῶν." His death, long expected by his friends, took place on November 17, 1861.

Adderley writes the sad news next day to Lyttelton, whom he calls, "Now my best contemporary friend," and who, equally with Adderley, mourned the loss of Godley. "I got just too late, summoned by one line in Godley's own hand, which I instantly obeyed; perhaps it was as well. . . . I have seen her [Mrs. Godley]. He died most happily, and with all his in-born courage and almost stern composure and thoughtfulness to the last. What a depth and soundness there was about his mind and feelings! Every recollection of him is striking, and a possession of permanence. We must collect a private memoir. I have an infinity of letters during twenty years full of the working of that noble mind. To me the loss is irreparable."

It is remarkable that Sidney Herbert, Godley, and Hawes all died in office while in various departments of the War Office, within a few months of each other.

Two monuments were dedicated to the memory of John Robert Godley by his devoted friends. One, the mural tablet placed in Harrow School Chapel, with a Latin inscription by the scholarly Lord Lyttelton, and appended to which are the distinguished names of those who erected it—" Pauci ex amicis quos sibi devinctissimos tenuit;"[1] and

[1] Inscription by Lord Lyttelton on a Tablet in Harrow Chapel—
JOANNES R. GODLEY
vir si quis alius
Fortis, magnanimus, rebus gerendis
Et in hominum moderationem natus,
Juvenis natale solum
Necnon Americæ nonnulla
Adcurate exploravit
Æqualium mentes ad majorum præcepta
Quibus coloniæ non tam regendae sunt
Quam creandæ
Inter primos revocavit:
Florentissimam in Canterburia ἀποικίαν
Excogitavit, deduxit, instituit,
Et dum vixit in corde habuit:

the other the collection of his letters, published for private circulation by Adderley, which Gladstone said was the best of all monuments.

These letters are addressed to Adderley, and dedicated by him to Lord Lyttelton. "To you especially," says the dedicatory preface, "but also to the rest of that inner circle of his friends whose names your Harrow epitaph records." He alludes to other "letters by Godley on political subjects, addressed to the Duke of Newcastle, all of which the Duke told me that, entertaining the opinion invariably formed of Godley by all his acquaintance, he had carefully preserved."

The death of the Prince Consort, on Dec. 14, 1861, was a personal loss to Adderley, he having a profound admiration for the Prince, with whom, as to high aims and strenuous endeavour, he had much in common.

The present Lord Norton contributes the following from his personal recollections :—

"The Prince Consort was present for the last time in public, when with the Queen, Princess Alice, and Prince Arthur, he reviewed the Eton College Volunteers in the quadrangle of Windsor Castle. I was Corporal to the Colours borne by Ellesmere[1] and Eldon,[2] and was fifteen at the time. We had

Redux in militaribus consiliis
Egregie operatus :
Sed infirma valitudine præpeditus
Ne ad summa progrederetur
Immaturam, ut loquimur, mortem obiit
XVII NOV. MDCCCLXI ÆT XLVII.
Hæc apud scholam cujus alumnus fuit
Pauci ex amicis
Quos sibi devinctissimos tenuit
Posuerunt.

C. B. Adderley	Lyttelton	Newcastle
T. S. Cocks	T. A. McGeachey	Roundell Palmer
Devon	Arthur Mills	R. H. Pollen
J. E. Fitzgerald	Monck	W. P. Prendergast
W. E. Gladstone	W. Monsell	H. S. Selfe
De Grey	G. A. Hamilton	John Simeon
M. J. Higgins		R. Thornton
Walter C. James		

Edward Twistleton   C. G. Wynne

[1] Present Earl of Ellesmere, then Lord Brackley.
[2] Present Earl of Eldon.

luncheon afterwards, and the Royal family came round to talk. Princess Alice stopped to look at Carrington,[1] our Colonel, who was very good-looking. The Prince Consort, who wore a grey great-coat, took Prince Arthur by the hand up the steps into the Castle—never to come out again."

NOTE-BOOK FOR 1861

In the House I worked this year in the Transportation Committee. Industrial School Bills ; Colonial Defences Committee, examining Lord Grey. Destitute Children Report.

As a Rugby Trustee I had much trouble about Dr. Temple (Headmaster, afterwards successively Bishop of London and Archbishop of Canterbury)—his part in " Essays and Reviews " [then considered by some to be of a sceptical tendency].

" Sir G. Cornewall Lewis put me on a Royal Commission about Durham University with the Bishop of Durham. Dr. Stanley [afterwards Dean of Westminster], Robert Lowe, etc. Our Report was decided *ultra vires* by the Judicial Committee, but was afterwards voluntarily adopted."

May 21.—Sophie Leigh's wedding to Granville Leveson-Gower.

The Royal Horticultural Gardens opened June 6—planned while I served on the Royal Exhibition Commissions under the Prince Consort.

There was a Volunteer Review of nine thousand Infantry and Cavalry at Warwick, July 23, the Duke of Cambridge staying at Stoneleigh for it. I was of the party, which included the Dukes of Rutland, Manchester, and Newcastle ; Lords Ducie, Hatherton, and Lyttelton. Luncheon at Warwick Castle, and great dinner at Stoneleigh.

On July 5, my fifth son, James Granville, was born [now Rev. the Hon. James Adderley, —" Father Adderley "—Vicar of Saltley].

[1] Now Earl Carrington, then aged 18.

CHAPTER XXXII

1862

OUTLINES OF WORK

IN the early part of the Session I regularly hunted every Saturday with Lord Lonsdale's and other packs near London, in company with the Speaker, Denison [afterwards Viscount Ossington], Cairns [afterwards Lord Chancellor]; he usually, and sometimes Lord Granville, arranging for the Speaker every Friday. [Sometimes they hunted with Lord Brownlow's harriers.]

We spent Easter at Paris—Julia, Annie, Charlie, and I; and I saw something of the Law Courts, and Monsieur Béranger and the Chambre.

In Parliament I raised a debate on Canada refusing the Militia Bill, Disraeli supporting me.

Disraeli wrote July 22, 1862 : " I quite approve of your moving in the Canada question : the Appropriation Bill, in all its stages, will give you a choice of opportunities."

Adderley's view was that Canada should form an army herself for her own protection, and that unless she did so, or contributed to the support of the British troops, that they should be withdrawn. He had constantly urged that self-defence was the proper sequence of self-government. On July 11, 1862 (see Hansard, vol. 168) Adderley asked whether the First Lord of the Treasury (Lord Palmerston) "intends the 12,000 British troops now in Canada to remain there during the winter wholly unaided by the Canadians themselves." On July 25 Adderley, raising the debate on the defence of Canada in a long speech, said : " The Canadians had a Militia of 5,000 men only, who were under drill six days in the year. . . . The Mayor of Montreal had spoken out honestly after the dinner at which Lord Monck was present, illustrating the old adage, *in vino veritas.* He said, ' Canada might esteem itself a most fortunate community in being protected by one of the most powerful nations in the world, which sent them as many as might be required of ships and red-coats without rendering them liable in purse or person. No matter how many red-coats, the more the better, if they took not a single sou out of their own pockets.' Such were the magnanimous words of the Mayor of Montreal, after Lord Monck had tried to rouse a patriotic feeling among the rich inhabitants of that city." Mr. Roebuck joined in the debate from the point of view of complete separation from the mother-country. Sir G. Cornewall Lewis, Secretary of State for War, while admitting that the Canadians had shown lack of energy, deprecated any undignified threats to Canada of withdrawing our troops. He proceeded to confess that he looked forward to a time when there should be ultimately complete separation from the mother-country. Disraeli said "the sending of 3,000 men to Canada, as was done in June last year, was, I think, to some extent an intimation to the colonists that we were prepared to undertake the monopoly of their defence. It daunted their ardour, and has tended greatly to the unfortunate state of things which now prevails in that quarter. I do not, as my right honourable friend near me (Adderley) knows, by any means agree with him in all the conclusions upon colonial questions at which he has arrived. He has, however, I think, done good service in bringing forward this subject to-night in a speech which I may be permitted to say was one of very considerable ability."

NOTE-BOOK FOR 1862

I was on the Sewage Commissions and Weights and Measures Committee, trying to introduce a Metric System ; and went with the House of Commons to inspect the new sewers in London.

I was on a Jury in the International Exhibition, and had to pacify all French Exhibitors by *mentions honorables*.

There was a grand Review in May of Warwickshire Yeomanry, Militia, and Volunteers, and a Volunteer Review in July at Ingestre ; and a sham fight in August between Staffordshire and Cheshire on the borders of the two counties.

Our visits this year were to Hatfield [James, second Marquis of Salisbury] ; Charlie and I to Voelas [Mr. Wynne] for grouse shooting ; to Broughton Castle [his brother-in-law, Lord Saye and Sele], where we met the last Lord Pomfret ; and in November to Pitchford [Mr. and Lady Louisa Cotes, *née* Jenkinson], whence we lionised Wroxeter and Shrewsbury.

Home work was giving a park at Saltley to Birmingham Corporation, etc.

Charlie [present Lord Norton] distinguished himself as an Eton boy, and characteristically in capturing a gang of poachers under powers of a recent Act kept in his pocket, as they returned through Lea Village at break of day with spoil.

1863

I thought the Session opened dully in political apathy. [The legislature may with some truth be said to have met but for the purpose of congratulating the Prince of Wales on his approaching marriage, and providing him with an allowance.[1]]

I got interested in the Convict question, bearing on colonial interests, which had always so much occupied me.

On March 9 I moved an Address for carrying out Penal Servitude Acts, and the 11th I beat the Government, carrying the Act for flogging garrotters. [Second reading, by 131 to 68.]

The Act empowered judges to punish the crime of robbery with violence by one, two, or three floggings—not to exceed fifty lashes—besides imprisonment. Though not in accordance with modern humanitarianism, it was considered a great achieve-

[1] Paul's " Modern England."

ment at the time, and brought Adderley into marked prominence—the last thing he valued. The Bill indeed embodied the general feeling, and was a vent for the universal resentment against the series of brutal robberies from the person which had been frequent during the previous year, and which, as the victims were often more than half strangled, went by the name of garrotting. Government opposed the Bill, and Sir George Grey (Home Secretary [1]) used the unfortunate argument that some of the culprits would be too weak for corporal punishment. "It was easy," says Mr. Herbert Paul,[2] "to raise a laugh at the 'ferocious valitudinarians,' for whose health the Home Secretary was so much concerned." The Bill passed by large majorities in the Commons and without a division in the Lords, despite an earnest protest from Lord Chancellor Cranworth. "It may be conjecturally argued," continues Mr. Paul, "that without the Flogging Bill garrotting would have revived. That the crime was suppressed before the Bill came into existence is a simple historical fact." Certainly, Lord Bramwell's severe, but well-merited, sentences of penal servitude on garrotters in the previous year had already had a salutary effect, and the "epidemic of garrotting" may be said to have ceased in consequence of it before the application of the Garrotters Act. Be that as it may, it was for many years rigorously enforced. It was said at one time to have fallen gradually into disuse ; but in the last few years the lash has been frequently ordered, while quite recently (April, 1908) Mr. Justice Lawrence sentenced eight garrotters to the lash within a few days.[3]

---

[1] Right Hon. Sir George Grey, of Falloden, G.C.B. ; to be distinguished from Sir George Grey, Governor of the Cape.

[2] "Modern England," vol. ii. p. 342.

[3] "The action of Mr. Justice Lawrence," said *The Daily Mail* (April 4, 1908), "will no doubt be hotly canvassed, and by some be severely condemned. But it must be remembered that there has been a serious epidemic of crimes of violence in South Wales, accompanied in many instances by the most brutal assaults upon weak and helpless women. It must also be remembered that to the really hardened criminal the modern prison has no terror. . . . There are unfortunately criminals so entirely destitute of moral

Lord Norton used to recount how that, on going down the street, he was saluted by the Prison Governor, who said, " I thought you must have heard the man howling ! "—the first man flogged under the new rule. Lord Norton used to add : " Really the Home Office ' cat ' was *too* strong ! " He suggested that only such a " cat " should be used for flogging as was approved by the Board of Trade.[1]

Further Notes for 1863

I took the Chair in Committee on a group of Bills— Blackfriars Bridge, etc.—and worked at the improvement of weights and measures.

I gave lectures at the Library I opened at Adderley Park, Saltley.

Grillion's Club held its Jubilee this year. [Founded 1813.]

Lord Leigh successfully set up worsted spinning and weaving at Coventry, in the deserted ribbon mill.

Gladstone splendidly opened our Wedgwood Institute, throwing poetry into smoke.

I attended the Edinburgh Social Services—Prince Albert present.

I gave an inaugural address at the opening of Coventry School of Art.

Deaths : Sir George Cornewall Lewis, in the Easter recess ; Edward Ellice, in September ; Sir Joshua Jebb.

We gave a ball in June at 35, Eaton Place.

1864

Adderley was very busy this year in Parliament, as well as in local work in the country. Nor did he neglect recreation. He again hunted regularly every Saturday in the early part of the Session with Speaker Denison, and Sir Hugh (afterwards Lord) Cairns, and Sir R. Airey.

sense and reason that the only motive which appeals to them is fear of pain. . . . It may be untrue that garrotting was stamped out by the use of the 'cat,' but the fact remains that fear of the 'cat' has in all probability prevented hundreds of thieves and robbers from repeating the exploits of the men who, forty years ago, made the streets of London so dangerous. The alternative is to detain these violent offenders in prison for life, and it may be doubted whether this would not be even more cruel than the infliction of a sentence which carries with it not one tithe of the suffering that the wrong-doer has caused to his hapless victim."

[1] The severity of the " cat " is said to depend on whether the man who wields it closes his little finger.

A letter of Lord Derby's among Adderley's papers, dated " St. James's Square, March 17, 1864," has reference to the doings of Robert Lowe (afterwards Lord Sherbrooke), then Vice-President of the Committee of Council on Education, and constantly in " hot water " with his opponents. The advocates of the denominational system of education looked on Lowe's administration and his revised Code regulations with great misgiving, and asserted that he resorted to " dodges " to secure the furtherance of his own views, while his demeanour in office certainly gave much colour to their accusations.

> DEAR ADDERLEY,
>   I write to say that I shall be glad if you can call here at 12 o'clock to-morrow to consult as to the best mode of dealing with Mr. Lowe's last new dodge. Your observation as to the retention of the objectionable principle of putting the endorsement on the wrong side of the account is quite correct.
>   Yours sincerely,
>   DERBY.

The criticisms of Mr. Lowe's opponents were formulated in a motion brought forward by Lord Robert Cecil (April 24, 1864) : " That in the opinion of this House the mutilations of the Reports of Her Majesty's Inspectors of Schools and the exclusion from them of statements and opinions adverse to the educational views entertained by the Committee of Council, while matter favourable to them is admitted, are violations of the understanding under which the appointment of the inspectors was originally sanctioned by Parliament." Mr. Lowe resigned, preferring resignation to explanation, and content to bide his time till the future should give him an opportunity for vengeance on his opponents.

The British establishments on the Western Coast of Africa were severely criticised by Adderley (July 18), and he gave notice that early in the next Session he should move for a Select Committee to inquire into the whole subject, " with a view to preventing the recurrence of present evils." Governor

Pine had "grand notions," and had written home that it "was useless talking of peace," and that "the silence of the King of Ashantee must be broken." "My Government," wrote Governor Pine, "is not a Colony but a Protectorate, so that I cannot call upon the natives or the inhabitants to supply either their labour or their money." Adderley pointed out that "our country was spending vast sums in maintaining wars in protecting one barbarous tribe against another—and this in a deadly climate which the highest authority had described as being a hotbed of disease. Moreover, during war, the abolition of the slave-trade was suspended, and the abolition of the slave-trade was the avowed object of our Protectorate."

Among Adderley's correspondence at this time are letters from Disraeli and John Bright, relative to the appointment of a West African Committee. The expression of their respective views as to Colonial principles is remarkable; and it is interesting to note that Disraeli was characteristically unwilling to risk crossing the temper of the country. He wrote:

HUGHENDEN MANOR,
September 13, 1864.

DEAR ADDERLEY,
I agree with you very much in your general views respecting our Colonies, but I can't conceal from myself that the country is not yet ripe for them. It has been so long accustomed to the idea of what they call Colonial Empire, and the power and profit which they erroneously associate with their obsolete conceptions, that it is in the highest degree painful and perplexing for them to contemplate the altered relations which now exist between the metropolis and its settlements. I think we could count on no united party support in favour of a resolution which on such matters asserted a principle; but a Committee of Inquiry, as you contemplate, is another affair, and in my opinion it would be a feasible move. I am therefore in favour of bringing forward the subject. . . .

Yours sincerely,
D.

Bright wrote :

ROCHDALE, *August* 25, '64.

DEAR MR. ADDERLEY,

I have given very little attention to the African question since the Committee of 1853, and am afraid I should not be of much use to you. I think the whole subject needs inquiry, and that a Committee may now do good ; for there is evidently a more reasonable temper in the House on questions of this kind than formerly prevailed, and the evil principles so long taught by Lord Palmerston seem to be losing their influence. . . . If you wish to have me on your Committee I will not refuse to serve upon it ; though I think it will take a good deal of time and labour. Mr. Baxter, I think, would be a good man on such a Committee. No other name occurs to me just now. He is acute and well-informed, and a good man of business.

To conclude the matter, we may here add that on Adderley's motion the West African Committee of Inquiry was formed in the following February (1865) ; that it ended its labours a year later, when Mr. Cardwell announced (February 8, 1866), that, as the result of its inquiries, orders had been given for the final abandonment of McCarthy's Island, and as regarded the more general recommendations of the Committee the Governor of Sierra Leone had received instructions to make arrangements for the reduction of the establishment of Lagos ; and that the objectionable state of the law which was proved to have existed with regard to domestic slavery was to be met either by alteration in the law or by a restriction of the area of territory.

NOTES FOR 1864

Local work : i.e. North Warwickshire Friendly Society, Sutton Coldfield Grammar School, Rugby Commission Report—got rid of Justice Clerk's fees, National Grants to Colleges—Saltley College first met for three dioceses united (of Worcester, Lichfield, and Hereford).

Feb. 13.—Dined with Disraeli.

March 5.—Dined with Lord Salisbury.

In the House of Commons worked at Gaol Bills and Prison

NOTES FOR 1864 (continued)

Discipline. Opposed Sir G. Grey (Home Secretary), Penal Servitude Amendment. Moved resolution to rescind the School Endowment Minute — Great whip on both sides, Government gave in and rescinded Minute. *I obtained in Gold Coast Debate appointment of West African Committee.* New Zealand debate, etc. Moved not to expose British troops in Canada unless supported by colonial forces.

Promoted Metric System of Weights and Measures ; supported Northcote extending flogging for Rape.

March 13.—I got a wretch, Hall, off being hanged—interview on Sunday with Sir George Grey [Home Office] for reprieve from hanging due the next day at Warwick—just in time.

April 22.—To Stoneleigh with Lord Carlisle and Lord Houghton for Shakespeare Tercentenary at Stratford.

May 28.—Dined with Sir E. Bulwer-Lytton.

June 22.—Dined Sir Roundell Palmer [afterwards Selborne]—Wensleydales, Lord Zetland, Fortescues, etc.

Sept. 28.—Beresford Hope and Lady Mildred came to Hams. Weigall the artist came to paint my portrait for the Birmingham Corporation, and Julia's for me.

Oct. 17.—Sir William Hartopp died. I went later to Four Oaks on executor's business, I being appointed Eddie Hartopp's guardian.

Among visits this autumn one was to Shugborough [late Earl of Lichfield]. Met there the Abercorns [1st Duke and Duchess] and the Elchos [present Earl of Wemyss and his first wife, *née* Anson].

1865

Early in January Crewe Hall (Cheshire) was destroyed by fire. Lord Crewe—very eccentric—wrote to his sister, Lady Houghton, while the house was in flames, " You used to complain this was a cold house—you wouldn't say so *now* ! " That very evening he wrote and commissioned an architect to build it up again. He said that he knew that as soon as the news got into the papers all his friends would write and suggest different architects, so he settled the question at once ! [When Hams Hall was burnt, many years later, Lord Norton said he acted on Lord Crewe's plan and began to rebuild immediately.] .

The Hon. Lady Adderley
Lady Norton

from a portrait by H. Weigall

At the General Election in July, Adderley was re-elected for North Staffordshire, but lost the head of the poll, the Liberal candidate Buller taking it, ousting Lord Ingestre, the second Conservative member. Disraeli wrote to Adderley after the election :

"You did your duty, and more, as is your custom, but the result to me was astounding. How came Ingestre to be so unaware of his position? and what causes occasioned it? You can answer these questions when we meet again on the Opposition Bench.[1] Pray make my compliments acceptable to Mrs. Adderley and believe me,

"Always yours sincerely,
"D."

Lord Ingestre insisting on standing on this occasion cost Adderley £4,000, as colleagues shared their election expenses, the whole of which amounted to double that sum.

On the death of Lord Palmerston in October, Earl Russell succeeded as Prime Minister.

NOTES FOR 1865

I took part with Bright in opening the Exchange, Birmingham.

Cobden died.

I took part in many debates, etc., etc. Duke of Marlborough introduced my Tithes Bill in the Lords to enable mother-churches to sell their tithes in districts cut off from them, and making District Vicarages, to tempt them to buy.

Lord Denbigh's funeral came in the midst of electioneering.

He was in William IV.'s and Queen Adelaide's Courts, with Lord Howe—two good Warwickshire men.

We visited Lord Houghton [Monckton Milnes], the Archbishop of York [Thomson] and the poet Swinburne being of the party, for the opening of the Industrial Exhibition for working men at Wakefield.

Lord Houghton and Sir Roderick Murchison were afterwards our guests at Hams for

[1] Lord Ingestre, eldest son of the Earl of Shrewsbury. The Shrewsbury family were too confident of their influence in the county.

Notes for 1865 (*continued*)

the British Association at Birmingham.

We went to Compton Verney for Lord Willoughby de Broke's coming of age, to Titsey for our nephew Charlie Leveson Gower's christening, and to Pitchford, for a ball at Shrewsbury, when we got upset !

Matilda Hartopp married Lord Edward Pelham Clinton in August ; we dined with Lady Hartopp (Dowager) the evening before : the Duke of Newcastle, all the Clintons, and all the Hartopps were present.

CHAPTER XXXIII

1866

FRANCHISE AND REDISTRIBUTION

THE year 1866 "began thankfully," writes Adderley, "for all ten children around us. But I thought the political prospects dull, not knowing what the coming year was to bring me of interesting official work."

Adderley was on the Paris Exhibition Committee, the Prince of Wales being in the chair. In connection with the Exhibition he went to Paris at Easter. His notes record :

We went to Paris at Easter. Sitting one day on the terrace at St. Cloud over the Seine, two officers came beside me and discussed the possibilities of siege and bombardment—which came to pass four years afterwards.

At Paris he prepared what proved one of his most successful speeches in Parliament—namely, on the County Franchise Bill.[1] Lord Dunkellin carrying

[1] In the " Life of Lord Iddesleigh " an interesting conversation between Adderley and R. Lowe with reference to the Franchise Bill is thus recorded : " *Feb.* 6, 1866.—Mr. Adderley mentioned that some careful inquiries had been made in certain boroughs, from which it appeared that 26 per cent. of the present £10 householders were of the artisan class, and that the extension of the suffrage to £6 householders would give the artisans 78 per cent. He says this was mentioned before Sir C. Wood, and that Wood said the Government information goes beyond that. Lowe said to Adderley : ' If you stand firm to your guns and oppose the Bill, I will undertake to bring you men enough to give you a majority of fifty against it.' A. said : ' What Bill do you mean ? ' L. said : ' Any Bill that lowers the franchise by one sixpence.' "

his amendment in favour of a borough franchise based on rating instead of rental (June 18), the Government was ousted towards the end of June, Adderley a second time contributing his share to the fall of Lord John Russell and to the elevation of Lord Derby, thirteen years having elapsed since the former occasion.

How much Adderley was in the confidence of his chief is shown by an interesting letter of Lord Derby—it was written in the month before the dissolution—in which he explains what is in his mind in regard to the Franchise and Redistribution of Seats :

ST. JAMES'S SQUARE,
May 10, 1866.

DEAR ADDERLEY,

I regret that you should have been prevented from attending our meeting on Tuesday. We had a long discussion, in the course of which all the fifteen present delivered their opinions *seriatim* ; and I understand the unanimous decision to be to meet the second reading of the Seats Bill by a resolution setting forth what appears to be the vices of its principle ; such as the mode in which they carry out their scheme of grouping, by clubbing together in every instance existing boroughs, and not availing themselves of a fair opportunity of admitting some considerable unrepresented towns by uniting them with small existing constituencies ; their plan for the rectification of boundaries, which I look upon as most objectionable ; to which might perhaps be added the reduction in the numbers of English representation. But I much regret to hear that since the meeting a strong objection has been expressed by many of our friends, under what I consider a very mistaken view, against any obstacle being placed in the way of the second reading of the Seats Bill. I might, indeed, be disposed to concur with them, if the second reading did no more than affirm the principle of Redistribution which we admit, and if the defects of the Bill were such as admitted of correction in Committee ; but that, as you will at once see, is inapplicable to the two first objections, and especially to the first, which does not admit of being dealt with in detail. Nor shall we have the opportunity of raising the question on going into Committee, after which I hardly think we could move an amendment applying to one of these alone. The difficulty is very great, and I do not see any mode of preventing defections, whatever course we take, which will destroy the effect produced by our unanimity on Lord Grosvenor's motion. I am far from objecting to meet the Government half-way on fair terms; but I have no reason to suppose that they, on their part, will make any such concession as we can be expected to accept; nor that we can force any such upon them; nor that, if so forced, they would accept them. As the Bills now stand (and I am not sanguine as to any extensive modification) they will simply be the extinctions of the Conservative party (and I may add of the real Whigs), for a period probably much exceeding the duration of my life at least. I know the dislike and apprehension with which many of the Whigs look on the measure, but I have no confidence in their breaking to any extent with their party. I need not ask you to consider this letter as confidential. I hope you will be able to attend the meeting to-morrow.

Yours sincerely,

DERBY.[1]

Lord Derby, on becoming Prime Minister, offered Adderley a post in the Government. He wrote:

ST. JAMES'S SQUARE,
July 4, 1866.

DEAR ADDERLEY,

I have accidently delayed longer than I intended requesting you to do me the favour of

[1] This letter indicates some want of accuracy in Mr. Herbert Paul ("Modern England," vol. iii. p. 36), as regards the motives and principles of both parties. He hints that the Conservative objection was a mere pretence; and (p. 87) he seems to ascribe to *Gladstone* some things which *Lord Derby* evidently had in his mind in May 1866.

accepting the office of Vice-President of the Board of Trade. It is, as you are aware, like your late office, a Privy Councillor's place, and changes now in contemplation will make it still more important than it has hitherto been. Pray let me have an early answer, as no time is to be lost. We shall have to go down to Windsor to be sworn in on Friday.

Lord Derby, the same day, gave Adderley the choice of being Vice-President of the Board of Trade " to be made separate " or Under-Secretary for the Colonies. " I chose the latter," notes Adderley, "as being acquainted with the subject. I reminded Lord Derby that he had refused me this office before [in 1852] because my views were then considered dangerous." [His colonial views had not changed in the meantime, but had been generally adopted.]

NOTES (*continued*)

On Buxton's resolution condemning Governor Eyre's suppression of the Jamaica rebellion, I defended Eyre, to my chief Carnarvon's disgust. J. Stuart Mill denounced me in a speech which he called in his biography his best.

The story of the Jamaica rebellion and its sequel has been often told. In the previous October a wild and mutinous outbreak of the negroes[1] had taken place at Jamaica, followed by deplorable circumstances. It was thought by many persons in England that the Governor, Eyre, had shown too much haste and severity in his treatment of the rebels in proclaiming martial law, under which Mr. Gordon, a coloured member of the House of Assembly, was summarily tried and hanged, after having been found guilty (it was alleged illegally and on insufficient evidence) of having incited the ignorant natives by seditious speeches and misrepre-

[1] *The Annual Register* (1865, p. 265) states : " Nothing could exceed the brutality with which the infuriated negroes perpetrated their atrocities."

sentations. On the other hand, the steps taken by the Governor met with the entire approval of the Legislative Council and House of Assembly, while he himself claimed that his prompt and vigorous, if severe, measures had saved Jamaica from further revolt. Feeling ran high in England for and against Governor Eyre. By his opponents, among the most prominent of whom was J. Stuart Mill, he was denounced as a murderer ; and a strong agitation was got up against him throughout the country. Mill was earnestly supported by Huxley, Tom Hughes, Herbert Spencer, and Mr. Goldwin Smith. Eyre's partisans formed the Eyre Defence Fund Committee, among the subscribers being Carlyle, Charles Kingsley, Tennyson, and Ruskin. Strange combinations of dissimilar personalities united to do Eyre honour—Kingsley and the Earl of Cardigan, of Balaclava fame, were associated in giving a banquet for him on his landing at Southampton in August, 1866. Adderley was on the side for supporting authority, and was of opinion that no Governor in the future would dare to act on his own responsibility in an emergency, however dangerous, if Governor Eyre were not upheld.

Writing three years later, Adderley, in his "Colonial Policy," thus treats the subject of the Jamaica Rebellion : " Royal Commissioners were sent out to report on the circumstances of the insurrection and its suppression ; and their report affirmed the gravity of the rebellion, and praised the Governor for the promptitude and vigour with which he at first put it down, but condemned the excesses and barbarities which took place in the process of punishment. ′ Governor Eyre was recalled, and has ever since been the subject of persecution by a private committee in England, but without effect. The object of the prosecutors has been to obtain a decision of what is law in cases where law fails, and where the officer in command, in the paralysis of law, has to exercise his own discretion *ne quid detrimenti res publica capiat*; and very naturally, all they have obtained is an elaborate conflict of opinions, with successive abortions of legal proceedings. Exaggerated expressions have been used, both by those who have made themselves special mouthpieces of a common condemnation of the horrible excesses committed in suppressing the insurrection, and by those, on the other hand, who indignantly vindicate from injustice an honourable officer who had a difficult task to perform, and certainly failed no further than in insufficient control, while all around him was savage passion and inveterate animosity, and who in long service has proved himself as humane, as able and courageous " (" Colonial Policy," p. 234).

Adderley was not acquainted with Eyre at the time, and it was not till eight years later that they met, when Eyre called on Adderley in London. Whatever may have been the mistakes and short-comings of Eyre as a Governor, one cannot but feel compassion for him on reading a letter of his to Adderley dated June 3, 1872, of which the following is an extract : " Since your friendly support was given to me," he says, " I have undergone the ordeal of persecution and prosecution, carried on through a series of years in every varied form that our very elastic law admitted of, in almost every possible court of England, and upon nearly every charge that the ingenuity of lawyers could devise—both in criminal proceedings and in civil actions. I have the satisfaction of knowing that in no single instance was any one of the multifarious accusations sustained, a result at least justifying those who, like yourself, so nobly supported me when the outcry against me was the loudest. . . . As it is, Jamaica was saved and I am ruined—an example which will afford little en-couragement to public men to undertake personal responsibility in grave national emergencies."

Towards the end of 1866 the Canadian delegates arrived in England and were received at Stowe by the Duke of Buckingham, who, a few months later, was to succeed Lord Carnarvon as Secretary of State for the Colonies and to become Adderley's chief in that department. Adderley was present at Stowe to assist the Duke in receiving the delegates.

1867

We began the year by receiving Sir John Macdonald[1] and the Canadian delegates on a visit at Hams : I, afterwards, dined with them at my chief, Lord Carnarvon's, in London.

I worked hard at my office, representing the Colonies in the House of Commons. There was little party discipline,—no opposite division from Lord John Russell or Gladstone,—Grosvenor making " Cave of Adullam."

We gave many receptions, and among others to the Bernstorffs [Prussian Minister]. In March Carnarvon, with Lord Cranborne and General Peel, resigned on Dizzy's Reform Bill.[2]

I had just carried the Canadian Confederation Bill through the Commons. (See *Annual Register*, 1867.) [" Lord Carnarvon," says Lord Norton in his " Imperial Fellowship," " had the satisfaction to present this great measure to the House of Lords, and it was my good fortune, as Under-Secretary, to have to carry it through the Commons."][3]

I afterwards carried the International Railway Bill under the Duke of Buckingham, Carvarvon's successor.

On July 6 an amusing incident, recorded by Mr. William White in " The Inner Life of the House of

[1] Right Hon. Sir J. A. Macdonald, G.C.B., many years Prime Minister of Canada. See page 237 for his letter twelve years later.
[2] The " Second Reform Bill," giving household suffrage in towns and the franchise in the country to all who paid an annual rental of £12.
[3] Lord Norton's " Imperial Fellowship," 1903.

Commons," took place, when Disraeli, who had de-
puted Adderley to reply to Mr. Horsfall's motion,
ended by leaving Adderley in the lurch. Why the
Under-Secretary for the Colonies should have been
selected for the ungrateful task does not appear.
He had certainly no connection with the theme of
the debate. Adderley did feel Disraeli leaving him
in the lurch, but he saw the humour of the situation,
and used to laugh heartily in telling the story. Mr.
White makes so merry a yarn of the episode that
we quote it here verbatim :

"On Monday night we had another sell ; but this
time it was the Conservative party that was sold—
sold in the most open, flagrant manner. Mr. Horsfall, the Conservative member for Liverpool, moved
that Liverpool, Manchester, and Birmingham should
each have a third member. Mr. Adderley was put
up to answer Mr. Horsfall—(put up, mark, for no
Under-Secretary would presume to rise unless he
was asked to do so by his chief)—and he made a
speech in his voluble but somewhat washy manner,
and proved to his own satisfaction, if not to the
satisfaction of anybody else, that the thing could
not, and asserted that it must not, be done—
Disraeli, the while, sitting close to the Under-Secretary. Now what was the nature of his reflections
all this time ? He looked, from a distance, as if he
was either profoundly thinking or not thinking
at all, so still, so immovable were his features.
Had he, then, resolved to grant all that his hench-
man was trying to prove could not be granted, or
was he revolving in his own mind what he should
do ? This can never be known. It would seem
that he must have determined beforehand to grant
Horsfall's request ; but, if so, why did he let
Adderley speak ? But, either way, it is clear that he
had consulted nobody. The grim, sardonic, silent
man ! his ways are indeed past finding out. Perhaps,
though, he really only determined to give way after
Adderley had spoken. Colonel Taylor was in constant communication with him, and he may have
whispered possible defeat in his leader's ear, or
Disraeli may have retreated in order to save himself

from defeat. After Adderley's speech there was a good deal of talk, but it was all on one side—that is, for the Amendment. At last Disraeli rose, and there was silence profound until his intention to concede began to ooze out, and then there came tittering, gradually growing into loud mirth mingled with louder cheering. And what did Adderley do? Poor man! Well, for a time, he looked exceedingly miserable. At length he rose and left the House, and did not return till the division was over." [1]

It may be added that an allusion by Adderley to " Mephistopheles " is to be found in a subsequent letter.

Adderley appears to have corresponded with Lord Grey on colonial matters before receiving from the latter the following letter, dated November 1, 1867, which is characteristic of Lord Grey's way of dealing with those whose opinions differed from his own.

DEAR MR. ADDERLEY,

I write one line to say I will not attempt to answer your last letter, because I don't want to take up your time to no purpose; and it is clear that I can no more hope to alter your opinion than you will change mine, as I think your view of all the facts totally erroneous.

Yours faithfully,

GREY.

FURTHER NOTES FOR 1867

I presided over a Liberal-Conservative Working Men's Association in the Exchange at Coventry; and I in vain attempted the abolition of hiring farm-servants at " Mops."

Our chief domestic event was Charlie's coming-of-age [eldest son]. Balls, dinners, cricket-matches, etc., at Hams.

Alarmed at my even course of prosperity. Evils all around, and some I might have mitigated!

[1] "The Inner Life of the House of Commons," by William White, vol. ii. pp. 71-72.

CHAPTER XXXIV

1867–1868

LETTERS TO LORD LYTTELTON

ADDERLEY'S intimate friend, Lord Lyttelton, went out towards the end of 1867 to New Zealand to visit his property, and the settlement which he and Adderley, some twenty years earlier, had jointly helped to form. Adderley wrote to Lyttelton:

HAMS,
December 30, 1867.

Before you had actually started I heard of Selwyn's taking Lichfield.[1] I even thought of telegraphing to you, but it was too late. I much regret it, as he vacates a post no one can fill as he did, and he takes a post I am not so sure he will thrive in. His brother told me the Queen asked him three times, "and he knew how to obey orders." I said "I never heard him so described!" He has taken his post at Lichfield, deserting Eccleshall, and intending to be the focus of all episcopal influence. What alarm this must have spread already! He will visit New Zealand again before he settles down here. I hope next Tuesday to have him and Sewell here [Hams]. As to this country, it is simply Fenianised. We are all becoming special constables, and the Home Office warns all to look sharp for the winter. I long to hear of your voyage and reception,

[1] Bishop Selwyn had been Bishop of New Zealand for twenty-six years; and it was there that he accomplished his great work, and where his administrative powers were most valuable. He was appointed to the See of Lichfield in 1868, and died there in 1878.

and impression of New Zealand. I hope you will find Bowen [Sir George, the new Governor] starting auspiciously, and Grey [Sir George] retiring peacefully, and the Colony fairly co-operating with our best and most liberal wishes towards them. I want much to hear what they really will do in the way of local government, and whether they will reduce their provincial governments in the municipal direction. Are they really prepared to undertake wholly their own defence? The Pan-Anglican having wholly broken down, they will have a clear source for a thorough Colonial Church, and set the example of all other Colonies. If Bishop Patterson succeeds, I should think he will be up to the occasion. But what a miserable endowment to start upon! I thought Selwyn would have made more of it in that way by now. Pray give my kindest remembrances not only to Selfe, and Spencer,[1] and οἱ ἀμφι, but to Fitzgerald,[2] whom I grudge to New Zealand, and all other mutual friends you meet. . . .

Politics are dead here since you left. Gladstone has let out in five speeches in two days all that he had bottled up, and that Dizzy's lumbago and wife-billing had averted before.[3] It does not look like a troublous Session, except for conspiracies at home and rumblings abroad. On the contrary, even Bright can make no hand of it; and as for things to be done, they are too perplexed for any definite handling yet, and must wait for the new Parliament. I hope Grote's[4] gum and Spencer's Blackstone kept down, with petroleum pills [for sea-sickness]. You would be taken up for carrying about such pills here, now there is so much Fenianising by chemicals which are being prohibited.

[1] Lord Lyttelton's son, the Hon. Spencer Lyttelton.
[2] James Edward Fitzgerald, afterwards Prime Minister (see pp. 168, 306, 307).
[3] Gladstone, among other recent speeches, had made a great speech at Southport on December 19, when he proclaimed an Irish policy, a policy of higher education, reform of religious institutions, and land reform. Lord Morley calls this "the standard raised." Mrs. Disraeli had a month earlier suffered from serious illness, and was now convalescent.
[4] The historian.

Strange times! Wars, rumours, and earthquakes. I hope you will perform your Antipodean return ticket safe from all; and we shall all want you back, though we Dizzyites won't let you be Colonial Minister just yet. . . .

COLONIAL OFFICE,
January 1868.

We have been fighting the Treasury daily, trying to get them to make a clear account with New Zealand, and say quits on Bowen's fresh start [on becoming Governor]. But they are so hungry for money in the Abyssinian desert that they will try to pick up even crumbs—more fools they. For the rest, we are in the thick of a Hudson's Bay plot with Canada, which addresses the Queen to act on the 146th section of the Confederation Act, and annex it at once. Sir E. Head [1] died suddenly in the midst of our discussions, and we have a Yankee, Sir E. Lampson,[2] and Watkin to deal with—not so easily. Sewell [3] has been with me at Hams, and FitzHerbert [4] has just arrived. I am in great hopes we may start Bowen well.

I fell in with Gladstone in the train, and had a talk with him, in which he told me I ought to be hung for some of my colonial shortcomings—e.g. having so many troops in Colonies, especially in what he called the weak point in England's fortunes—North America.[5] He was looking well, and

[1] Right Hon. Sir Edmund Walker Head, eighth (and last) Baronet, K.C.B.
[2] A native of Vermont, U.S.A., created a Baronet in 1865 in connection with the completion of the first Atlantic Telegraph Cable.
[3] See pp. 114, 115.
[4] "Early in 1868 the New Zealand Finance Minister, Mr. Fitz-Herbert, arrived in England for the purpose of conferring with the Imperial Government, and he executed his instructions in the fairest and ablest manner" (Adderley's "Colonial Policy," p. 156).
[5] This was chaff. No one was more keenly in favour of withdrawing British troops from Colonies than Adderley, and he and the Duke of Buckingham gradually worked for that end where possible. Lord Granville, succeeding as Colonial Secretary, carried out the same policy. (See FitzMaurice's "Life of Lord Granville," vol. ii. pp. 22-24, where Adderley's "Colonial Policy" is quoted.)

the blow on the eye had done no harm. Lord Derby is still laid up with the gout—having received two royal visits, and, I suppose, drunk . . . champagne. He is very cross about the Fenian bothers, which are most troublesome and expensive. Even our ships of war are patrolled at night. We are deciding on Virgin Gorda,[1] one of the Virgin group, for our new naval West Indian Station, on St. Thomas' being blown up.

Ever affectionate,
C. B. A.

COLONIAL OFFICE,
February 28, 1868.

We are in a Ministerial crisis, but Gladstone won't be in again just yet. The new arrangements are taken well, and the Whigs are down in the mouth, and still hampered by their old narrow circle. Dizzy will die hard; indeed, I doubt if Mephistopheles can die, though he may twist Faust's neck.[2] We are hard at work in this shop [Colonial Office] annexing Hudson's Bay and snubbing Howe's repealers, who are over here. His friend Seward, with his Fenian allies, are insolence itself. We are full of ideas of consolidating the West Indian Islands into two or three governments, and thus get better men as governors, judges, etc. Perhaps one or two bishops only for all. I think Virgin Gorda will be our new packet station. Get us all the information you can pick up about them. As to Parliament, I suppose Chancellor Hunt[3] will be simple in his Budget, and act only as Dizzy's sub. The Irish debate will be the chief.

[1] *À propos* of the Virgin Islands, Lord Norton used to tell a story of Sir John Pakington, whose ignorance of geography when he was Colonial Minister was well known. When suddenly accosted by a lady saying across the dinner-table : " *You*, Sir John, can doubtless inform us where are the Virgin Islands ? " his native wit came to his assistance in concealing his ignorance, and he readily replied, " As far as possible, my dear lady, from the Island of Man."

[2] Disraeli became Prime Minister on Lord Derby's resignation, and did not fall till the end of the year.

[3] The Right Hon. Ward Hunt.

CHAPTER XXXV

DISRAELI SUCCEEDS DERBY

Notes 1868 (*continued*)

This was my last year in the Colonial Office with the Duke of Buckingham as chief—rough, hearty, and full of work. I had many subjects to deal with: West Indian Naval Station, Hudson's Bay, New Zealand, etc.

I beat Bright on the Nova Scotia motion.

The Union of Nova Scotia with Canada had been effected in the previous year (being part of the Act which Adderley carried through the House of Commons). Some of the people of Nova Scotia strongly disliked the Union, though more of them had desired it; and Bright, representing the disaffected, attacked the Act, which he said was in the nature of "a fraud upon the Imperial Parliament," and asked for a Royal Commission of enquiry. Adderley denied that the people of Nova Scotia had been "entrapped," and said that this country was now asked to undertake a most questionable interference with the local affairs of North America, that a Royal Commission would be an unpromising remedy for the grievances, and that the recommendation to appoint one, under the circumstances, was "about the most insane thing the House could be asked to agree to." Cardwell brought his great experience of North American affairs to bear in support of

Adderley, but Bright was very angry with Adderley's speech, and insisted on going to a division, which resulted in the defeat of his motion by 183 to 87.[1]

In March Lord Derby resigned for Disraeli to be Prime Minister. Disraeli, wishing to oust Lord Chelmsford from the Lord Chancellorship in order to substitute Cairns, treated all offices as vacant, and filled them all up as before with the exception of the Lord Chancellorship.

Disraeli accordingly wrote at this crisis to Adderley:

> 10, Downing Street,
> *March* 3, 1868.
>
> Dear Adderley,
>   I hope you will do me the favour of filling, under the new Administration, the office which you filled in the Government of Lord Derby. Our great friend wants us all to stick together.
>   Yours sincerely,
>   D.

It was about this time that Disraeli remarked to Adderley: " There are two rules, when in office, to be always borne in mind: in the first place never speak a word which you can help speaking, and in the second place never write a word which you can help writing." The latter part of the advice Adderley treasured up, and on a future occasion acted on it to Disraeli's satisfaction.

Notes (*continued*)

Gladstone defeated Disraeli on the Irish Church Disestablishment Bill in April.

---

[1] Bright had previously more than once said Adderley would go down to posterity for his great colonial services, but afterwards wrote, Adderley "is a very *dull* man !"

I took Sir Hercules Robinson and Sir Etienne Carter to Stoneleigh [on a visit to Lord and Lady Leigh] where Jefferson Davies, late President of the Southern States, also came.

I accompanied Disraeli to the Council at Windsor for the Queen to dissolve Parliament.

I was elected again with Buller [Liberal] without contest.   Staffordshire was now in three divisions.

The Ministry resigned, forestalling defeat, the November elections having gone against them. [Sir Charles Adderley consequently was out of office.]   Gladstone was sent for by the Queen from a ball at Hawarden, and became Prime Minister. Bright was made a Privy Councillor.

1869

The great public event of the year was Gladstone's disestablishment of the Irish Church.

R. Lowe's strange Budget, *ex luce lucellum*, attacked by the East End match girls.   They asked Mr. Lowe, " What would Lucy say ? "

The Rugby Trustees were two days in my house in Eaton Place drawing new Statutes under the Act, and blotted their fame by electing Dr. Hayman Head Master.   [Lord Norton habitually took the greatest interest in his duties as a Trustee of Rugby.]

I went to Windsor to be invested by the Queen as K.C.M.G. [Knight Commander of St. Michael and St. George] and became " Sir Charles," at Lord Granville's request.[1]

[1] This Order of Knighthood, founded in 1818, and originally limited to natives of the Ionian Islands, Malta, and the Mediterranean, had been recently reorganised and made assignable to persons who had rendered valuable service in colonial or foreign affairs.

This was a graceful attention from the new Liberal Colonial Secretary to the late Colonial Under-Secretary in the Conservative Administration. When Sir Charles Adderley walked into the House of Commons for the first time after receiving his knighthood, Disraeli said, " I am glad our opponents decorate our bench."

Lord Granville wrote, April 15, 1869 :

MY DEAR ADDERLEY,

Please to read the last paragraph of a speech I made at a dinner of the Colonial Society, reported in *The Times* of the 11th March. You will see there a reason why I venture to ask you whether you would allow me to offer to you the Knight Commandership of the St. Michael and St. George. I have written with the same object to Lord Lyttelton.

Yours sincerely,

GRANVILLE.

Lord Granville had said on the occasion alluded to in his letter : " The Duke of Buckingham [when Colonial Secretary], pressed by the extreme difficulty of obtaining the Order of the Bath for men who by services in the Colonies had a just claim for honour, procured the Queen's sanction to a reorganisation of the Order of St. Michael and St. George and its extension to the whole of the Colonies, and a complete remodelling of its statutes. This was only done on the eve of the Duke's resignation. . . . My duty," continued Lord Granville, " for whatever time I may be connected with the Colonial Office, will be to maintain the high character which has been impressed upon the present Order, and to confine the gracious mark of the Sovereign's favour to those who have done real and great service to the Empire " (*Times*, March 11, 1869). Lord Norton used to say that the motto of the Order should be (from Horace) *Imperi porrecta majestas*, and not the meaningless, *Auspicium melioris ævi*.

Sir Charles Adderley's chief work this year was in writing his admirable " Review of Earl Grey's

14

Colonial Policy of Lord J. Russell's Administration " [1853] and a subsequent " Colonial History." [1] It should be read by all who wish to follow the gradual expansion and history of our Colonies up to the year 1869. It was in allusion to this work, and to other essays on colonial policy, that the Right Hon. Joseph Chamberlain said that not only did Lord Norton render " great services to the State, but in his writings he left on record a statement of facts and principles which have been useful to all his successors."

AMONG DOMESTIC EVENTS FOR 1869:

Our son Charles caught Scarlet Fever in September while visiting the Dilkes at Maxstoke Castle [near Hams] where his mother and I went to nurse him. . . .

[After this Charles, the present Lord Norton, became engaged to Miss Caroline Ellen Dixie, daughter of Sir Alexander Dixie and sister of Mrs. Dilke—the marriage took place in 1870.]

1870

Gladstone's second year of great changes. The First Irish Land Act.

My time was chiefly in the chair of the Sanitary Commission in Lord Northbrook's place [afterwards Viceroy of India] and in the Report on it which has been a digging for all Acts on the subject since.

Now began Prussia's conquest of France, which France drew on herself.

I had an amusing drive on Lord Tollemache's four-in-hand on Derby Day to the Tollemache [Dysart] place, Ham House, Twickenham; *Gladstone on the box.* Young Tollemache drew him out at

[1] Reviewed by Mr. Reeves in *The Edinburgh Review*, 1870, vol. 131, p. 98.

tea-time, asking him to account for some speech, which he did to this boy as fully and more amiably than to men.

[Among serious thoughts chronicled :]

I see a guiding Hand more and more strengthening my faith. Life is given to prove the conquest of selfish nature—to acquire the Spirit of Christ, to live in Him, that is to live *out of self*.

1871

The absorbing interest was Prussia surrounding Paris, and, soon, the Commune horrors.

I was finishing up my Sanitary Commission. Stansfeld[1] brought in *Local Government* Bill on my report, credit was given me for the *title* which disarmed opposition. Poor Law and Health were put in one department.

I helped to defeat Sir John Lubbock's attempt to open school endowments.

I raised debate on Washington Treaty : Roundell Palmer, Gladstone, and Northcote making great speeches.[2]

[1] Sir James Stansfeld became the first President of the Local Government Board, August 1871, previously President of the Poor Law Board.

[2] August 1871, " Hansard," vol. 208. Sir Roundell Palmer said : " It must be satisfactory to the House to find that on the colonial branch of the subject, on which the right hon. gentleman (Sir Charles Adderley) is entitled to speak with the greatest authority, the Treaty of Washington is entirely approved by him. I feel indebted to him for having, with the assistance of the Government, brought the subject forward, because I cannot think that it would have become the House to separate without devoting some time to a review of this matter." Mr. Gladstone said : " My right hon. friend, the member for Staffordshire, has been the critic of the Treaty of Washington upon this occasion ; but, subject to some few exceptions, I do not think that even his judgment on it has been very unsatisfactory . . . for as to the points on which he bestowed most of the time, viz. the points that touch the interests of Canada, he gave a very weighty opinion that Canada had reason to congratulate herself on the result of that negotiation."

I stayed away from the combined attack of Conservatives and Radicals on the Government—White's motion on National expenditure—and I threw over the Duke of Sutherland's Stoke-on-Trent Purification Bill as unfair, etc., etc.

A most pleasant fine day was spent this summer with Corry [ex-First Lord of Admiralty] going over Chatham and Sheerness.

The London season was fertile in agreeable dinners and parties—at Dorchester House, Holland House, the Bernstorffs, etc. [Count Bernstorff was elevated from Prussian Minister to German Ambassador, on the unification of Germany. He died in 1873. He and Countess Bernstorff were intimate friends of Sir Charles and Lady Adderley.]

Notes of Domestic Events

1871

The marriages of Eddie [Hon. Sir E. Chandos Leigh and Miss Rigby] and of Jimmy [Hon. and very Rev. James Leigh, Dean of Hereford] with Miss Butler—" Fanny Kemble's " daughter.	Deaths of intimate friends : Dugdale of Merivale, Sir Thomas Dyke Acland [his father's friend and contemporary] ; Lord Aylesford [sixth Earl] ; C. Buxton.

1872

Thanksgiving at St. Paul's on the Prince of Wales's recovery—a fine National Church gathering.

My chief work in Parliament was assisting Stansfeld passing the Public Health Bill, which was based on my Sanitary Report; moving resolution for Reform and Industrial Schools to be in Education Department, Sir John Pakington supporting me ; but majority was against.

À propos of Sir Charles Adderley's Sanitary

Report, and the Bill based on it passed in Gladstone's administration, it is recorded that on one of the last days, or rather nights, of March, Disraeli, "in mid-debate" in the House, hurriedly handed to Sir Charles Adderley a scrap of paper— still preserved and docketed—on which he had written, "Give me in writing your point you were $\frac{1}{2}$ mentioning this evening, D." Sir Charles, knowing his chief's liking for brevity, and re- membering the advice he had given him on a former occasion, wrote in reply a few short, but concise notes on sanitation, while others, applied to by Disraeli, bored him by replying at great length.[1] The result was Disraeli's famous " Sanitas Sani- tatum " speech, delivered at Manchester a few days afterwards in which he alluded in complimentary terms to Sir Charles Adderley's sanitary measures. " A great scholar and wit," said Disraeli, " three hundred years ago said that, in his opinion, there was a great mistake in the Vulgate—which, as you know, is the Latin translation of the Holy Scriptures—and that, instead of saying, 'Vanity of Vanities, all is Vanity !—*Vanitas Vanitatum, omnia Vanitas !* '—the wise and witty king really said, ' *Sanitas Sanitatum, omnia Sanitas !* ' . . . Pure air, pure water, the inspection of unhealthy habitations, the adulteration of food—these, and many kindred matters, may be dealt with by the Legislature, and I am bound to say the Legislature is not idle upon them ; for we have at this time two important measures before Parliament, one—by a late col- league of mine, Sir Charles Adderley—is a large and comprehensive measure, founded upon a sure basis, for it consolidates all existing public Acts and improves them," etc.[2]

[1] The circumstances appear to be incorrectly told by Sir M. Grant Duff (Diaries, July 10, 1893), as from his account it would seem that Disraeli was Prime Minister at the time, and that he "sent round to the various departments to ask what they were doing, when many of the ministers replied at great length," whereas on April 3, 1872 (the date of the "Sanitas Sanitatum" speech), the Gladstone Government was in, and Sir Charles was, of course, not "President of the Board of Trade."

[2] "Selected Speeches of Lord Beaconsfield," vol. ii. p. 511.

Government was twice beaten, and I helped, by voting with them, to save them from a third beating by Admiral Erskine on April 19, on the Pacific Islands debate.

[Among domestic events :] Margaret Leigh married Lord Jersey; Gilbert Leigh came of age [the late Hon. Gilbert Leigh].

Among contributions to the Visitors' Book at Hams this autumn was the following anonymous one (September 1872) :

All-beauteous nature, whimsical though kind,
To different creatures different tastes assigned.
In peaches wasps delight; and boys in jams;
In turkeys, Aldermen; but *all* in *Hams.*

1873

I took part in many debates, and served on the Noxious Trades Committee. Gladstone, beaten on the Irish Universities Bill, resigned, but returned.

Arthur Sullivan stayed with us for the Birmingham Musical Festival.

In the autumn we visited the kind Tollemaches at Peckforton Castle. [Mr. (afterwards 1st Lord) Tollemache and his second wife.]

My locked-book shows a growing want of sympathy with my party, and wish to retire from Parliament. [It was rather a want of sympathy with any party.]

CHAPTER XXXVI

1874

PRESIDENT OF BOARD OF TRADE

A SUDDEN dissolution in January; I got in again without a contest. The elections going against Gladstone, he resigned [Disraeli became Prime Minister again].

Annals of Our Time for January 7 chronicles an allusion to Sir Charles Adderley, by Mr. Grant Duff, in a speech addressed to his constituents at Elgin, in which he expresses an opinion that for a Conservative Cabinet to be possible—not as a mere stopgap, but to live with its own life—not one or two men like Lord Derby are necessary, but half a dozen ; and I do not see the men, . . . an assertion which I make without forgetting the merits of politicians like Mr. Cave or Sir Charles Adderley." [1]

I was sitting with the Rugby Trustees, electing Jex Blake to the Head-mastership, when Disraeli's letter was brought to me offering me the Presidency of the Board of Trade.

Disraeli's letter, which bears a broad black edge as mourning for Lady Beaconsfield, is dated 2, Whitehall Gardens, February 23, 1874.

[1] *Annals of Our Time*, vol. ii. p. 1133.

DEAR ADDERLEY,

If agreeable to you, I will advise the Queen to appoint you President of the Board of Trade.

Yours sincerely,

B. DISRAELI.

(He had hitherto usually signed " D." or "Disraeli," without the " B.")

The announcement of this appointment unfortunately got into the local Warwickshire papers, and was copied into others before the Queen had ratified it. This breach of etiquette was said to have much displeased Her Majesty. The Queen, however, merely remarked, with some emphasis, to Disraeli, who reported the occurrence to Adderley : " I *know* who your President of the Board of Trade is ! " but did not resent the premature announcement as she once did in the case of a Bishop.

When accepting the Board of Trade Adderley, with characteristic humility, told Disraeli he " knew nothing about it." Disraeli replied, " You know as much about it as Ward Hunt does about the Navy."

No sooner was I in office than I had a severe attack of rheumatism in the legs. Of course I had numerous speeches to make officially in the House, and Bills to conduct.

Plimsoll constantly attacked me on shipping, and ran me hard on a second reading [Hansard 170.173]. I had interviews with the Cabinet on Board of Trade questions and Bills. London Gas Company required legislation.

My pleasantest work was with the Trinity House, and I went on several cruises on board the yacht *Galatea* with them, inspecting lighthouses and lightships. Once we were caught in a sea-fog and anchored at sea, ringing bells all night to avoid a collision—repaid by a delicious landing in the

morning on hills smelling sweet with thyme—
never forgotten.

I gave a Greenwich dinner to colonials.

Our neighbour, young Lord Aylesford, gave his
last flare-up at Packington—a ball in a temporary
pavilion to the Prince and Princess of Wales.

This year died my intimate friend Charles Wynne
Finch; and the highly intellectual Edward Twistleton[1] by suicide.

This brilliant man of letters and of many attainments is described in a letter of Adderley to Lord
Lyttelton, October 7, 1874 : " Edward Twistleton
has died very suddenly at an hotel at Boulogne after
a day's illness—though I think he went there feeling
ill ; and he wrote thence a peculiarly affectionate
letter to my wife and myself, as if a special instinct
of leaving us was on him. You know what a quiet
and criticising intellect his was, and what a store
of literary knowledge, ancient and modern, of all
languages he had. An hour with him was sure to
be a treat and a fillip. It is as great a mental loss
as Godley. How our lights seem going out! Their
successors are for the next generation. One cannot
renew the light of one's own early days, but must
be content to set with them shortly [Adderley
survived over thirty years]. Only this week last
year he was here, and I engaged him to write a
continuation of ' Hallam's Literature '; but he said,
' Life was too short. . . .' Pity such a fountain
should only have sent forth spray—worth little but
its own sparkle ! Yet I suppose his conversation
and influence among his literary friends was his
métier. He was the whetstone to make others cut

[1] The Hon. Edward Twistleton (see " Dictionary of National
Biography "), born 1809, died 1874, brother of the sixteenth Lord
Saye and Sele, is said to have served on more Commissions than any
man of his time. Twistleton erected the monument to Keble in
Westminster Abbey. Adderley accompanied Twistleton to the
unveiling of it, both expecting a large concourse of people, but
found, to their surprise, no one present except Dean Stanley and
the sculptor !

—I wish you would give me, out of your classical store, a line for his tomb. I might suggest it to Saye and Sele [Adderley's brother-in-law]. As to his sceptical turn, I believe his was a form of intellect which will have its own judgment. His morals were sensitively high, and I don't believe a low or impure thought could ever rest in his mind. Anything unjust, or unkind, or dishonourable positively nauseated him. I used to think of ——'s scepticism, I would prefer it to the faith of many, and I have always thought the earnestly incredulous Jews were infinitely worthier than the merely nominal professors of Christianity. So do I disburden my mind to you in this sadness to-day."

This was the outpouring of one friend to another, each himself imbued deeply with religious faith. Lady Adderley, who had been the intimate friend of the late Mrs. Twistleton, an American lady, noted for her beauty and singular charm,[1] had written to Lord Lyttelton about Edward Twistleton: " It is very sad, but I cannot but hope, from much that I have seen of poor Edward during this long illness [Mrs. Twistleton's], that the heart is more opened to convictions than Mr. Claughton [2] imagines. Every allowance must be made, in first approaching him, for a most reserved and inaccessible nature, and a great deal of eccentricity, but he is most affectionate, and kind sympathy will do much."

[1] Ellen, daughter of Edward Dwight, Member for the Province of Massachusetts, died 1862.
[2] Afterwards Bishop of Rochester.

CHAPTER XXXVII

1875

MERCHANT SHIPPING BILL

THOUGH not in the Cabinet, I had charge of the chief Government measure, the Merchant Shipping Bill.

My other official subjects were : Marine Insurance Bill—not proceeded with ; Railway Regulations ; Gas Bill ; Trade Marks ; Dover Harbour.

The Merchant Shipping Bill got choked.

On July 22 Disraeli withdrew the Bill—Plimsoll shook his fist at him in the House. I had a scene with the ministers in Disraeli's room.

The Unseaworthy Ships Bill was then introduced by me and passed [a temporary measure].

With regard to the withdrawal of the Merchant Shipping Bill,[1] which elicited the fury of Mr. Plimsoll, Adderley remarked in a letter to Lord Lyttelton :

" I warned the Cabinet over and over again that their delays in putting their own Bills on before,

---

[1] This measure gave protection to seamen in the Merchant Service against the danger of being sent to sea in vessels unfit for voyage. Mr. Samuel Plimsoll, M.P. for Derby, had taken this up as his special subject, believing that many lives were lost by the unprincipled conduct of certain shipowners whom he accused of sending men out in rotten, but well-insured, vessels.

would involve them in a Plimsolliad and gratuitous discredit, as the Bill was progressing, and, as Hartington said, four days more at the outside would have finished it."

Adderley, not being in the Cabinet, was under a disadvantage in these very delicate circumstances.[1] It is said that Disraeli, when asked why he did not offer Adderley a seat in the Cabinet on making him President of the Board of Trade, gave as his reason : " Because Adderley will be Adderley still."

The following account of this episode, so notorious in the annals of the House of Commons, is contributed to these pages by " One behind the Scenes," and contains some little-known touches :

" On the day of the Plimsolliad Sir Charles Adderley had had an interview with the Cabinet upon coming to the House, and had told Dizzy plainly it would be monstrous on his part if he did not recognise Plimsoll. Sir Stafford Northcote, who represented the Board of Trade in the Cabinet, was told to go down and tell the Commons at four o'clock that a measure would be brought in securing survey of unseaworthy ships. This he did, and Plimsoll was in ecstasy, when Dizzy entered and vetoed any inquiry, and told the House that such was the congested state of public business, that due consideration could not be accorded to Plimsoll's wishes. The Irish party around Plimsoll told him to remonstrate, which he did, going up the middle of the House and calling out at Mr. Bates, M.P., ' Villain,'[2] and shaking his fist at Dizzy's nose, who was reclining on the bench, and never moved a muscle, until Lord Henry Lennox had taken Plimsoll on to the terrace to cool his passion. Then Dizzy arose and told the Speaker that, after the extraordinary conduct of the member for Derby,

[1] Sir Stafford Northcote wrote to Adderley (September 19, 1875) : " The misfortunes of last Session were largely due to the fact of the President of the Board of Trade not having been able to make himself disagreeable in Cabinet."

[2] Mr. Plimsoll's words were : " I am determined to unmask the villains who send to death and destruction . . . (Loud cries of order and much excitement)."—Hansard, July 22, 1875.

he could not do less than admonish him.[1]   Next day
Sir Charles Adderley was sent for by Dizzy, who
confessed that he had erred, and told Sir Charles
he must get him out of the mess.   A short Bill
was then brought in, temporarily empowering the
Board of Trade to appoint surveyors to stop ships
over-laden and unseaworthy."

During the year that Sir Charles Adderley had
been President of the Board of Trade he had
mastered the details of his office, and, modest as he
had been on first undertaking his new duties, he
now felt himself as capable as any man to carry
through the work which he had begun.   That he
had "done his duty, and more" towards the passing of the Merchant Shipping Bill was acknowledged
by those most likely to know the facts.   Mr. Farrer,
Permanent Secretary of the Board of Trade (afterwards created Lord Farrer), wrote to him of "the
single-heartedness, unfailing temper, and unwearied
zeal with which, under every discouragement, you
have worked at the most difficult and delicate business I have ever known at the Board of Trade";
and we may here anticipate events by alluding to
his triumphal carrying of the Bill in the following
year.   It may be added that Sir Charles Adderley
had a great respect for Mr. Plimsoll's high character
and philanthropic aims, though he considered him
"too blindly against shipowners"—too prejudiced
in his wholesale condemnation of them.

But Disraeli, it was believed by many of his own
party, at the close of the summer session of 1875,
felt his *amour-propre* wounded by the "Plimsolliad"
which had attracted the eye of the country to his
own miscalculation ; and certain members of the
Cabinet who had had a share in the miscalculation
were, it was now rumoured, inclined to blame Adderley as not having managed well.   Among those who
"read between the lines" in the following episode

[1] Mr. Herbert Paul's account proceeds : "Having refused to
apologise, he was directed to attend in his place that day week to
receive the Speaker's reprimand.   When the time came Mr.
Plimsoll expressed regret for his irregularity, and declined to
retract his charges.   He had succeeded in his object. . . ." See
also *Annals of Our Time*, vol. ii. p. 1174.

were, not only Adderley himself, but his friends, Lord John Manners (the late Duke of Rutland), Spencer Walpole, Ward Hunt, Lord Harrowby, and others.

After the prorogation of Parliament Disraeli began to evolve a scheme which, while Adderley was to be treated with all possible respect and consideration, he was to be offered up as the scapegoat of failure—in other words, he was to be the Jonah cast out of the ship.

On August 20 he wrote to Adderley :

MY DEAR SIR CHARLES,
        The Queen has decided on reconstructing the Board of Trade and raising this department to the class of the great offices of State. I should be sorry if this important change deprived me of your services, for I have ever entertained for you respect and personal regard, and I contemplate making some proposals which, if accepted, would allow me to place you in a post not inferior in official esteem to that which you now occupy. But I find myself on this head in a considerable difficulty. The appointment of the new President of the Board of Trade could not be long delayed, because he would have a right to expect, and so, too, the country and his colleagues, that he should have the Recess to prepare for the onerous duties which await him. I find it impossible, from a variety of causes and circumstances, to attempt at this moment the other changes which I am desirous of accomplishing. Still I have thought it best to be candid, that you should be the very first person made acquainted with Her Majesty's intentions. Believe me,
                        Sincerely yours,
                        B. DISRAELI.

It seems strange that Disraeli should have committed himself to asserting that the Queen, to whom he had confided his new idea, had actually *decided* on adopting his somewhat mysterious scheme of elevating the Board of Trade to some novel position of dignity ; more especially when we consider that, as a matter of fact, the scheme ended in nothing.

The directness of the reply which Adderley sent to Disraeli's letter must have been disconcerting to its recipient :

(Copy)   *August* 22, 1875.

DEAR DISRAELI,

I write at once, on receiving your letter, to say that I feel, of course personally, that the step you have taken at this moment must throw on me the blame in public estimation of the failure of the Board of Trade measure of this Session, and will be taken by those who don't know the facts, i.e. by the world at large, as my condemnation. Against this I must protest as a great injustice. The subject was one which was certain to get embarrassed by delays. I frequently wrote reminders through Northcote (my only access to the Cabinet) that Plimsoll's Bill lay behind, and that his wild agitation would become more difficult to deal with than the Bill. I have, since coming down here, put together a memorandum on the whole position, and I am convinced that a revival of the Bill, which might have been carried before Whitsuntide, with adjunct subjects, is the right course now. But I say no more. The matter is very secondarily one of personal consideration, and if my secession will do any good, I can assure you that whatever means my acquaintance with the office, and I will add my devotion to it, have given me of being of service in its important interests, I shall offer these still, as far as I may be able.

Faithfully yours, . . .

A few days later Mr. Spencer Walpole wrote :

August 30, 1875.

MY DEAR ADDERLEY,

I am quite concerned to hear that Disraeli should have thought it advisable to make any

[1] The Right Hon. Spencer Walpole, formerly Secretary of State for Home Department.

changes in the Board of Trade which would deprive the Queen and the country of your loyal, able, and long-continued services. But surely something may, and certainly something ought to be done to keep you in the Board of Trade. It is most unfair to throw on you the blame of the withdrawal of the Merchant Shipping Bill; and when others forced that withdrawal upon you by their own miscalculations, the credit of the Bill which has been passed [the Unseaworthy Ships Bill] should be yours and not theirs. I have no patience with such shabbiness. I can quite understand your feelings about retiring from the House of Commons under such circumstances. But I for one, and I believe many others, shall deeply regret it. . . .

On September 13 Adderley wrote confidentially to Lord Lyttelton : " I expect daily to see the announcement of the Board of Trade. being reconstructed on a larger scale, etc. I am to have an equivalent office to my present . . . but I feel inclined to throw up not only office but Parliament altogether, after thirty-five years' work in it on subjects all of which have prospered and turned out usefully. I can hardly fancy sitting by while another, be he who he may, conducts the measure I had in hand, and which dropped from no fault of mine. Nor do I like sitting in back benches away from former colleagues. Lord John Manners deprecates my notion [of retiring from Parliament], and says I shall incur at my own hands, by suicide, the condemnation which I don't deserve, and should not get by dismissal."

Weeks passed, and nothing more was heard of the scheme for "reorganising the Board of Trade."

Meanwhile Sir Stafford Northcote, who had now returned from a holiday in Switzerland, whither he had gone "to escape his letter-bag," went to stay with Disraeli at Hughenden, and, much in Disraeli's interests, told him he heard Adderley had made up his mind to leave Parliament ; whereupon Disraeli empowered him to write to Adderley offering him the Headship of the Civil Service Commission, vacant by the death of Sir Edward Ryan, a post which, although a Privy Councillor's place, debarred its holder from a seat in the House of Commons. Northcote thereupon wrote to Adderley from Hughenden, October 12 : "Since I have been here I have had a good deal of talk with Disraeli about the Board of Trade. When he wrote to you some weeks ago he was thinking over some arrangements which would have involved considerable changes."

So now we have it. "Disraeli was *thinking over*," which Disraeli had expressed : "the Queen *has decided*."

Sir Stafford then proceeds tentatively to make Disraeli's offer.

Disraeli next proposed, in addition to the Civil Service Commissionership, to recommend Adderley for a peerage at no remote date. At least "I would bind myself," he wrote, "that I would not leave office without advising the Queen to accomplish our common wish" (the Queen's and Disraeli's wish).

Lord John Manners, Ward Hunt, and other friends, still advised Adderley not to leave the House of Commons, and Adderley went to consult his old ally, Lord Harrowby, at Sandon. Lord Harrowby was, as his father, the friend of Pitt, had been before him, a man of wide political influence. He had, moreover, "a particular affection and respect for Adderley."[1] He wrote to Disraeli, who shortly afterwards sent his (Disraeli's) intimate friend Lord Bradford to Adderley with a message : "Anxious to consult your interests. Don't think yourself deserted by your colleagues."

Sir Stafford Northcote now told Adderley that Mr. Stephen Cave was intended for the Presidency of the Board of Trade, while he told Cave that Adderley was resigning. Adderley, on hearing that Cave, a personal friend for whom he had so high a regard, was to be the new President of the Board of Trade newly constructed (as he believed), and with newly added powers, did not hesitate further.

---

[1] Letter of Lord Sandon, December 5, 1882, on Lord Harrowby's death.

15

He even wrote to Cave urging him to accept, while he wrote to Disraeli accepting the offer of the Civil Service. Cave wrote in reply to Adderley, and at the same time sent him a copy of a letter he had written to Disraeli, accepting the Board of Trade, which after all was offered to him *without any additional powers, and without even a seat in the Cabinet.*

(Copy of letter from the Right Hon. Stephen Cave to Disraeli.)

CLEVE HILL, BRISTOL,
October 18, 1875.

DEAR MR. DISRAELI,

Northcote has communicated to me your proposal that I should take the Board of Trade with another Parliamentary Secretary [Hon. Edward Stanhope, Vice Mr. George Cavendish-Bentinck]. He has assured me that Adderley, who is a much better man than I am, is satisfied with the arrangement, otherwise I could not for a moment entertain it. Personally I would much rather be left where you kindly placed me, as I cannot but be sensible that I am invited to undertake a task of no ordinary difficulty, and one which may probably break me down. I have told Northcote that I think the Presidency of the Board of Trade should be accompanied by a seat in the Cabinet. I am sure it cannot be properly worked without it. At the same time I do not wish to add to the difficulty of the situation, and therefore I hold myself unconditionally in your hands for the present, and will of course do my best. I am very indifferent to office provided my credit is saved, and if my retirement would make matters easier I am equally ready to retire."

This copy was enclosed to Adderley with the following letter:

Tuesday, October 19, 1875.

MY DEAR ADDERLEY,

Many thanks for your letter, which is exactly what I knew you would write. You have probably received by this time one I wrote to you. I should not have congratulated you had I not been assured that the peerage was a certainty. . . . I daresay I might have stood out for the seat in the Cabinet, but I don't like bargaining with people who are in a corner, and if one fails after all, which I fully expect to do, one would justly be kicked all the harder after setting so high a value on oneself. My wife is very angry with me for thinking of the Board of Trade, which she thinks will certainly kill me. My best consolation is that not a thousandth part of the people one fancies mark what is done amiss really trouble their heads about one. I must say I would rather be improving apricots with Sir W. Temple (was it not ?) than be trying to infuse honesty and humanity into traders by land or sea. Perhaps Disraeli may think that so unwilling a horse, as my letter to him shows me to be, is not worth driving. I shall not cry over it. But I am sorry to think that our walks in the small hours of the morning are over, and that you will no more insidiously tempt me from divisions. . . .

However Mr. Cave, becoming aware of all the circumstances two days later, withdrew his acceptance of the Presidency of the Board of Trade. He wrote to Adderley :

Thursday, October 21.

I have bolted ; Disraeli has never answered me, and I have recalled my letter, and said I felt so strongly that the President should be in the Cabinet that I would rather not take office, but, having declined a more important post, I did not think it right to retain those I now hold, so I offered to resign them, which I think he will accept, as he wants to place G. C. B. [George Cavendish Bentinck]. I only wish I had done this at first instead of showing the vacillation I have done. But I know I am an impostor, and if I took the Board of Trade I should be found out. In great haste.

Sincerely yours,

STEPHEN CAVE.

The episode concludes with a letter from Disraeli to Adderley, which, if taken in conjunction with his original letter, makes interesting reading :

October 23, 1875.

DEAR SIR CHARLES,
My original letter to you was solely prompted by a feeling that you ought to be the first person made acquainted with a plan which was then known only to the Sovereign and myself, and I never contemplated for a moment that while the changes, which were always contingent, were in embryo you should feel under the necessity of withdrawing from the duties of an office which were so peculiar and so pressing as those of the Board of Trade. [Yet in his original letter Disraeli says : " The appointment of the new President *could not be long delayed, as he would expect to have the Recess to prepare* for the onerous duties which await him." Adderley was therefore expected to vacate in the Recess.]
Not having succeeded in my first and main object, I offered you the Head of the Civil Service Commission, and, when you accepted it, the Presidency of the Board of Trade to Mr. Cave. He did accept that, and has since declined it. The position of affairs is now serious for the Government, and I cannot think deservedly so. The functions of the Board of Trade are in urgent public request. I must therefore, now, ask you to retain your post, and act not provisionally, and give your best energies to putting your office in a train to meet Parliament. I will give you one great assistance. I will relieve you of your present secretary [Cavendish Bentinck], and if, as I trust, you comply with my wishes, I will place as your subordinate one of the most rising members of the House of Commons [namely the Hon. Edward Stanhope].
Yours sincerely,
B. DISRAELI.

Thus everything remained as before with the

exception of a new Vice-President, and, as Adderley's notes tell us :

A new Merchant Shipping Bill was drafted by me, which next Session [1876] I carried triumphantly alone and unaided, my second, E. Stanhope, being laid up with illness.

FURTHER NOTES FOR 1875

I and Edmund [his brother] sailed with the Admiralty in the *Enchantress* to Poole Harbour about a Naval Cadet school ashore ; and to the Channel Islands, and settled to abandon Lord Palmerston's Alderney Harbour.

Gray, Head of Marine Department of Board of Trade, accompanied me to the Eastern Ports in special train—a grand reception.

I went with Edward Stanhope to Liverpool, with Gray to Bristol, Plymouth, etc., about Marine surveyors ; I gave prizes in the *Worcester* training ship. At a grand dinner in Trinity House—Royalty abounding—the Lord Chancellor proposed my health.

Our visits this year were to the deaf and dumb Lord Carbery—Ball at Burleigh—Disraeli there for coming of age of Burleigh [afterwards Marquis of Exeter] ; to Ravensworth Castle [Lord Ravensworth] ; and to Studley Royal [Lord Ripon].

1876

The New Merchant Shipping Bill which I carried through was the largest measure carried during this Ministry. I had to fight Plimsoll on several clauses, but he only beat me in one, and I carried my load-line against him, though it goes by his name.[1]   His was the popular side, too blindly against shipowners, whom I brought to reasonable terms for sailors' safety.

The more difficult "Maritime Contracts Bill" Sir Stafford Northcote took up, but dropped.

The storms of debate over the Merchant Shipping Bill were likened in their violence to storms at sea— certain wags said Adderley was "at sea" in more senses than one.   He had in fact less experience of a tempestuous ocean than of its figurative counter- part in the House of Commons.   He successfully weathered the storms there and steered his ship safely through them to "the haven where he would be."

I had a most agreeable voyage with the Admiralty in the *Enchantress* to visit officially the German Naval posts—Wilhelmshafen and Kiel.   The Em- peror [William I.] ordered hospitable reception for us everywhere.   All the German officers speak English, and their best ships are built in England [1876].

The Prince of Wales returned from India, ar- riving off the Needles with three war-ships—a lovely morning; the Princess met him in the Royal Yacht, and as he went on board and kissed her all the bands struck up "Home, Sweet Home."

Disraeli made the Queen Empress of India, and she made him Earl of Beaconsfield.

Domestic events were :

Arden takes honours at Oxford; the marriage of our daughter Isie with Vauncy Crewe; the sad

---

[1] In after-years he frequently alluded to the fact that "Plimsoll's Load-line " was in reality his own.

death of my best friend, Lord Lyttelton ; the death of my old Christ Church friend, George Drummond ; our Church at Lea was begun to be restored and improved, Julia giving a legacy she had recently received.   My worry at home was the Lea vicar attacking my right to land which my ancestress, Dorothy Adderley, had charged with the vicar's income.   I finally settled the question by exchange of land, and making conveyance to the living.

Our principal neighbour's place was now deserted by the A's. . . .

CHAPTER XXXVIII

1877

OFFICIAL INTERESTS

THE year began with deluges and storms. Dover Pier was half destroyed, which gave the Board of Trade much scheming. This was a year of official enjoyment: moderate work of great interest, and with able permanent staff, such as Farrer [afterwards Lord Farrer], and Edward Stanhope for second [Vice-President of Board of Trade], and Charlie [present Lord Norton], my private secretary. I think I was liked in the office, and I was in kindliest relations with all. Often I was sent for to the Cabinet on various Bills Seaman's Discipline Bill, etc.; Marine Insurance was my dread. I took the chair of the Select Committee on polling hours. Beaconsfield disputed my right to appoint Miller to the Railway Commission [a post worth £3,000 a year], but Cairns [Lord Chancellor] backed me, and a compromise was made.

Lord Beaconsfield contended that the Railway Commission was not subordinate to the Board of Trade, and that the appointment rested with the First Lord of the Treasury; but the name of Mr. Miller (Q.C.)[1] being submitted to the Queen and

[1] The late Sir Alex. E. Miller, C.S.I., was Legal Member of the Railway Commission from 1877 to 1888.

Her Majesty's consent and signature being obtained, Lord Beaconsfield had no choice, as the Lord Chancellor pointed out, but to agree to the appointment. The truth was that Sir Charles Adderley's secretary and eldest son Charles, taking advantage of the fact of his having received no instructions not to proceed with the appointment of Mr. Miller, hastened a special messenger to Osborne, obtained the Queen's signature, and thus thwarted Lord Beaconsfield and secured the appointment of Mr. Miller. Although Sir Charles Adderley was not responsible in this matter, it was the second time within two years that he had been the means of crossing Disraeli. It is said that Disraeli never forgot it.

The war between Russia and Turkey opened in this spring. Struggles of debate through whole nights in the House of Commons began. Lord Derby gave a splendid banquet in the Foreign Office, where Schuvaloff [Russian Ambassador] met Musurus [Turkish Ambassador].

On Sunday, July 1, Arthur, our third son, was drowned. I had on Saturday, June 30, dined with the Duke of Cambridge—all the ambassadors there ; and early on Sunday morning joined Julia at Eton, and attended Communion in St. George's Chapel with Jem [his fifth son James, then a boy at Eton]. On our returning to London next morning we were met at Paddington Station with the terrible news— Arthur drowned ! Charlie and Arden brought the body to Hams. Sad reopening of Lea Church with Arthur's funeral.

This dearly loved son was drowned in the Falls of Bruar, near Blair Athol. He was reading at Pitlochry with his brother Reginald and Mr. Fairley, their tutor, during the beginning of the Long Vacation from Christ Church, Oxford. They were looking at the view from the head of the Falls. Arthur Adderley had gone to a spot by himself, and stepped in, and was instantly carried away into the torrent beneath. Mr. Fairley, hearing the splash and seeing him in the water, ran down and jumped into the lower dam to stop the body, but in vain. The falling water kept the body under, and it was not found for many hours afterwards. No young man was ever more beloved by relations, friends, and all who had anything to do with him in college or in home life, old or young, or by servants or his poorest neighbours. Among notes written by Lord Norton some years later, alluding to the gloomy views of death dwelt on by some religious persons, the following refers to this son :

Arthur's temperament was more joyous. . . . He seized the *life* view ; and R. too, when he suddenly lost him, dwelt more, even at the time, on the Communion they had just had together than on the terrible event itself. Arthur's was the stronger mind, but he left that impress on ——'s character, intense love and faith overcoming sorrow and death in the almost visible presence and communion of a Divine Saviour of transcendent love.

Another note tells of the stricken mother. Brave as always in spirit, Lady Adderley gradually failed in health after the shock of this bereavement, when the seeds were sown of the malady of which she died ten years later :

It broke her heart. . . . Many others she loved as dearly, but this wound never healed up in her depth of feeling.

Queen Victoria wrote on this melancholy event :

WINDSOR CASTLE,
July 4, 1877.

The Queen trusts Sir Charles and Lady Adderley

will not think she intrudes on their terrible sorrow by writing, but she cannot remain silent on hearing of the awful misfortune which has just befallen them, and she wishes to express her deep and heartfelt sympathy with them, and how her heart bleeds to think of the overwhelming and stunning shock which they must have experienced on hearing the terrible intelligence. Most truly does the Queen hope that their health may not suffer, and that they may be mercifully supported by Him who alone can give comfort and peace of mind.[1]

[1] Autograph letter.

CHAPTER XXXIX

1862-1886

HAMS THEATRICALS

By a melancholy coincidence, a portrait of Lady Adderley appeared in *The Whitehall Review* among a series called "Leaders of Society" in the very week of her great sorrow. Lady Adderley was the last person to claim to be classed as a "Leader of Society," but this chronicle of her husband's life would be incomplete without reference to Lady Adderley as a hostess at Hams, not only when distinguished politicians were entertained there, but when the very remarkable series of amateur theatricals annually took place. Ever since 1862 these had come to be looked upon as a necessary part of a Warwickshire Christmas. The houses in the neighbourhood were filled, and many came from afar to witness these performances, which attained a social celebrity. After the death of Arthur Adderley there was a break before they were resumed, as Lady Adderley wrote to a friend, "for the sake of the many unselfish children I have left."

Among the originators of these theatricals, in the early days, were Lady Adderley's brothers—the Hon. Chandos Leigh [1] (of "Old Stagers," Canterbury, fame) and the Hon. James Leigh,[2] the "Jim Boly" who helped Sir Francis Burnand to found the Cambridge A.D.C.—were noted for their theatrical ability. But, "not content with mere family talent,"

---

[1] Now Hon. Sir Chandos Leigh, K.C.B., K.C.
[2] Now Dean of Hereford.

236

said *The St. Stephen's Review*,[1] " the Hams Company has always numbered among its members the rising amateurs of each generation." In a long list appear the names of Charles Weguelin, William Anson, Stephen and Alfred Scott Gatty, J. F. Clerk, Foster Alleyne, Lionel Benson, Claude and Eustace Ponsonby, Captain Gooch, Augustus Spalding ; and of later years, last but not least, the names of Arthur Bourchier, Charles Colnaghi, Alan Mackinnon, and Lionel Monckton stand prominently forth. In fact, most of the principal " Windsor Strollers " and "Old Stagers " of twenty years ago were to be found among the company at Hams, " Father Adderley " himself in his early youth being the " life and soul " of the troupe. The pages of the *Hams Theatrical Chronicle* are indeed a record of amateur performances remarkable alike for their long continuity and for the artistic care and skill which were displayed in their production.

[1] For January 1884.

CHAPTER XL

1878

FINALLY ACCEPTS PEERAGE

January 23.—Given the freedom of the Shipwrights' Company at a banquet in the Grocers' Hall, with W. H. Smith and Lord John Manners.

February 27.—Dined with Duke of Cambridge—all the ministers.

There were Ministerial changes owing to Disraeli's Eastern Policy. On his venturing the passage of the Dardanelles, Carnarvon resigned. Disraeli wanted the Duke of Somerset in his place, and Cave and Ridley in office and Plunket attached. Disraeli offered me the Governship of New South Wales, £7,000 a year [or more]. I refused, and said nothing would tempt me abroad. On March 8 Disraeli offered me a peerage for the third time. On Sunday, March 31, a messenger came from Disraeli to say the Queen yesterday offered me a peerage, which I finally accepted, in consequence of changes on Lord Derby's resignation. The Queen said a peerage was due to me " by long service and social position."

Three days later it was announced that Sir Charles Adderley was created Baron Norton, of Norton-le-Moors, Staffordshire. He was succeeded in the

RIGHT HON. SIR C. B. ADDERLEY, K.C.M.G., FIRST LORD NORTON

p. 238]

Presidency of the Board of Trade by his friend, Lord
Sandon, the eldest son of Lord Harrowby—an
appointment which gave Lord Norton especial
pleasure.

On closing the episode of Sir Charles Adderley's
career at the Board of Trade it may here be recorded that when Mr. Joseph Chamberlain succeeded, two years later, to the Presidency of that
department in Gladstone's Government, he told Sir
Charles's son that he found "several splendid
measures pigeon-holed" in the office (they were
drafted by Adderley) and asked why the Conservative Government had not passed them—one of them
being the Carriage of Grain Bill,[1] which he himself
passed, and which (he added) "had put the first
feather in his cap."[2] The answer was that Mr.
Chamberlain had in Gladstone a chief who appreciated those who served in office under him, and
made use of their services.

On April 13 I made a farewell address to former
constituents of North Staffordshire, after thirty-
seven years, followed by the novel feeling of having
nothing to do after a great deal of work lately. I
took leave of the Speaker and all the officers of the
House of Commons and of the Board of Trade, after
being four years President. At the Civil Service
Engineers' dinner I made my last ministerial speech,
praising Lord Salisbury's circular [who had succeeded Lord Derby], which riled Gladstone so much
he nearly left the room in anger with me; but my
speech was well received, especially by Lord
Granville.

The sun probably did not go down on Gladstone's
wrath. At all events on April 20 he wrote to
Norton: "I am glad to find an unforced oppor-

[1] Or Grain Cargoes Bill.
[2] Mr. Joseph Chamberlain permits this record of his conversation.

tunity of offering you my hearty congratulations on your assumption of a peerage. In no quarter will you leave behind you any sentiments except those of friendly recollection and regret, and for my own part I shall gratefully remember what good service you have done at an important juncture from within the Conservative Government to the cause of a sound colonial policy."

The Indian troops being brought to Malta without Parliament being consulted was loudly attacked, but Beaconsfield assumed the Protectorate of Cyprus.

I got this year my last cruise in the Trinity House yacht *Galatea* with Lord Caithness—picking up Edmund at Ryde. Nisbet and Waller were the Elder Brethren. We ran along the south coast to the Scilly Isles, where we were received by Governor Dorien Smith at his abbey.

On June 4 I spoke for the first time in the House of Lords on the Public Health amendment.

CHAPTER XLI

1878 (*continued*)

SPECIAL ENVOY TO MADRID

[IN July] I was sent as special envoy to Madrid to represent the Queen at the funeral of Queen Mercedes of Spain. Charlie [1] and Arden accompanied me as attachés. Lionel West, English Minister to Spain, joined us on the way. On our arrival at the frontier a guard of honour was in attendance, and at the entry of every province a captain-general always accompanied us through. We arrived late at Madrid in consequence of our reception all the way along. Sir John Walsham received us, and the German and Italian envoys in uniform. We called in ceremony on the foreign ministers and President of the Council, and they returned the call at our Hôtel de la Paix ; and later dozens of ambassadors came. Next morning I went early to see the Museo with Major de Winton—who represented the Prince of Wales ; the rest of the day was spent in leaving two hundred cards on every official and ambassador, special or ordinary. At two I had an audience of King Alfonso, presenting the Queen's letter, making a short speech in French. The King said that, of all the kind messages sent

---

[1] His eldest son, secretary to the mission.

him, there were none that had touched him so much
as Her Majesty's, and especially referred to the first
and other telegrams, which went to his heart. I
was told by Sir John Walsham that the Queen's
first telegram completely overcame the King, and
that he sobbed convulsively. "The Queen of
England's letter," said the King to me, "comes from
the heart, and is not a mere formality." [When
Lord Norton afterwards informed the Queen of
this it gave Her Majesty especial pleasure.] The
King told me to present Charlie and Arden to
him, and asked about Arden's uniform.[1] The heat
was intense, and a gold cuirass uniform hardly
tolerable. Lionel West and Sir John Walsham
dined with us in the evening.

The following is an extract from a draft of a report
of the proceedings which Lord Norton wrote on his
return, in obedience to the Queen's wish conveyed
to him by General Sir Thomas Biddulph :
"The Queen," wrote Sir Thomas, "would like,
if you will kindly do it, to have a report drawn up
by you, not exactly official, detailing all the circumstances to which you allude, which report the
Queen will keep as a record of your mission, and
of one of the most melancholy events which has
ever come to Her Majesty's knowledge."
After giving an account of his reception by the
King, Lord Norton's report continues :
"Nothing could exceed the dignity and self-
possession of the young King, combined with a
most winning and engaging manner, deeply afflicted
as he most evidently is, yet rousing himself for
all necessary public duty. Perhaps I may mention
here a note the King sent by me to Lord Rosslyn,
which is signed ' Votre affligé Alphonso,' and which

[1] The Manchester; the King said he would like his own
regiment to have a similar uniform.

expresses a consciousness of inability yet to realise the full extent of the great loss he feels he has sustained. The Duke of Sestos most obligingly showed us over the Palace, and there I saw full evidence of the domestic happiness and love which has been so soon and so abruptly taken from the King, in the arrangement of the private rooms, and all the traces of cultivated social life. I was permitted to go into the very room where this beloved Queen breathed her last. Not a thing had been allowed to be touched since the fatal moment. The very candle by the bedside remained as if just extinguished, and the last worn dressing-gown was hanging near. I was told much of the late Queen's kindness to all about her, and attention to the poor of Madrid, and the many charities she personally attended to—short and young as her life as Queen had been. The eloquent sermon of the Bishop of Salamanca,[1] though so highly in her praise, seems to have been no flattery. The King returned to the Escurial on the evening of the 16th. On the 17th the grand funeral service took place at the great church of San Francisco. Besides the large concourse of high officials, ecclesiastic, diplomatic, civil, and military, there were so many of the chief nobles and ladies present, though everybody had been driven from Madrid by the intense heat, that no less than 5,000 were excluded from an absolute deficiency of room. The Church was entirely draped with violet cloth embossed in gold with the Spanish, Orleans, and Bourbon bearings, and illuminated with innumerable candles. The music was Spanish, most exquisite in itself, and most exquisitely executed with all the highest art of Spain. A white marble cenotaph in the middle of the dome represented the depository of the body, itself already resting in the chapel of the Escurial. The 18th was occupied by farewell official visits, and on the 19th the King sent for all the Envoys at 8 a.m. to the Escurial, where we were presented to the Princess of the Asturias and to the Duke and Duchess of Montpensier. A breakfast was prepared

[1] Or the Archbishop of Toledo.

for us after we had been over the noble work of Philip II., and had seen the chapel where the Queen's remains lie temporarily, while a magnificent tomb is being built for them. They may not be put in the Mausoleum, where all the kings from Charles the Fifth [1] are placed in gilded casket sarcophagi, because no royal issue had been born ; but the King would not allow his beloved Queen to be buried with the other branches of the Royal family, and she will have a chapel for her tomb alone.   The King will soon retire to his château in the Pyrenees, and intends shortly to occupy himself with the Army in the North." [2]

The Queen sent a message to Lord Norton through Sir Thomas Biddulph, July 31, 1878, to thank him for his report, " which is quite what Her Majesty wished to have to keep with her papers."

In October I was President of the Social Science Society at Cheltenham.

Sir Stafford Northcote came to Hams for a Grand Reception at Birmingham.

[1] Charles V., "whose embalmed features were perfect when his coffin was lately opened " (Lord Norton's Diary).
[2] King Alfonso survived Queen Mercedes seven years, dying November 25, 1885, having left by his second marriage a son and heir, the present King Alfonso XIII.

CHAPTER XLII

1879

WORK AND CORRESPONDENCE

WORK in the House of Lords : Employers' Liability, Industrial Schools, etc.

Beaconsfield asked me to speak on Agricultural Depression, and Lords Winmarleigh and Skelmersdale asked me to carry the Poor Law Amendment Bill through the Lords ; which I did.

Julia was presented this year as Lady Norton ; the Queen pressed her hand in recollection of her great sorrow of Arthur's death.

I was President this year of the Birmingham Music Festival. [The President had the right of *encore* ; Lord Norton only gave one—" I waited for the Lord," sung by Madame Trebelli and another. The artistes were grateful that there were no other *encores*, but the audience was dissatisfied.]

During the Session I tried, at Archbishop Tait's request, readings at Lambeth, but it came to nothing.

Lord Leigh anticipated the new game-laws by giving his tenants hares and rabbits.

We made a tour of visits to friends in Devonshire and Cornwall : Aclands, the St. Germans, Robartes, Boconnac, Lord Devon, Lord Fortescue, Kennaway, the St. Aubyns.

Two letters among Lord Norton's correspondence at this period are respectively from two very dissimilar persons—Sir John Macdonald, Prime Minister of Canada, and Professer Max Müller, but are curiously similar in tone. Sir John Macdonald writes (September 7, 1879): " I wish it were possible for me to revisit Hams. [It was twelve years since his former visit.] I fear that time has greatly altered the original from whom the photograph you so kindly mention was taken. I trust that time has dealt leniently with you. It is possible I may return to England next season, and I shall indulge the hope of being able to see you then."

Professor Max Müller writes (January 19, 1880): " I felt surprised and pleased you should remember my visit to you, though I can assure you your charming house has left a very lively recollection in my mind. But nearly a quarter of a century, I fear, has passed since those bright days, and I am afraid you would hardly recognise, in an old grey-headed man, the young German student who was then introduced to you by Lady Mary Feilding. Unfortunately that *mauvais quart d'un siècle* has also made me much less *vagabundus* than I was then, and it is but seldom that I tear myself away from my home, my family, and my books. If, however, my presidential duties should call me and Mrs. Max Müller once more to Birmingham, it would certainly be a great pleasure to both of us to accept your kind invitation."

1880

I was offered the Governorship of Bombay; I declined ; Sir James Fergusson accepted.

Lord Norton corresponded with the Right Hon. W. E. Forster on Educational matters. Mr. Forster wrote (April 4, 1880): " There is no little annoyance in a political life, but the kindly feeling of a political opponent like yourself makes up for a great deal. I am very glad you are coming to see the Bradford High School. There are strong opponents to these high schools in Bradford, though I think the feeling of the town is with me in their favour ; but when you come we must take care that one or two of these opponents go with you to the school, so that you may hear both sides."

NOTES

The elections in the spring resulted in Beacons-field's defeat and resignation, Gladstone becoming Prime Minister, with Bright and Chamberlain in the Cabinet.

I worked in the House of Lords—Employers' Liability, etc., and drafted a Bill on Juvenile Offenders.

Among home matters, a Wesleyan minister asking me for site for a Wesleyan chapel at Bodymoor Heath, Julia started a mission there under Miss Ball, which proved a most successful and useful work.

Sir William Harcourt, Home Secretary, came to Hams for a Birmingham meeting ; I drove him and others with four horses to see Saltley Reformatory, etc. He afterwards sent Litchfield, Commissioner of Charities in New York, to see Saltley.

Sir William Harcourt wrote to Lord Norton :

SECRETARY OF STATE, HOME DEPARTMENT,
September 7, 1880.

DEAR LORD NORTON,
I am extremely grateful for your letter. The subject is one which profoundly interests me. Since I ordered the returns a fortnight ago, I have been appalled at the numbers of children of nine, ten, eleven, and twelve years of age sent to prison for a week, or a fortnight's hard labour for first

offences. What chance is there for the future? I have discharged them by the score as quick as I could, but not soon enough to prevent the prison taint passing upon them. Many of the offences are of the most trivial character—" bathing in canals," " throwing stones," " damaging grass," " stealing turnips," " obstructing streets." At the same time I recognise the difficulties of magistrates still, as to the manner of dealing with unruly and mischievous boys whose parents will not pay the fines. We seem to want some legislative provision for dealing with such cases without making the children gaol-birds. If there could be some sort of child's lock-up where a child could be treated as a naughty boy, for small offences, instead of being treated as a criminal, it would be a great thing. The Jurisdiction Act of 1879 seems defective, as it does not allow the birch except for *indictable offences*, and the protracted periods in Industrial Schools and Reformatories are often not appropriate; besides, these are already over-filled by the School Boards. I should be very grateful if you would give me the benefit of your great experience as to the best remedy for the present state of things. I assure you there are thirty or forty of these committals every day. I am glad to see, by the Manchester papers, that the matter is being discussed there.

Yours very sincerely,

W. V. HARCOURT.

1881

BIRMINGHAM CORPORATION

Lord Salisbury was chosen leader of the Conservative party in place of Lord Beaconsfield.

I undertook a Reformatory and Industrial School Bill, to unite the two; moved Reformatory Resolution in the House of Lords.

I won my Appeal before the Master of the Rolls

against the Birmingham Corporation for fouling the river Tame. [The litigation was first begun in 1854.]¹

I presided over the Birmingham Cattle Show in November.

The Birmingham Corporation having begun a great reservoir of 80 acres near our Whitacre Lodge [at Hams], the Contractor bringing fifty navvies put in wood huts, we got up a Chapel, School, and preacher with success. Tried also, with Fawcett's help, to start a savings bank in the grounds ; but navvies, though they had high wages, would not save.

Domestic events :

Our second son, Arden, married [August 30th, 1882] Grace Stopford Sackville. He had, by the terms of his great-uncle's will, on attaining the age of 25 [in 1879], come into possession of Fillongley.

The late Earl Fortescue, one of Lord Norton's most intimate friends, wrote some verses in the Hams Visitors' Book [October 11, 1881] concluding with this advice to his host :

> But mindful be, still working while 'tis day,
> *Work duly to relieve with needful play.*

1882

A transition year to me owing to serious illness. Going up to London in February for the Session, pain and shivering came on ; severe illness from internal abscess—Erichsen's knife seven inches into me ! Many friends came to see me daily. Lord

¹ See p. 143.

Selborne, Bromley Davenport, and Villiers [Rev. H. Montagu Villiers, of St. Paul's, Knightsbridge], who brought me Communion. [Another frequent visitor in the sick-room was the late Earl of Kimberley.]

I worked in bed with pamphlets on Education and the Penal Code, sending questions to Committee.

In April to Brighton, made worse by walking too soon. At last in wheeled chair, daily preparing to speak in House of Lords. On recovery I sat on Commission for Protection of Girls, Lord Cairns in the chair. ·

Parliament was stormy as the weather. Many M.P.'s suspended. The Egyptian War the chief event. We dined with the Wolseleys just before Lord Wolseley was sent out.

July 28, our fortieth Wedding-day.

In August to Homburg. Doctor let me drink waters too soon, which threw me back. Very pleasant Kursaal. Many friends—Lady Wolseley, who heard there the news of the victory of Tel-el-Kebir. I saw schools everywhere. The American Macpherson interesting.

Lord Norton used to say that in consequence of this illness in his seventieth year he broke some of the habits of his life. He gave up smoking altogether, and soon got accustomed to the change.[1]

He continued his daily ride in London, however, till eighteen years later,[2] his extreme short-sighted-

[1] Up to this time he had been a great smoker. It had been his custom to smoke on the balcony at 35, Eaton Place, late in the evening, however cold the weather. It was on one of these occasions that the late Lord Shrewsbury, sitting out after dinner with Lord Norton, caught the chill which proved fatal to him (May 1877).

[2] Archbishop Benson, at one time, usually joined Lord Norton to ride with him in Rotten Row late in the afternoon.

ness, it may be added, being the cause of some anxiety to his fellow-riders.[1] He took daily walks, and was noted for his fast walking. *A propos* of this habit, Lord Norton related that once, when Disraeli and he were walking together on their way to the House by Wellington Barracks, Disraeli, in the midst of a debate with him, had at last to pant and say, when he could find breath, " If this pace continues—my dear Adderley—our interesting conversation—must end." Exercise Lord Norton considered essential to everybody's well-being. That two of our most illustrious statesmen [2] took none, was a matter of concern to him. " All *animals*," he would comprehensively remark, " require exercise."

Towards the end of this year Lord Norton lost his venerated and beloved friend Lord Harrowby,[3] aged 84. " A rare and beautiful character," his son Lord Sandon wrote of him to Lord Norton.

He had been my chief friend in political life in Staffordshire since 1841, and had recently said to his son [Lord Sandon], that few recollections gave him more pleasure than having brought me forward for the county. [When he himself was Lord Sandon, M.P.]

Lord Norton, on his part, always spoke with warm

[1] *A propos* of his short-sightedness, it is remembered that once, when a large party of guests were assembled before dinner in Eaton Place, in the dusk of a summer's evening, and the moment arrived for Lord Norton to take the lady of highest rank in to dinner, he selected by mistake, out of many ladies of rank, one who had none —a friend of his daughters, unknown to the other guests, who asked each other who she could be. Lord Norton did not discover his mistake until dinner had proceeded for some time, when the answers of the lady puzzled him so much, and his questions appeared to her so random, that explanations became necessary, and to his surprise he discovered that she was not Lady ——— !

[2] Lord Salisbury and Mr. Joseph Chamberlain.

[3] 1882. Dudley, second Earl of Harrowby, K.G., born 1798. The Lord Sandon of Lord Norton's early years in the House of Commons.

gratitude of the start in his career which he owed to Lord Harrowby, at a time in his life when his future seemed undecided.

1883

On New Year's Day Lord Norton received the following letter from Lord Derby, the son of his former chief. Lord Derby had left the Conservative party, and had recently taken office under Gladstone, as Secretary for the Colonies:

KNOWSLEY,
December 31, 1882.

DEAR NORTON,

Your letter has given me great pleasure on various grounds. I believe we have always thought pretty much alike on colonial matters, and certainly we have both taken more interest in them than most men engaged in public life. There is no office which I should have liked so well as that which I now hold, and if it leaves leisure for Grillion's what more can one want? Things seem pretty quiet just now; but Q. how long will it be before our African black sheep begin to jump over the fences? That is the quarter of the globe in which I fear most trouble. Colonies are like children—the smaller they are the more bother you have with them. All good wishes for 1883.

Very truly yours,

DERBY.

Lord Derby always expressed great regard for Lord Norton's opinion. " Your hints are always useful," he wrote on one occasion.

1883

VISITS IRISH REFORMATORIES

I went with Reformatory and Industrial Schools Commission to Ireland. Received by Lord Spencer at a dinner and ball. At the Lord Mayor's dinner some guests were just out of prison, some going in !

We went in deep snow to the Reformatory in the Wicklow Mountains.

In the House of Lords I spoke on Colonial and Educational questions, and I opposed Lord Salisbury's Merchant Shipping Bill; Stuart Wortley's Friendly Societies Bill I carried through the House of Lords.

There was a great Anniversary Meeting and revival of the old Mendicity Society at Apsley House. [Lord Norton became chairman of this most excellent society, and worked in its interests till his death.]

Whitacre Water was now formally opened: 80 acres of water 25 feet deep—a lake-feature in the scenery near Hams.

The Duke of Buckingham, Lord and Lady Hertford, and Lord Lorne [present Duke of Argyll] came to Hams for the Birmingham Cattle Show; and Lord Lorne, lately returned from the Governor-Generalship of Canada, spoke on Canada to a crowded audience in the Town Hall at Birmingham. Sophie Leveson-Gower, W. Childe-Pemberton, and Hussey were also of this party.

Lord Norton, one evening, discussing with Lady Hertford a proposed improvement to the entrance at Hams, said, " I am too old to make alterations; I must leave this for my son to do." Lady Hertford replied, " But Hertford has lately made an improvement at Ragley, and he is older than you." Seven years later, after Hams was burnt down, Lord Norton made the alteration, and he lived twenty-two years after this conversation. In a few weeks Lord Hertford was killed by a fall from his horse.

Other autumn visitors to Hams were the Archbishop of Canterbury [Benson], Lord Alwyn Compton [then Dean of Worcester] and his wife, and later, Sir Stafford Northcote for the Birmingham Institute and Conservative Banquet.

During Archbishop Benson's visit, Lord Norton took him over to Saltley to see the Reformatory. The Archbishop afterwards wrote :

January 21, 1884.

It is very good of you to keep up my acquaintance with the Saltley boys. It was such a *moment's* word, and the poor boys (since you say it was their own idea) bring to one's mind Wordsworth's saying :

> They talk of unkind hearts, kind deeds
> With coldness still returning ;
> Alas ! the *gratitude* of men
> Hath oftener left me mourning—

so undeserved it is, as is also your great kindness, my dear lord, in a far higher degree. . . . I earnestly pray that your long labours for their class may be rewarded by a long succession of rescued boys and rescued futures.

1884

My old friend, Lord Hertford—so lately with us at Hams—died in January from an accident in the hunting-field at Ragley. Julia so fond of Lady Hertford.

CHAPTER XLIII

1884 (*continued*)

FRANCHISE BILL CONTROVERSY

THE chief public events were: The Soudan War (I met Lord Wolseley at Broughton Castle [Lord Saye and Sele's] just before his going out); and the Franchise Act for extending household suffrage to counties.

The Franchise proposals led to great controversy. At Lord Salisbury's, Jersey and I in vain opposed Conservative resistance to the measure.

This was in the summer of 1884, when the Lords, following Lord Salisbury's exhortations, did not give Mr. Gladstone's Franchise Bill a second reading, in spite of Lord Norton's advice, in which he was supported by Lord Jersey. Lord Salisbury was determined that the Franchise Bill should not become law *unaccompanied by a Redistribution of Seats Bill*, by which town and country should be as far as possible distinctly represented. The Conservative majority in the House of Lords was large, and the Liberal majority in the House of Commons was large. The Liberals now everywhere proclaimed that the House of Lords and the Conservatives were hostile to the Franchise Bill, and Mr. Morley, in a speech at St. James's Hall, proclaimed that the House of Lords should either be " mended or ended." [1]

It was felt by Lord Norton, and some other Conservative peers, that the continued opposition to the Franchise Bill would be so permanently disastrous to the country, and to the Conservative party, that every effort should be made to work for a peaceful solution of the matter. This was the state of things in the autumn, when the controversy led to a remarkable political episode in which Lord Norton was the central figure as the intermediary between Gladstone and Lord Salisbury, between the Government and the Opposition, between the Commons and the Lords ; and Lord Salisbury, who in June had disregarded Lord Norton's advice, eventually followed it in November. The course of affairs which led to this result is illustrated as follows by Lord Norton's correspondence and notes.

On the evening of October 25, 1884, Lord Norton received two important letters at Hams from Lord Salisbury [2] and Mr. Gladstone respectively.

---

[1] " ' If,' said the Conservatives, ' you do not show us your Redistribution Bill until your Reform Bill has been passed we shall be at your mercy, because on our rejecting your measure you can dissolve Parliament without any Redistribution Bill at all.' ' If,' the Liberals replied, ' we produce our Redistribution Bill before the Reform Bill has been passed, you can compel us, through the House of Lords, to substitute your scheme for ours, or to have no Reform Bill.' "—Paul's " History of Modern England," vol. iv. p. 332.

[2] It may here be mentioned that Lord Norton always entertained the warmest regard and admiration for Lord Salisbury, whom he had known as Lord Robert Cecil in his early Parliamentary career. Lord Norton used to recall the great impression made by Lord Robert Cecil's first speech in the House of Commons when he supported J. S. Mill ; and he used to say of Lord Salisbury that he would go down to posterity as the man who preserved the peace of Europe under the greatest difficulties. On the other hand, Lord Salisbury had always the warmest regard for Lord Norton.

Lord Salisbury wrote :

October 24, 1884.

DEAR NORTON,

I have not seen Winmarleigh's [1] memorandum, but I quite agree with you that *the* thing to struggle for in the distribution is the separation of rural and urban districts. But how are we to get the Government to assent to this principle? And until they do show some signs of being willing to do justice on this point, I do not think we can safely drop our swords. Gladstone's present contention is that, whatever else is sacrificed, we are not to commit the profanation of forcing him to contradict himself.

Ever yours truly,
SALISBURY.

It was believed by prominent members of his own party that Lord Salisbury at this time " staked everything on an early dissolution," and an arrangement by which the Government would remain in office to carry through the Redistribution Bill would be directly opposed to Lord Salisbury's object.

" I am afraid," wrote a Conservative Earl at this time to Lord Norton, " that it would be hardly possible to prevail upon our House to pass the Franchise Bill, unless there should come a great change over Lord Salisbury's mind."

Be that as it may, the same post which brought Lord Salisbury's letter brought one unexpectedly from Gladstone, opening the door to compromise. Gladstone, recalling a conversation he had had with Lord Norton at Grillion's, gave Lord Norton an opportunity to assist him in his efforts towards an understanding.

[1] In October the venerable Lord Winmarleigh drew up a memorandum, which he sent to Lord Norton, stating the position of affairs, and pointing out that the widespread, though unfounded, impression that the House of Lords was hostile to the Franchise Bill might be a serious obstacle to the Conservative party, in view of a general election, and advising, in conclusion, that a division should not be taken on the second reading in the House of Lords, but on a clause enacting that the Bill should not become law until accompanied by a law of redistribution, etc.

October 24, 1884.

MY DEAR NORTON,

You will have observed, I think, with regret, that last night the terms demanded from a large majority of the House of Commons [the Liberals], were the unconditional acceptance of the views of the minority [the Conservatives], who likewise represent the majority in the House of Lords. We, on the other hand, say we cannot do that; you must know we cannot do it; ask us something that we can do. This they [the Conservatives] positively decline.

When I saw you [at Grillion's] you said your desire was that the separation of rural and urban interests should be aimed at by the Redistribution Bill. I consider your anxiety to be just. I think that within the limits of reason and convenience, which will not allow the matter to be pursued into every detail, that separation should be studied and effected.

I believe there is nothing in reason which you could ask that would not be readily granted.

Perhaps you noted Carnarvon's recent suggestion : that three or four men, on whom much reliance would be placed by both parties, should meet together and consider the outlines of redistribution. Some good might, I believe, come of such a plan. He said he feared it would not act because of the private prejudice of his opponents. I have been doing what I could to put onward[1] his suggestion. I have not yet heard that any of his friends have done the same, or are doing anything similar. But I still hope from the followers, if not the leaders.

Yours sincerely,

W. E. GLADSTONE.[2]

---

[1] The word "forward" is erased, and "onward" substituted—a characteristically subtle distinction.

[2] In August, according to Mr. Herbert Paul, "Mr. Gladstone assured the Queen, in a private memorandum, that he was most anxious to close the controversy by any honourable means, and to prevent a still more serious dispute from arising. In September a Conservative newspaper committed a fortunate indiscretion. *The Standard* published the Ministerial scheme for the rearrangement

It was late on a Saturday evening when Lord Norton received these letters at Hams forwarded from London, and he at once determined to act. Next morning, record Lord Norton's notes :

On Sunday (October 26) at day-break I went from Hams to London, and in several conferences helped an arrangement between the leaders of both parties to unite the Franchise and Redistribution of Seats Bills. Sir Erskine May told Gladstone it would be an epoch in his next edition of " Constitutional History," and Lord John Manners wrote to me, " The political truce was to a great extent due to you."

This brief record of the incident conveys but little idea of the correspondence and interviews necessary, or of the time and trouble involved on Lord Norton's part, towards bringing about a settlement which was not concluded for several weeks after the eventful Sunday when the negotiations opened. Nor did the first day's labours produce much apparent result.

To undertake this journey on a Sunday, to forgo his morning services at church, was entirely contrary to his life-long rule and practice ; but he felt that every day gained brought the negotiations a step nearer in the direction of peace.

On arriving in London, Lord Norton at once went to Lord Salisbury and Sir Stafford Northcote and showed them Gladstone's letter. A memorandum of Lord Norton's states that they, " taking Gladstone's proposal to mean a conference of leaders, refused to tie their hands, and said they could not bind their followers, but that I might tell Gladstone that if he would introduce the Redistribution Bill in the Commons as soon as the Franchise

of seats. . . . Secrecy being no longer possible, why should not the details be arranged between the two parties before a Redistribution Bill was brought in ? The Queen, in October, suggested private communication between the leaders."—*Modern England*, vol. iv. p. 334.

is passed, so that by adjourning over Christmas it might be discussed in the Lords *before the Franchise is out of hand*, they would be easy with the Distribution, and pass the Franchise's second reading. Gladstone did not take this as much advance towards compromise, but said he did not mean a conference of *leaders*, but of men of weight in both parties to discuss what difference really lies between them as to the principle of Redistribution which he is anxious to make as conservative as possible."

Gladstone, in the early stage of negotiations, would not have any other go-between than Norton, saying that he was the only one of his opponents he would trust. Lord Norton used to relate how on this Sunday afternoon he was greatly struck with Gladstone sitting quietly immersed in the study of his Bible, only occasionally stopping to write a note to Lord Salisbury for Lord Norton to take.

The whole correspondence at this time is of great interest. It is docketed by Lord Norton "Gladstone's letter to me, and consequent correspondence which led to the compromise on the Reform Bill between the Lords and Commons."

Sir Stafford Northcote wrote to Lord Norton on October 27, the day after .the Sunday on which the negotiations had opened, for further explanations of Gladstone's intentions. Lord Carnarvon wrote the same day :

HIGH CLERE CASTLE,
October 27, 1884.

MY DEAR NORTON,

Your letter, with its most important enclosure [Gladstone's letter], has determined me to go to London this evening to do my utmost to bring about some understanding. I feel sure I may for the present retain Gladstone's letter, which may be useful, but I will take care of it and return it. Pray do everything you can to keep the door open. Time seems to me of great consequence and I dread the effect of a heated debate in the Commons.

Yours most truly,
CARNARVON.

Several letters from Lord Carnarvon followed, discussing the arrangements as they progressed or were delayed from time to time.

Lord Jersey wrote on November 1 :

"If I may use the expression, I should say that you have got the right sow by the ear. I really think you have succeeded in bringing about a good prospect of the settlement of the unhappy difference. You may rely on my being ready to assist you in your good efforts, and I sincerely hope that, for the good of the country, you may succeed." [1]

Lord Salisbury wrote on November 12 :

MY DEAR NORTON,

We shall probably follow your advice so far as not to take any division on the second reading of the Franchise Bill. Our great division will probably be on going into Committee on Thursday the 20th. I should have no objection to a suspensory clause, if I knew the Government would accept it ; but for us to insert it at this stage at least would not be prudent. I should prefer to delay proceeding with the Franchise Bill beyond a second reading, until a Redistribution Bill had been sent up to us. I believe that when we have declared for such a course Government will introduce their Bill.

By November 18 matters had practically been arranged. On that day Lord Salisbury announced in the House of Lords that, as a result of a communication of Mr. Balfour with the Government, Lord

---

[1] The following facts are chronicled in *Annals of Our Time* (Irving), vol. ii. p. 1456 : "*November* 6.—Mr. Gladstone, in a brief speech, moved the second reading of the Franchise Bill. An amendment insisting on its being accompanied by a Redistribution Bill was moved by Colonel Stanley, but before the House met next day it was evident that overtures for a compromise, if not actually made, were anticipated, and that on each side they would meet with a favourable reception. . . .

"On *November* 7 the second reading was carried by 372 against 232.

"*November* 11.—In spite of a distinct change of line in the debate, the conciliatory disposition manifested in the early stages having almost disappeared, the Franchise Bill was read a third time without discussion."

Hartington had stated that the Government would receive in trust a communication from the Opposition that they would go into consultation on the Redistribution of Seats Bill, and would not ask for the assurance as to the passing of the Franchise Bill as a preliminary to such a consultation. The Bill was then read a second time without a division.

On December the 1st Gladstone introduced the Redistribution Bill in the House of Commons, and on the 5th the Franchise Bill was read a third time in the House of Lords, and became law, just before the House adjourned on the 6th. Thus the private negotiations, in which Lord Norton played so prominent a part, had attained their object with complete success.

Lord Norton used to relate how Gladstone asked him, "Do you say that it is wrong to go to the country without the redistribution?" and how, when he answered "Yes," Gladstone did not reply, but Lord Norton knew he had convinced him.

When Gladstone met Lord Norton next at Grillion's, some time afterwards, he said, "The last time we met here led to important consequences— the compromise about the Franchise Bill."

Mrs. Gladstone was wont to say of Lord Norton, " He is the *kindest* of dear William's *enemies*." But in truth the feeling that existed between Gladstone and Norton was one of warm friendship. It was rooted in the profound regard which each had for the other's character, and in the common sympathy which their religion inspired while politics divided them.

To one who made a remark in disparagement of Gladstone, Lord Norton said in tones of severe rebuke : " Sir, it is evident you do not *know* Mr. Gladstone. If you knew him half as well as I do, you would raise your hat at the mention of his name." And on a similar occasion he said : "God grant I may be near him in the next world!" The veneration which Norton felt for Gladstone, however, did not preclude an occasional sally. On Mrs. Gladstone replying one day to his inquiries after her husband, "Oh! he is still completely taken up with his Genesis,"[1] Lord Norton exclaimed, " What ! Has he not yet begun to think of his Exodus ? "

Gladstone, on his part, showed affection and consideration for Norton on more than one occasion. Once, in the early days of their friendship, he came across the House to Adderley, who was next to Disraeli, and touched him to attract his attention, only to tell him that some severe remark which he (Gladstone) had made in a speech the night before was not intended to apply to him or to wound his feelings. Disraeli, when Gladstone had gone away, said to Adderley, " What was that lunatic saying ? "

[1] Gladstone published " The Dawn of Creation and Worship " and " Proem to Genesis " in *The Nineteenth Century* in the following year, 1885.

CHAPTER XLIV

1884 (*continued*)

SOME VISITORS AT HAMS

LORD HOUGHTON paid his last visit to Hams in January 1884. ["Is there any one," inquired Lord Norton, "whom you would like to see here?" "Yes," replied Lord Houghton, "I should like to see *Joseph Van Arteveld.*"][1] He was most anxious that we should go together and see J. Chamberlain, who was much pleased with our visit, and afterwards kindly sent me all sorts of interesting Board of Trade papers, and Memoranda of the Session to read.[2]

Lord Houghton wrote in the Hams Visitors' Book on this occasion the following lines on Lord Beaconsfield and Mr. Gladstone:

We spoke of two high names of speech and pen ;
How each was seeing, and how each was blind ;
Knew not mankind, though knowing many men ;
Knew naught of men, but knew and loved mankind.

Mr. Shorthouse, author of "John Inglesant," wrote

[1] Sir M. Grant Duff's Diaries (March 19, 1892).
James and Philip Van Arteveld, father and son, were distinguished demagogues and leaders of the Flemish people in the fourteenth century. Had the insurrection of Philip been successful, Froissart observes that "the whole of the nobility and gentry would have been destroyed!"
[2] Mr. Chamberlain was President of the Board of Trade in Gladstone's Administration, 1880 and 1885.

beneath on the same day, in allusion to the house he was visiting:

Earth is hallowed by the homes of the pure.

Among other subjects I spoke in the House on the Emigration debate, recommending the boarding out of young paupers in Canada.

Speaker Brand retired, most ably succeeded by Arthur Peel.

I wrote two articles in *The Nineteenth Century*: (1) on the Education Code, (2) on Imperial Federation, then very ignorantly harangued about.

I presented, on the part of the Shipwrights' Company, a bust to Lord John Manners; and dined, in my citizen capacity, at the Lord Mayor's reception of heads of Companies, with lace-makers and drapers.

Lord and Lady Carnarvon came to Hams for the Conservative Banquet at Birmingham. Coote came to meet them, from Ireland, where he had gallantly acted as magistrate. Lord Carnarvon, when Viceroy, afterwards took him into the Household.

Among domestic events, Reginald, by the advice of the Archbishop [Benson], joined Canon Mason at All Hallows, Barking, for clerical work among the poor; James [afterwards known as "Father Adderley"] passed his Law Examination well; then joined the East London Mission [Oxford House, Bethnal Green, just founded].

We went to Titsey, for Ronald Leveson-Gower's coming of age in September. In the midst of the rejoicings a telegram arrived saying Gilbert Leigh killed in America [eldest son of Lord Leigh]. James

Leigh [now Dean of Hereford] left at once for America to bring home the body [of his nephew]. Funeral at Stoneleigh, October 22.

Among other deaths, my old friend Bromley Davenport died suddenly in command of Yeomanry at Lichfield. [June 15—the result of his exertions to restore peace in the Yeomanry riot at Lichfield.]

Notes for 1885

General Election on the New Franchise. The new county votes were led by demagogues, and the old borough votes were Conservative.

Gladstone's Government defeated on Budget, June 8 ; Salisbury becomes Premier— Northcote made Earl of Iddesleigh.

I wrote letters to *The Times*, etc., against W. E. Forster's and Lord Rosebery's Colonial Federation. Bright, at the Speaker's Levée, came up to me and said, " If you go down to posterity it will be for what you have done for better Colonial Policy."

The Prince of Wales came to Birmingham—stayed at Calthorpe's [Perry Bar]. We were of the party.

I set up the old " Mendicity Society " by a Concert which was given for it at Apsley House. The Duke of Welling-ton, with the Rev. H. Montagu Villiers, established a Club in Lowndes Mews.

Julia had a great success in Eaton Place for her Charity, with a comic Operetta by W. Childe Pemberton [Arthur Bourchier, James Adderley, and A. MacKinnon].

Jim, giving up Bircham's office, prepares for Ordination, the Archbishop taking kindest interest.

Lord Fortescue came to Hams to look round the Birmingham Schools with me.

On Lady Selborne's death, the Lord Chancellor wrote to me : " My chief thought now is to rejoin her." [Lord Selborne wrote (April 12) : " Her life on earth was an anticipation of that into which she has now passed, and all that remains for me on earth is to prepare for following her." He survived ten years.]

1886

The two chief events in Lord Norton's life this year were : (1) his being nominated by Archbishop Benson to the House of Laymen, and (2) his being put on the Royal Commission on Education.

With regard to the House of Laymen, the Archbishop wrote (January 30): " I trust you will allow me the great honour of nominating you. I am the more anxious about you being a member of it because your diocese, having no Diocesan conference, has otherwise no representative. In the first year I think I had better fill up only five of the ten nominations assigned to me." Lord Norton became a prominent member, Lord Selborne being in the chair.

On the Royal Commission Lord Norton struck up acquaintance with two very dissimilar personalities: Cardinal Manning and Dr. Dale, the Nonconformist minister, for both of whom he had great respect. It was his habit to take Cardinal Manning home in his carriage every day from the Commission. Their views coincided in so far as they were both averse from education by the State, as in France, without religion. But it is said that Dr. Dale's view as to religious education, viz. that religious education must be given by *religious teachers only*, did much to cool Lord Norton's ardour for religious teaching in Board Schools. A cordial correspondence sprang up between them. Writing some years later, Dr. Dale alludes to "friendly intercourse with yourself, from whom I differ in some things, but with whom I profoundly agree in things of transcendent importance." It was in the essence of Christianity that the dissenting minister found a common bond with one of the staunchest laymen of the Church of England. A letter of Dr. Dale in juxtaposition with one of Cardinal Manning will be given at a later date.

NOTES FOR 1886

My health never so good, though nearing 72.

January.—Salisbury out and Gladstone sent for.

February.—The meeting of Parliament, after the new Ministry of Gladstone and Rosebery, formed.

The blank announcement that the Irish Policy could not be started till April 1.

May.—The country absorbed in Gladstone's Irish Government Bill. Liberal split. *Chamberlain resigns.*

May 30.—Two (to me) interesting parties : (1) the Speaker's (Peel) Dinner to Radical M.P.'s —he asked me to help him at his *sans-culotte* dinner. I sat between Cremer of Shoreditch and Durant of Tower Hamlets ; see notes of interesting conversation [not to be found]. (2) Congress of Education party at Lord Stanley's of Alderley. I had long talk with Bright.

June.—Gladstone defeated.

July.—General Election. Salisbury in again.

NOTES FOR 1886 *(continued)*

Wakefield Congress. I read paper on "Free Schools."

Canon King made Bishop of Lincoln. [Bishop King became one of Lord Norton's intimate friends, the only one, he said, to whom he felt he could speak unreservedly about spiritual things concerning himself.]

I set the Shipwrights' Company on lectures in the Mansion House, which led to a Shipwrights' School.

Reginald conducted the Poplar Mission, he and Jim working in East of London, and preparing an Exhibition for next year there.

I wrote to *The Times* against the Bishop of Durham's Sunday closing of public houses in his diocese, as impracticable.

Autumn guests at Hams were : Phelps, American minister, Bishop of Southwell, Dean Gott.

DOMESTIC EVENTS

The death in January of Edward Grove Cradock (Principal of Brazenose), in consequence of which my brother Edmund succeeding to the Knighton property [Leicestershire] had to take the name of Cradock instead of Adderley.

Lord Norton notes "a powerful sermon" which he heard preached at St. Paul's, Knightsbridge, by the Chaplain-General for the Bishop of London's Fund. The subject was the "Loaves and Fishes." "He gave them to His disciples, *and they gave them to the people.* You wealthy," said the preacher, "have at least five loaves, and are bound to give them. Christ will bless the gift and *make it adequate.* The giving and receiving have a mutual destiny, which requires the mutual action in attaining it, and the greatest blessing is with the givers, as Christ's ministers. In His works of love He made men His agents as well as recipients. Wealth spent on self cankers and curses its owners, and widens the gap between rich and poor — both meant to work life's probation together—thus embittering the absence of the intended blessing."

CHAPTER XLV

1887

LADY NORTON'S DEATH

THE dreadful year of Julia's painful sickness and death. The year began with hopes of her recovery. On February 3 she for the last time left Hams, where she had been the centre of good and happiness to all for forty-five years. By May there was no hope. The end came on the 8th. . . . Most loving, most unselfish, firm, courageous, and true, she died as she lived, in perfect faith, in self-abnegation, devotion to others and earnest trust in God.

The pages of one of Lord Norton's note-books describe, during many weeks, the daily fluctuations of the long and harassing illness which preceded this melancholy event, and express the hopes and fears, the religious thoughts and aspirations, with which his heart is full. All his life he firmly believed in the ministrations of angels to men. "Are our guardian angels," he now asks himself, "told to minister direct to each heir of salvation? Do they waft our prayers to Him? . . . Are they necessary to His omnipresence?" He desires to realise the omnipresence more fully. "It strikes me," he notes, "how the *rapidity of communication* is one of the growing consciousnesses of these days, uniting with other consciousnesses. . . . Walpole,[1] whose recent loss of his wife makes me draw to him in sympathy and converse, told me of two instances: Lady Caroline Townshend and (the most different character) Lord St. Leonards,[2] who both told him of having at a moment of collapse—one in a fit and the other in drowning—seen their whole lives before them *at one glance* . . . and our Lord's description of His coming as the lightning gives one some idea of the omnipresence."

On the day before Lady Norton's death Mr. Gladstone wrote (May 7, 1887): "It is with deep sympathy that I learn the circumstances under which you write, but I think the author of the book[3] before me knows where to look for solace and support, even in the presence of those troubles which divide asunder bone and marrow. May all the consolation that comes from above support you according to your great need."

The Archbishop of Canterbury (Benson) was one of the first to express his sorrow and sympathy. "I know," he wrote (May 10), "your hopeful faith will not be dimmed for one hour, but I hope it may be a little comfort still to be sure that there are so many who not only honour and love you, but also pray for you and for the joyful reunion. . . . All our actions are so visibly incipient and unfinished, that we should be quite unable to understand anything if death did not come to mark this world's life itself as merely incipient."

Cardinal Manning wrote on May 18: "You have, I am sure, all consolation, for I know that you seek it in its only source. I hope that you may receive it abundantly." Mr. Phelps, the American minister, wrote (May 15): "Only in the sublime faith to which you are happily no stranger is to be found the assurance that the loved dead are not lost, but only gone before into the happier country. My brief acquaintance with Lady Norton, which I

[1] Right Honourable Spencer Walpole married the daughter of the Right Hon. Spencer Perceval, who was assassinated in the House of Commons in 1812.
[2] Lord Chancellor Sugden, 1st Lord St. Leonards.

had hoped would be prolonged during my stay in England, had impressed me very strongly with a sense of her loveliness of character. I remember, with great satisfaction, the pleasant days last summer at Hams in the home she made so attractive, and has left so desolate." Lord John Manners wrote : "I think of all the many proofs of kindness and good-will you have shown me and mine during our long friendship, and truly grieve for you." Among the letters of condolence none touched a more beautiful note than the letter of Bishop Ellicott of Gloucester and Bristol, one of the most practical as well as learned of prelates : " There must be the blessed reunion ; there is, too, I am persuaded, far more *communion while we are here with those we have lost* than the hurrying world is at all aware of. This becomes spiritually felt, at times strongly realised—and comfort is silently vouchsafed to us."

Lord Norton resumed his occupations and duties as soon as possible.

My chief work in this year was on the Education Commission.

I was visited at Hams by Walpole and Selborne, with whom I went to see Cardinal Newman [a neighbour at Birmingham].

I laid out Saltley roads, and stopped the burial of non-parishioners.

Annie is now my right hand [his eldest daughter].

HAMS, *October* 21.—Strange momentary depression at my usual waking hour, 5 o'clock. Bethought me of John, 14th chapter. How much more incomprehensible it would be that any man should have *imagined* such words than that they should have been supernaturally brought to the writer's memory! I feel sure that many things have been supernaturally brought into my mind through life—often and often.

CHAPTER XLVI

1888

AN INTERESTING CORRESPONDENCE

THE Education Committee was now in its third year. Towards the end of it, Cardinal Manning wrote the following letter, which is of interest, as specifying his views :

December 2.

MY DEAR LORD NORTON,

Let me thank you heartily for your article on the "Two Education Reports." I have seen nothing so much to the point. The Primate's Conference was premature and immature. But there was a good minority of 45, which, when the County Councils are at work, will rapidly multiply. Till then Voluntary Managers will not understand the rate question.

The Dale Conference was deplorable, and so was *The Times*, which says that the exclusion of Voluntary Schools from the rates is essential to the settlement of 1870, which "fell down from Jupiter." There was no "settlement" and no compromise, but only an occasional and fragmentary Act, forced through by religious jealousy, and demanded by a perilous national evil. All this piecemeal legislation will compel future legislation, or, as you say, the nation will be educated by the State, like France and America—the worst form of education, fatal to faith, conscience, and national independence. You

have sounded the first bugle, and I hope many will take up the same note. As I read it I thought we were sitting side by side again. Believe me always,
Very truly yours,
HENRY E. CARDINAL MANNING.

Beside the Roman Catholic it is interesting to place the Nonconformist view, as explained by Dr. Dale in a letter which chronologically belongs to the year before.[1] Lord Norton had sought— apparently a vain and hopeless research—to find some concordat between Christians of various faiths and denominations. Dr. Dale points out the utter impossibility of such an attempt, and argues in favour of merely secular teaching in day-schools, leaving religious teaching to the Sunday schools.

MY DEAR LORD NORTON,
I can quite understand that what I said in reply to your earnest appeal, by which I was greatly touched, seemed unsatisfactory. Let me deal with the matter in concrete form. In the first place, no concordat between Evangelical Christians and Unitarians on the subject of religious teaching is possible. . . . Unless our Lord is spoken of with reverence, awe, and wonder, which His Divinity should inspire, I think that to talk to children about the earthly history must discourage faith rather than contribute to it.
In the second place, no concordat is possible with the Roman Catholics. They are obliged, with their views of the Church, to meet the proposal with an unconditional refusal. The attempt, as far as it was made in Ireland, was a failure from the beginning.
In the third place, no concordat is possible between Nonconformists and that party in the English Church, which at present is most vigorous and powerful, and is showing the most earnest religious life—I mean the High Church party. [Dr. Dale proceeds to discuss the essential difference between the Church and Nonconformist views of Baptism,

[1] July 1, 1887.

18

and, further, to point out that the Low Church party can only be said to approach the Nonconformists in doctrine when the former "appear to explain away the clear teaching of her (the Church's) formularies."] This, however, [he continues] is only an illustration of the difficulty of a concordat. We may all see the same sun and stars, but our astronomical theories—our teaching about them—may differ. The difficulty of securing masters and mistresses who will teach so as to reach the hearts and consciences of the children, is also serious. My conclusion is, let the school be secular. Let the Churches find how to draw the children to church. I have great faith in Sunday schools. . . . Mr. T——'s evidence shows that the overwhelming majority of children in public elementary schools are also in Sunday schools; and if the clergy would give the strength to Sunday schools which they now give to day schools I believe that the difficulty would be solved.

NOTES FOR 1888

The Archbishop opened Oxford Hall in Bethnal Green.

Lord Mount Edgecumbe and Lord Halifax stayed at Hams for the Birmingham Festival.

Dinner at Grillion's to Lord Lansdowne, returned from Canada.

1889

Lord Norton and other prominent members of the House of Laymen were at this time attempting a coalescence of some sort between the Church of England and certain Nonconformist bodies, especially the Wesleyans. The terms and trusts of John Wesley's will, which were brought to Lord Norton's notice by Sir Stephen Gatty, late Chief Justice of Gibraltar, seemed to raise, if not hope of unity, at least grounds for amicable discussion. These trusts were still (in 1889) binding in Australia and some other Colonies with regard to Wesleyan property under the authority of the Wesleyan Church then in conference in England. John Wesley had made certain specifications with regard to the tenure of the minister's office. This tenure was not to exceed three years, " except in the case of the *minister being an ordained clergyman of the Established Church of England*." It was this exception in the trusts of Wesleyan property which interested Lord Norton.

This " is one of the many proofs," he wrote, " that Wesley's chief anxiety was lest his great Church revival should turn to Church disunion. Nothing would have horrified him more than the idea that this his revival of the Christian Church was affixing his name to a large section of it. Wesleyans are not followers of Wesley if, in the present state of the Church of England, they maintain their distinction by way of rivalry, and allow lawyers and chapel-shareholders to cause division. The exposure of the deed [John Wesley's] gives a good opportunity for the Church to open wider still her arms, and identify her Ministry with the irregular auxiliaries who are at this moment using the same forms and liturgy of the Church in needless separation from her."

Lord Norton corresponded with Dr. Rigg, head of Wesley College. Dr. Rigg held out no hopes of union. Writing to Mr. Gatty (February 6, 1889) Lord Norton says : "The clause was meant, no doubt, as Dr. Rigg admits, to release from the itinerary rule any of those ministers who might be ordained clergy of the Church of England, and it shows the anxiety of Wesley to get his ministers ordained and to avoid separation. Dr. Rigg's letters unconsciously show how much pride of office has to do in maintaining separation of Christians using the same liturgy and in nothing but minority to be distinguished from Low Churchmen. In the United States there is no difference between the Episcopal Church and Wesleyans, many of whom are ordained. He shows how bitter the jealousy and hatred is on the part of the Wesleyan Ministry towards the Church, and the joyful anticipation of revenge for the *spretæ injuria*[1]—a very

---

[1] *Spretæ injuria* : an allusion to the coldness and want of sympathy with which the Church of England originally treated the Wesleyan movement, when, after the death of Wesley, the Wesleyans made some overtures to the Church.

Christian spirit of enmity! But, as Disraeli said, 'all criers for fraternity want the *elder brother's* place for themselves.' The confusion is that all the varieties of Dissent each want it and cannot allow even the necessity of precedence in time, if nothing else, but are ready to join in the group of claimants against the actual primogeniture.

"Rigg does not want union won by mutual concession. I think the *congregations* are inclined, but not the ministers nor demagogues. The spirit of sect is inherent in all human nature. This is the egotism which dictates all human action unsublimated. The worst feature is the intrusion of sectarian egotism within the Church itself, and even its hierarchy. What else is the excellent Bishop King of Lincoln doing in most injurious controversy with the Primate, on unspiritual doctrine, to the scandal of the Church, and causing the enemy to blaspheme?"

The intimacy between Lord Norton and Archbishop Benson grew with advancing years.[1] They frequently corresponded. From time to time Lord Norton would consult about the plans of his sons Reginald and James, in whose labours the Archbishop took special interest. "You are blessed," the Archbishop wrote, "in the aspirations and self-denial of two such sons. It is the kind of thing also to make people feel there is something in the 'Classes.'" James (who was ordained priest on March 17) took a prominent part in working with the Bishop of London and John Burns for a solution of the Dock Strike of 1889.

To start a diocese for Birmingham out of the overgrown diocese of Worcester was an object

---

[1] They had indeed much in common, and what his son says of the Archbishop in the following passage is equally applicable to Lord Norton. "The habit of gazing upon God fashioned in him the spirit of humility. It is quite true that when once he had made up his mind that a thing was right he was almost masterful in his determination to carry it out."—"The Life of Edward White Benson, Archbishop of Canterbury," vol. ii. p. 760.

which both Lord Norton and Archbishop Benson had at heart. Lord Norton offered £1,000 this year towards the scheme which, to his disappointment, was not proceeded with after a meeting at Birmingham in the following year. He nevertheless did not cease to work for it, and, unlike the Archbishop,[1] lived to see it accomplished some fifteen years later, to his great satisfaction.

The Archbishop, in a letter, after referring to the meeting at Birmingham when he was Lord Norton's guest at Hams, thanks Lord Norton " warmly, and more than warmly, for your precious friendship to me in all things."

A letter from the late Earl of Kimberley is noteworthy as representing the ideas in 1889 of so distinguished a member of the Liberal party with regard to the possibility of future democratic changes in the English Constitution, such as are, in our own day, aimed at by many of the same party. Lord Norton had sent Lord Kimberley a pamphlet which he had published twenty years before entitled, "Europe incapable of American Democracy," in which the following remarks occur : " If such a change as democratising the English Constitution could be effected while our form of Parliamentary Government by Queen, Lords, and Commons remained, the result would be far more democratic than anything existing under the constitution of the United States. Theirs would be a limited and balanced democracy compared with ours. The independent powers of the President, the co-ordinate authority of the Judiciary with the Legislative, are checks and safeguards in their case, which would have no equivalent in the reckless race of imitation. Unless our whole machinery of government were radically altered, it is remarkable that the House of Commons, in whose apparent interest reform is

---

[1] " It was a matter of constant regret to him [the Archbishop] that neither then, nor in his lifetime, was [this] object ever accomplished."—"The Life of Edward White Benson, Archbishop of Canterbury," vol. ii. p. 296.

sought, would be the first to suffer and probably to succumb."

Lord Kimberley wrote:

35, LOWNDES SQUARE,
July 27, 1889.

MY DEAR NORTON,

I have read your pamphlet. I think there is much force in what you say as to the results of grafting (if it be possible) the " American Democracy " on our institutions. It is perfectly true that a democratised English Constitution would be far more democratic than the United States Constitution. Have we not already gone far in this direction ? My feeling is, and has been for some time, that we shall have to resort to some system of checks similar to those which fetter the American Democracy. I do not believe in the practicability of governing our Empire by a single assembly when anything may be done by a bare majority. The democracy will, even for its own protection, want some security against the freaks of a single assembly. Of course we have still the House of Lords, but it has very little real power, and will, if it continues to exist, be reduced to a political nullity, like the Crown (though no doubt the Crown retains much social influence, it has no power to resist the Democracy). Perhaps the solution may be found in some arrangements like those of the Swiss Constitution, which, whilst thoroughly democratic, impose a very effectual check on both government and legislature. If you have not read Sir J. Adams and Mr. Cunningham just published, I strongly recommend you to do so. . . .

OTHER NOTES FOR 1889

County Councils began this year. I was made a six-years' Alderman. I began visiting Warwick Prison, and was struck by the number of re-commitments.

Began a new church at Washwood Heath—Chapel of Ease Saltley.

Work in House of Lords over the new Education Code, Poor Law, Protection of Children, etc.

Ronny Leveson-Gower, just engaged, died suddenly.

Bright and the Duke of Buckingham died the same day [March 26-27].

CHAPTER XLVII

1890

HAMS BURNT

WE went to London April 21. Next day Hams was burnt.

Fire broke out in an upper room, and the house was completely gutted, only the outer walls being left standing. The books, pictures, and the carved chair presented by Cape Colony nearly forty years before, were saved, with the sculpture and frieze of Thorwaldsen, which was, however, much blackened by the smoke. Hams Hall, a square substantial structure, was built in 1760, at a time when houses presented externally few features of architectural merit. Inside it was roomy, comfortable, and well arranged, and, above all, it had associations for Lord Norton which no other house could give.

The shock of the destruction of his old home was borne by Lord Norton with remarkable composure. At the same time we gather from his note-book that—seeking as he always did the spiritual aspect of life and events—the instability of earthly things was especially brought home to him, and he felt in this trial a fresh loosening of the ties which bound him to material interests. As soon, however, as he received the telegram announcing that Hams was burnt, he determined to rebuild it on the old model. He immediately set to work about its reconstruction, and, at the age of seventy-six, personally supervised this in minute detail of arrangement and decoration.

I began to rebuild at once—no architect necessary,

279

Holland & Hannen were the contractors, and the Sun Insurance office paid me the whole of the sum in one cheque.   I put more water-tanks both on the roof and on the ground.

Within a year Hams was completely rebuilt and restored; no trace of the catastrophe was visible, the house appeared throughout to be the same as of old, although in fact internally nothing of the original remained.

Lord Norton's constant interest in the Colonies, New Zealand in particular, led him to correspond (as we have said) with Mr. Fitzgerald, Premier of New Zealand, the brilliant and humorous Irishman whose career as a leading colonist he had watched for nearly forty years.   Mr. Fitzgerald was an enthusiastic Home Ruler, and was never tired of instancing the success of self-government in New Zealand as a reason for its being granted to his native country.

Lord Norton apparently could not resist sending Fitzgerald's letters on to Gladstone, and thus placed himself—as the sequel shows three years later—in the peculiar position of a Unionist propagating arguments in favour of Home Rule.   Mr. Gladstone was at first hopeful of making him a convert.

He wrote (August 21, 1890):

"I return Fitzgerald's letter with thanks. It opens very interesting subjects.   He was always a man of mark. . . . In virtue of your having framed the Canadian Act, even if it were nothing else, you will assuredly be remembered in the short but remarkable list of those who reformed our colonial system, and saved us from results which it is terrible to think of.   I am daring enough to hope that you will extend the spirit of your colonial policy in the case of Ireland.

"The anti-union Irish Protestants are a singular and (except the clique) an interesting race."

NOTES FOR 1890

Lord Feversham and I got a clause put into the Settled Act Bill enabling a tenant-for-life to take a half-year's rent to restore a burnt mansion.

Bishop Philpott, of Worcester, resigned. I earnestly set to work to make a Bishopric of Birmingham.

[Among visits :] A happy month at Fillongley [2nd son and daughter-in-law. From here he went over to see the wreck of Hams. "As I wandered about Hams," he wrote, " I felt *as if I had outlived myself*, and were looking over my late home, now passed from and deserted."] Went to Belvoir Castle—a most pleasant visit [his old friend, Lord John Manners, had succeeded as Duke of Rutland in 1887]. Belvoir twice burnt—the last time, in the beginning of this century, an entire wing, which had just been restored. The then Duke, who had taken the greatest pride and interest in restoring it, noted in his diary simply, " I thank the Almighty that none of my household were injured." To Sandon—delightful rides with Sandon [third Earl of Harrowby]. To Powis Castle [late Earl of Powis]. To Calke Abbey [son-in-law and daughter Sir V. and Honourable Lady Harpur Crewe]. In the magnificent park "Lady Catherine's bower," a relic evident of life gone out. Steps and bridge over valley and water to sylvan retreat, where ladies sat and men idled while a musician played. Now the whole place given over to game preserves, and not even drained that the rushes may give cover !

Country life is now threatened with much change. Old families going on all sides, places either breaking up or getting into tradesmen's hands. The present Lord Chancellor, Halsbury, and Lord Salisbury getting a Bill through the Lords to abolish entails and, by compulsory registration of titles, to facilitate dispersion of land.

[Among domestic events :] Dudley Leigh's marriage [present Lord Leigh].

[Deaths of friends :] Lord Cottesloe ; Lord Tollemache ; Mrs. Arthur Peel [*née* Dugdale]; Miss Percy, of Guy's Cliff ; My old keeper Mercer, whose father before him had been keeper in my great-uncle's time. The sad death of one man in the flames at Hams.

1891

I took advantage of my burnt-out-from-home winter to have my portrait painted by Jacomb Hood, highly recommended by Richmond as a most promising young artist, the Duke of Argyll being my colleague under the operation.

Work in Lords—Factory Bill, raising age of work ; Education Code. I got Lord Herschell to bring in a Bill against betting agents.

Lord Herschell had previously written :

May 9 [1891].

My dear Lord Norton,
    As the law stands under the Infants' Loans
Act, I think the Public Prosecutor is right. The
law went then as far as I think public opinion
permitted. Perhaps now it might go further, and
cast the onus on the money-lender in every case
of proving that he had reasonable ground to believe
that the person to whom he sent a circular was of.
full age. I will consider the matter.

Lord Herschell, after considering the matter, took
Lord Norton's advice, and brought in the Bill against
betting agents.

I sat on the Judicial Committee in the Bishop
of Lincoln's appeal.

I joined the Bishop of London's Fund Committee.

Raised the insurance on Hams, farms, etc., to
£100,000.

Easter Day, March 29.—Back at Hams. Put up
statuette of Gladstone in the hall of Hams, who
wrote : " Catherine told Acton, the sculptor, ' The
best likeness ever made.' " [1]

An epigram which Lord Norton wrote this spring
on the " Beerage," to which a new and fourth recruit
had recently been added, found its way into *Vanity
Fair.* It is mentioned by Sir M. Grant Duff as
having been well received at Grillion's, but he him-

---

[1] Mr. and Mrs. Gladstone had this summer the sorrow of the
death of their eldest son. Mr. Gladstone wrote to Lord Norton
(July 12) : "A bright spirit, gone from us, has gone only to greater
brightness. Surely in that immortal life—in that *Land of Promise*,
He will fill our desires with happiness ! "

self was only able to recall the last line. The verse ran as follows :

> Wilfrid, no more, except in jocund strain,
> Sing to your joyless water-gods in vain.
> Quadruple honours on the Beerage rain,
> And Bacchus wears his *ivy* [1] crown again !

I began negotiating with the Mayor of Birmingham about the fouling of the Tame—they to give me £5,000, and I to give up my injunction against them.

The following year's diary has this note : " £5,000 voted to me by Birmingham Corporation for Tame improvement, *with kindest expressions* as to forty years' litigation having terminated." In reference to this, Alderman Lawley Parker of Birmingham said that Lord Norton, after all the litigation with the Birmingham Corporation, settled the business finally in half an hour's conversation, giving the Corporation splendid terms, as if they were the dictators in the matter and not he—the reverse in fact being the case.

All up with the Birmingham Bishopric ! Controversy with Jesse Collings about his Allotment League. Two letters from Jo. Chamberlain pressing me to sell a site at Saltley to the Wesleyans [to build a chapel].

Mr. Chamberlain urged two reasons to induce Lord Norton to consent : (1) That the result of his refusal would be that every dissenter in East Birmingham would vote against the Unionist candidate at the next election. (2) That the Wesleyans were willing to pay a high price. Neither of these materialistic arguments appealed to Lord Norton. His unwillingness was based on moral grounds alone.

---

[1] Even for future generations it seems hardly necessary to explain that that ardent advocate of tee-totalism, the late Sir Wilfrid Lawson, is here apostrophised. " Ivy " is a (probably wilful) mispronunciation of the then new Barony of Iveagh.

" I cannot admit," he wrote, " the distinction between
giving and *selling* the means of what one considers
wrong. . . ." He had made a special study of
Wesleyanism, entertained the highest respect for its
great founder (if indeed John Wesley can be called
the founder of modern Wesleyanism), and, as we
have seen, at one time cherished the vain hope that
Wesleyans would join with the Low Church party
under the banner of the Church, as in America ;
and it was the hostility of modern Wesleyans to the
Church of their founder which made Lord Norton
the more unwilling to allow them a site at Saltley,
where the Church was earnestly and successfully
fulfilling her mission. " It is not," he wrote to Mr.
Chamberlain, "that I do not share in Wesleyan
religious opinions. I am more Wesleyan than they,
for Wesley most strongly deprecated his Church
revival being drawn into Church division. It is in
Wesley's spirit that I have spent £70,000 in Saltley
alone in making a full supply of places of worship."
A year later, however, Lord Norton, his " warm,
charitable heart " being unwilling to provoke bitter
and unchristian feeling, gave way and sold the site
to the Wesleyans.

[Among visits :] To Tatton—Lord Egerton took
us to the Manchester Canal, part opened in October ;
to Hatfield, to meet the Prince of Naples.

Lord Herschell's pleasant visit this autumn to
Hams.

Lord Herschell, who, in the following year, became
Lord Chancellor for the second time, paid several
visits to Hams. Lord Norton had for him a warm
regard, and they had musical taste in common, both
playing the violoncello with skill. Later Lord
Norton sent all his music to Lord Herschell—" It is
a pleasure to me to have it," wrote Lord Herschell,
" as a souvenir of our friendship."

CHAPTER XLVIII

1892

HIGH AND LOW CHURCH

ARCHBISHOP Benson wrote (August 12, 1892): " It would take even more than your ever-regarded command to keep me from thanking you for your kind letter of satisfaction in the Privy Council confirmation of judgment [the Archbishop's judgment in the case of Bishop King, of Lincoln]. I have received nothing which so makes me feel how strong the Church is in her great laymen. . . .

" I had an evening at the Christ Church Mission which made me feel that the advice about your son James was the soundest I ever gave. He is doing noble things in a nobly humble and faithful spirit. Evidences of God's blessing were on every side. I am delighted to think your essay is in the hands of the publishers."

This " Essay " was a little book entitled, " High and Low Church," the first edition of which was sold in a fortnight. Lord Salisbury wrote to Lord Norton : " The differences which separate the mass of High Churchmen and Low Churchmen have always appeared to me ridiculously small, and give one a great idea of the natural combativeness of the human race."

It is interesting to recall that Lord Salisbury, always a strong supporter of the Church of England, had, as Lord Robert Cecil, said in a letter to Mr. Adderley nearly forty years before that, unless the middle classes received due education in the teachings of their Church, " the Church of England could not last forty years."[1] It may be added that, during the intervening years, no one more than Lord Salisbury had worked towards preventing the catastrophe which he had dreaded.

Lord Norton believed that the area of agreement between High and Low Churchmen is much greater and more important than that of their differences, and he wrote this essay to impress that belief on others. " The divisions," he wrote, " caused within the Church by different apprehensions of the same fundamental truth by differently constituted minds, come short of schism, though there is often very unchristian exaggeration of such differences, causing hostile feeling, jealousies, or even mutual contempt." Again, " While High and Low Church are disputing about the process of ' New Birth,' or exact meaning of ' Real Presence,' or the prescriptive wardrobe of priests, or legitimate drama of worship, the world, in Renan's phrase, is escaping from the meshes of all belief. Young ladies are engaged in fusing their half-conceptions of sceptical theories in attractive little novels ; the rattle of a talking age is chattering the fancies of unthinking brains, and the flattery of shallow education and rejected reverence all swell the tide of this world's last development against the next world's unflinching claims."

The little book was on the whole highly praised by the Reviews. *The Guardian* said : " Lord Norton has now and again a raciness of expression which cannot but force attention from the most obstinate

[1] Lord Robert Cecil wrote to Mr. Adderley, November 14, 1855 : " I do not know if you have been applied to for the enclosed [a scheme in connection with St. Nicholas' College, Shoreham], if not I will ask you to read it. It speaks for itself. . . . It deserves the earnest support of Churchmen more than any scheme in existence ; for it is the only effort on a large scale to meet the danger which threatens the Church's existence as an establishment, viz. the hostility of the middle and lower middle classes. I have heard a very able M.P., an enemy of the Church, say that she cannot last forty years as things are now, and I think there can be little doubt that he is right. But this hostility mainly proceeds from the utter neglect of the Church of their education." Mr. Adderley then declined to subscribe to the scheme on account of the " extreme views " of some of its chief supporters.

of his opponents. Thus when he has occasion to dwell upon the intimate union of Church and State under the Stuarts, he indicates the results with striking concentration : ' But both Church and people soon remonstrated, the one crying Erastianism, the other Tyranny.' The following thought has seldom been more tersely or happily expressed : ' The great probation of life is the passage through outward objects in this world to inward fitness for the next.' Again, Lord Norton has surpassed himself in the creation of the phrase 'conscious photophobia,' to describe the condition of mind of those persons who object to the presence of lighted candles on an altar in the daytime. To hear his disease ticketed with so magnificent a name is almost enough to reconcile the victim to the illumination which has provoked it."

The Spectator, while criticising Lord Norton's strong language on the subject of " Voluntary Outsiders," as, for example, modern Wesleyans, whom it warmly defends, added : " Nothing can be more admirable than his attitude towards the recent ecclesiastical litigants. He sees perfectly well that unless the Church of England is to be comprehensive in a sense in which neither the Church of Rome nor the Calvinistic Churches of the Continent can possibly be comprehensive, it has no *locus standi* at all."

The extremists of either party in the Church were perhaps not likely to be satisfied with Lord Norton's charitable and earnest, though somewhat optimistic, attempt to bridge over the gulf existing between them ; but the effort came at a moment when it was though more possible to achieve success than at any time since the beginning of the Tractarian movement.

Archbishop Benson wrote (November 28, 1892): " How I wish that your warm, charitable heart and fund of good judgment could touch the feeling and sense of the obstinate ! "

The author of " John Inglesant " wrote : " I have had great difficulty in *finishing* your book, for it struck me, as soon as I began it, as so admirably timed and so useful to many people I knew, that I have not been able to keep a copy in the house, having sent so many away. I have, however, succeeded in keeping a copy at last until I finished it. I think the value of such a book, written at such a moment by an educated layman of position, cannot be overestimated. Were I to go into all the points where I find so much to admire I should tire you . . . but I must refer to your remarks upon Fasting Communion [Lord Norton considered that the High Church party attached too much importance to the *necessity* of Fasting Communion, discouraging Communion after an eleven o'clock service] and the advantage of communicating when the mind and spirit have been prepared by the beautiful service of the Church in Matins. It seems presumptuous to say so, but the amount of information and knowledge, and the wealth of illustration in your book, strikes me very much. . . . Your book seems to me to breathe the spirit of the Caroline Church of the latter half of the seventeenth century—the great century of the Church which, whether we consider the list of great divines, or the Communion literature which they have left us, is unique in the history of the Church of England."

Lord Norton, a strong Churchman, had no leanings in the direction of extremes. Most of his friends, as he advanced in life, most also of those within his home circle, were what are termed High Church. But his early evangelical upbringing never ceased to tinge his inmost thoughts. "Indeed," he wrote later, "a real sense of Divine Presence almost gives unconsciousness of any special manner of worship."

NOTES FOR 1892

I spoke against London County Council Technical Education; and also pleaded against exclusion of Reformatory Boys from Army and Navy.

CHAPTER XLIX

1893

AN INTERESTING CORRESPONDENCE

HOME RULE debate. A letter to me from Fitzgerald, in New Zealand, gave Gladstone an argument
for Home Rule. I had an interview with Gladstone,
and got up to defend him in the House of Lords.

This letter, received by Lord Norton early in
January 1893, was as follows:
" If I were called on to make a speech on the Irish
question, I would describe the state of all the
Colonies as I have known them in my lifetime.
The rebellion in Canada, the uprising at the Cape
at the attempt to force convicts upon them, the
Press of every Australian Colony and of New
Zealand for so many long years teeming with
abuse of the English Government. I could tell of
Governors hissed in theatres, and of one Governor,
[New Zealand], accused of burning down Government House.
" I would describe the speeches at public meetings
and the unrestrained vilification of every man
attached to the Government of the day. I would
then describe the colonial world around me now:
the exuberant and sometimes absurd display of
loyalty to the Queen and mother-country, and even
the growing desire of closer ties by federation—at

all events, by the mass (though I fear there are leaders who look at federation as only a step to separate nationality) ; and I would ask my hearers what has been the magic spell which effected this wonderful transformation scene ?   It is all expressed in one word—Home Rule.

"Now for fifty years two great experiments have been going on before our eyes.   One has been carried on in Ireland, the other in the Colonies. One, indeed, has been tried for many times fifty years—it has been a miserable failure. The other has been a miraculous success.   What shall we say of statesmen who persist in continuing the unsuc-cessful experiment, and refuse to try that which has marvellously succeeded ?   There is the whole case in a nutshell.

" As to the Irish leaders at the present hour one can only laugh when one does not weep !   For my own part I see an additional reason in the present sad state of Irish parties why, in the event of Home Rule being carried, the bond of union with England would be *greatly strengthened.*   For at present you have all, or nearly all, the active force of the country against you.   Now, under a local Government, there would be the traditional factions of the two parties —the majority and the minority, alias the *ins* and the *outs.*   The latter would *always look to England as a means of getting them their desire upon their enemies.* In a small arena I have seen that here.   When New Zealand was divided into provinces, the Provincial Government played the game of respon-sible government very prettily.   We were playing at party government like very intelligent schoolboys. We all were very jealous of the General Govern-ment.   But the *minorities* in the local Government always called on the Olympian deities at the seat of Government for help.   I see no reason why the same causes should not produce the same result in Ireland.   You would at all events have a large part of the Irish people loyal to England.   Indeed, you would have the *whole,* every man of them *loyal, only not all at the same time.*"

These curious arguments in favour of Home Rule

were somewhat unfortunately forwarded by Lord Norton to Gladstone, just before the meeting of Parliament.

Gladstone wrote (January 12, 1893):

"I thank you sincerely, both for your own letter, written with your usual generous kindness, and for the remarkable enclosure from Fitzgerald. Will you permit me to telegraph to him to inquire whether he will allow me to make public use of that part of the letter which I will term the colonial contrast?"

Permission being granted, Gladstone produced Fitzgerald's arguments in favour of Home Rule in his speech in the House of Commons, as Lord Norton's notes, quoted above, explain.

On the rejection of the Home Rule Bill by the House of Lords, Lord Norton and Gladstone corresponded further. Gladstone wrote from Black Craig, September 10, 1893:

"I thank you very much for your letter. It is just like yourself, that is to say, kind and generous throughout. Who the aspersing peers are I know not, and never shall know, for my eyesight disables me from reading the debate. All the better, I can neither wonder at nor complain of them, when a man like Argyll, my friend for forty years, and my colleague for twenty, accuses me (if I understand him aright) of having done what I did in order to get office—in face of the fact that my first act was, shortly after the election, to make known to the Government that if they would settle the Irish question they should have the best support I could give them, and that I never said a word against them (though they were a small minority), until they declared in February for *coercion*. No answer was ever made to my offer, but I *know* that there are among them men . . . who lament that it was not accepted. . . . Your vote is one of those that it was a special sorrow to me not to have.

"I was sorry to miss you the last time when I went to Grillion's, especially because I wanted to say with how much pleasure I had read your son's [James's] excellent, and, in the proper place, entertaining book [1] which you were good enough to send me. . . ."

James now formed an Anglican Brotherhood at Plaistow under vows. I consulted Archbishop Benson on the subject. The Archbishop wrote : " I have most carefully weighed the pros and cons as they present themselves to me about James's wishes. . . . I do believe in brotherhoods, both for the brothers' sakes and the Church's. I do think that they are rapidly becoming a necessity for the discharge of our work in dense populations. . . . His description of living, with laity and clergy, a simple life among the poor does not, at any rate, go beyond what is a deep need of our time."

In consequence of Archbishop Benson's advice Lord Norton (who had little sympathy with vows of celibacy, even although they were temporary) made no further demur, merely remarking to a friend, when his son James became " Father Adderley," " But I draw the line at calling my own son Father ! "

The Archbishop, Lord Halifax, and Professor Stokes were of a party at Hams this year for the Church Congress, after which the Archbishop wrote with regard to James Adderley's maiden speech at the Congress :

" With the rest of the world or Church, we heartily and affectionately congratulate you on Jim's *success*, if so horrid a word is justifiable in such a connection. It is a great thing to have Jim's gift of so going to people's hearts and conciliating all sympathies—and although it may be a question whether the details will work out as expected, yet the aim is unquestionable, and the spirit. May he be led in the right way, and delivered from all

[1] " Stephen Remarx," by Father Adderley.

temptation, spiritual and mental, which dogs the heel of 'Success'! We rejoice with you. . . ."

NOTES FOR 1894

Parish and District Councils started.
Gladstone resigns in March.
Rosebery Premier.
I spoke at Salisbury's anti-Home Rule meeting—also in Lords on Licensing Bill.

My chill of last November keeps me in Dr. Maclagan's hands.
Part of nave and aisle added to Washwood Heath Church.

1895

Lord Norton now brought out a little essay on Socialism. *The Spectator* praised it. Lord Selborne, the venerable Ex-Lord Chancellor, wrote (February 3rd):

I thank you very much for your little book on Socialism, which I read through without stopping as soon as it came to hand; and still more for your affectionate words, which I heartily reciprocate. Among many and dangerous delusions which are afloat at the present time, I look upon the Socialistic idea as perhaps the most serious —the more dangerous because of the plausible way in which it presents itself to the mind of some benevolent and well-meaning persons, as recommended from a Christian or philanthropic point of view. In the practical and political forms which it has hitherto assumed I think it is *anti-Christian* and the reverse of *philanthropic*—tending, in politics, to nothing short of universal slavery; in morals, to class-hatred, and, in more material things, to national decline and impoverishment.

I need not add that in your own general conclusions I heartily agree; though you perhaps treat what calls itself (or is called) *Christian Socialism* rather more gently than I should.

Ever most truly yours,
SELBORNE.[1]

[1] Lord Selborne died the following May 6.

CHAPTER L

1895 (*continued*)

GLADSTONE'S VISIT TO HAMS

DURING this summer Lord Norton had, perhaps, the greatest satisfaction and pleasure of his declining years. Mr. Gladstone paid a long-projected visit to Hams for three days, arriving on August 28. He was now in his eighty-seventh year, and his host was five years his junior. While many of Gladstone's former friends and supporters had lately turned from him, Lord Norton, his political opponent, drew closer and warmer the ties of long-standing friendship. Miss Helen Gladstone accompanied her father, and among the party were the Archbishop and Mrs. Benson, Lord Leigh and Miss Agnes Leigh, Dr. Talbot, Bishop Designate of Rochester, and Mrs. Talbot, Lord Peel, Sir Frederick and Lady Peel, and the Hon. and Rev. Henry Cholmondeley. Two days were occupied in expeditions to Drayton and Stoneleigh respectively. "Never did anything go off so perfectly well in every respect," wrote one of the guests afterwards. "Such a conjuncture of most interesting scenes with distinguished personages! Above all, the Drayton visit! An Ex-Premier visiting the home of one of his forerunners [the great Sir Robert Peel], contemplating the portrait of himself, painted sixty [1] years before, and, *pleno ore*, recalling scenes and events which other pictures

---

[1] Gladstone was thirty-two at the time the portrait was painted by Lucas. It was one of a collection of portraits which Sir Robert Peel brought together. All the heads of Government, from Walpole to the Peel Administration, are represented.

Lord Norton.   Archbishop Benson.   Mr. Gladstone.

AT HAMS HALL IN 1895.

p. 348]

or busts *et similia* brought back to his mind." Mr. Gladstone had not visited Drayton since 1835, when he was Under-Secretary for the Colonies under Peel. Before leaving Drayton he wrote in the Visitors' Book : "A day of the utmost interest and delight on visiting Drayton, after an interval of nearly sixty years." It was on this occasion that Lord Norton saw for the first time the pistols, preserved at Drayton, with which Peel intended to fight O'Connell.

Archbishop Benson noted in his diary [1] an account of Mr. Gladstone's conversations at Drayton. "I would have given anything," he says, "if I could have had a shorthand writing-machine with me. I never saw such an interest as Mr. Gladstone took in every point." Among other things, he told the story of Disraeli's giving, as his reason why he (Disraeli) had attacked Peel—as "a small dog barks at a large one "—" Because," said Disraeli, "Peel was the only man by attacking whom I could bring myself really forward." "Disraeli's career," added Gladstone, "is, taken from first to last, the most extraordinary of any political life I know of. No one can write it. I could write it better—I know more of it—than any one. Pitt's early life was full of a strange romance ; but, taken all through, Disraeli's was the most strange that ever was." Of Peel Gladstone said, "He and the Prince Consort had the 'conscience burdened with public duty' more than any two people I have ever known—a most noble sense of duty." Of politics Gladstone said, what all politicians say who have done with them : "There will never be ideal politics—men and parties being in far too vast an admixture. It is a sorry concern." [2]

Of the visit next day to Lord and Lady Leigh at Stoneleigh Abbey [3] Lord Norton notes :

[1] "Life of Archbishop Benson," vol. ii. pp. 658–9.
[2] *Ibid.*
[3] Archbishop Benson notes : "Stoneleigh is really grand—the ancient part, with its gables, its Norman doors, its undercroft, quite beautiful, humble, and simple, and fit for good monks."—*Ibid.*, vol. ii. p. 659.

"Ovation all the way from crowds to see Gladstone." *A propos* of this visit, Lord Norton said :
"When Gladstone meets any one his first thought
is, 'What does he know ? What can I get out of
him ?' When he met Lord Leigh he had heard
of Stoneleigh that it possessed some of the finest
oaks in England, so when he sat down by him he
began at once : 'Lord Leigh, have you any theory
as to the age of oaks ?' 'Yes, certainly I have ; I
possess several myself that are above a thousand
years old.' 'And how do you know that is so ?'
asked Gladstone. 'Well,' said Lord Leigh, 'I have
several that are called "Gospel Oaks," because the
Saxon missionaries used to preach under them more
than eight hundred years ago, and they would not
be likely to choose a young oak to preach under.
We may suppose that they chose an oak at least two
hundred years old.' 'Well, that is a very good
reason,' said Gladstone."[1]

"There never were three days so marvellously
organised," wrote the Archbishop to Lord Norton,
"and Mr. Gladstone really *is* a great experience ; we
saw him so easy and unreserved, so carrying the
great man without self-consciousness into quiet,
comfortable hours ; and his ready and exact memory
backs up such a freshness of thought and word that
I feel I have seen one of the sights of the age as
I never saw him before, though I have known him
so long."[2]

It was while at Hams that Mr. Gladstone planned
the visit of Archbishop Benson to Hawarden, which
at the close of the following year was to be the
scene of the Archbishop's sudden death.

Lord Norton notes :

Gladstone's visit to Hams—delight of all.

[1] See Augustus Hare's "Story of My Life," vol. vi. p. 406.
[2] It was under Gladstone's Administration that Benson was
appointed to the See of Canterbury. Lord Norton used to recall
that when the Archbishopric was vacant some busy-body said to
Gladstone, "Do you know that Benson is working for the Tory
party in Cornwall?" Gladstone replied, "A Bishop who does
that while Canterbury is vacant is the man to make Archbishop !"

Delicious reflections on the happy three days just gone.

[Again]: Gladstone's and Archbishop Benson's glorious visit—interesting all around.

Contact with such minds is *sursum corda*—refreshment and strength to mind and soul and faith. How soon may we meet where the fulfilled Passover is real, not typical Communion!

Mr. Gladstone himself wrote: "The visit to Hams fills—shall I say?—a fragrant place in my recollection. . . . Thanks again and again from one warmly yours."

The late Mr. Augustus Hare records in "The Story of My Life" a visit which he paid to Hams on November 30, 1895.[1] "This is a large house," he says, "of extreme comfort, and its owner, Lord Norton, who looks sixty although he is eighty-two, is one of the most agreeable hosts in England."

NOTES FOR 1895

I was elected Master of the Shipwright Company.

Restored Curdworth Church.

I gave £100 towards Keeper's Lodge in Adderley Park (People's Park), Birmingham.

Deaths: Lord Selborne, Sir Robert Peel, Granville, Leveson-Gower (brother-in-law).

[1] Vol. vi. pp. 406–409.

CHAPTER LI

1896

ARCHBISHOP BENSON'S DEATH

ARCHBISHOP BENSON, four days before his death in church while on a visit to Mr. and Mrs. Gladstone at Hawarden, wrote to Lord Norton from Ireland, where he was concluding a laborious tour:

" Belfast Castle, October 7, 1896. . . . It would need no temptation of company to bring me to Hams if it were possible. But terrible masses of work and engagements await me, and I am bound to go home for them as rapidly as I can, leaving Cheltenham before the function ends. I go to Mr. Gladstone on Saturday." . . .

1897

[LORD NORTON'S NOTES]

On Sunday, April 4, I called on Gladstone, just returned from the Riviera. I spoke of Archbishop Benson's happy death at Hawarden. Gladstone said, " The Irish visit killed him. It was a great opportunity for Irish clergy to make capital out of the Archbishop's visit, and they over-worked him." I said, " It was a noble act, his visit." Gladstone: " He had a superstition about Disestablishment. Nothing I ever did gives me more satisfaction. I don't know what you thought of it ? " I said I wished the funds etc. released had been secured to religious purposes. G—— said he had "tried to secure them to poor relief of various kinds. . . . The Tories applied the money to many wrong purposes." He said, "I go to Hawarden to-morrow. I am too old to get about—seven years older than you." "No," I said, "not five." He said, "I have been at places of our excellent friends where they had such fine linen on my bed that I could get no warmth."

"That *instinct*," Mr. Gladstone wrote, "on which you comment so acutely and so justly seems to tell me, not in words but by a mere inward voice, that it is the law of nature for a very old man to retire like the snail into his shell. I have some hope that you have various years to pass through before you hear this inner voice."

1898

Lord Norton lost in the spring of this year his two intimate friends, Mr. Gladstone, who died on Ascension Day, and Sir Thomas Dyke Acland, who died towards the end of May, in his 90th year.

Lord Norton wrote to Sir Thomas's daughter, Mrs. Anson :

May 31.

I feel I have lost a *relation*, as your dear father always called me—so long and intimately have our families lived together. He and I travelled together on leaving Oxford. His father and my father did the same. My dearest associations are with Killerton and all its belongings there. . . . The greatest kindness and warmest affections from my boyhood upward I have had from that genial quarter, and the spirit which has now gone shortly before me, and so closely upon Gladstone's—the kindred spirit which he always told me was linked

with his—has given me through my life a high
example, and a kindly influence of greatest value.
I shall in heart and mind be with you all, realising
the well-known and well-loved scene itself on
Friday.

Very faithfully yours,

NORTON.

NOTES (*continued*)

Six hundred Birmingham Conservatives came to
Hams.

I gave the proceeds of the sale of lease of Uppingham Hall to the Restoration of Curdsworth Church,
and £2,000 more to Washwood Heath.

I made another effort with Lord Salisbury to get
the Birmingham Bishopric, but failed.

The S.P.C.K. Centenary: I put up a memorial in
our Church (Lea) to Dr. Bray, who was Vicar of
Lea and the founder of the S.P.C.K. and the
S.P.G.

Lord Norton now published a little book called
"Reflections on the Course from the Goal" which
soon went into a second edition. It was intended
as the last message which a veteran statesman,
"standing upon the edge of life and looking back
upon its course, just before the step into its endless
consequence, has to give his fellow-men. The past
interests of the way seem a vanishing picture, and
nothing is really left of them but their impression
on the character now going for final presentation
before the Judge. . . . Now that the end has come
the travelling gear is laid aside and the wayside
thoughts have fled. The soul is disencumbering itself
to enter into the Actual Presence." "The central
thoughts of this testament of his," says *The Spectator*,[1] "published while he is happily still with us,

[1] *Spectator*, October 29, 1898.

are that by living in this world in conscious subjection of our wills, both actively and passively, to that of God, we may and shall develop natures which, beyond the grave, will pursue an eternal existence of perfect harmony with the Divine Will. . . . The religious spirit is to be shown not in withdrawing from or despising the world, but in the temper in which ordinary concerns are treated." On this point Lord Norton lays special emphasis. "In different ways," he says, "philosophy and asceticism falsely disconnect the idea of present from that of future life. Locke considered them separate concerns. A Kempis wrote : 'The highest wisdom, by contempt of the world, presses towards the kingdom of heaven.' But the course of life to the prize lies through all its joys and sorrows, its trivial duties or glorious exploits, its trials and enjoyments."

It was in this spirit that when Mr. Gladstone, on one occasion, intending to retire from political life, said : "I must now prepare for my end," Lord Norton replied : "*Your whole life* is a preparation for it."

1899

The following letter of Lord Norton has a special interest for members of Grillion's Club, addressed (February 11, 1899) to the veteran Sir Henry Dyke Acland,[1] the distinguished younger son of Sir Thomas Dyke Acland (the principal founder of Grillion's), brother of the Sir Thomas D. Acland who had died the year before, and uncle of the present Sir Thomas D. Acland, to whom the letter refers. Lord Norton now resigned the Secretaryship of Grillion's, his co-secretary, Mr. Arthur Mills, so long associated with Grillion's, having recently died.

DEAR SIR HENRY,

I moved and carried with warm unanimity at breakfast this morning that Sir Thomas Acland

---

[1] Himself created a baronet.

be elected an *extra* member of Grillion's Club. Poor dear Arthur Mills would have been horrified at such a break of all the laws of Medes and Persians. The Speaker [Gully] was present, and the breakfast very large, but the expression of affection to the memory of the genial founder of the club [the present Sir Thomas's grandfather] was enthusiastic and the new member himself is greatly liked. I am delighted that I should have this act to do—my last on resigning the Secretary- ship of that brilliant old foundation of the ever- youthful Acland, whose spirit still lives in the Club. The new secretaries are Sir Redvers Buller and Sir Robert Herbert.

Ever yours affectionately,

NORTON.

CHAPTER LII

1900

IMPERIAL FELLOWSHIP

THE strength of British colonial attachment to the Empire and readiness for co-operation as a part of the whole, revealed by the Boer War, had been a source of keenest satisfaction to Lord Norton. That self-government in the Colonies, which, fifty years earlier, he had strongly advocated, would lead to a feeling of fellowship with the mother-country rather than endanger it he had always firmly believed, and he rejoiced to have lived to see, in the rally of British Colonies to Imperial Fellowship during the closing year of the nineteenth century, so complete a proof of the truth of his belief.

Lord Strathcona wrote :

March 20, 1900.

MY DEAR LORD NORTON,

Your letter to *The Times* is an admirable one, and I need hardly say to you that, with the sentiment conveyed in it I am entirely in sympathy, as are, I am sure, the whole people of Canada and of the other outlying constituent portions of the Empire. We all know that in the formation of the Dominion, and in many other ways, you did yeoman service, and your continued support in everything tending to knit the more closely the several parts of the Empire we in Canada greatly appreciate.

Lord Norton's letter to *The Times* (February 22, 1900), referred to by Lord Strathcona, comments on some remarks of Lord Rosebery in the debate of the previous Thursday. " This Empire," Lord Rosebery was reported to have said, " rested much on prestige, and our Colonies now came to our support [in the Boer War] because they believed they were associating themselves with a powerful Empire ; but if we deprive them of that belief, the life of this Empire will be short." " This is applauded," Lord Norton critically remarks, " as a wise warning that if the Colonies are led to suspect that we cannot raise troops enough to assert our own supremacy in South Africa they will have misgivings as to our capacity to provide for their safety.   Here we still see lingering ideas, even in leading minds, of our Colonies as *dependencies* far below their lofty spirit of *fellow-citizenship* which at this moment they are so gloriously evincing.   They are not fair-weather friends, so long only as 'we show ourselves strong enough to provide for their safety,' but they are proud to own the common nationality—all providing for the safety of all."

In July 1901 Lord Norton was one of six peers who voted for the Bill introduced by Lord Grey to get rid of the King's Declaration as to Religion on ascending the Throne.   Lord Halifax wrote to Lord Norton (July 26) : " I think we six were the only sensible people in the House of Lords on Monday. . . . Tweedmouth's speech ought to have convinced every one what a horror the Declaration is."

In August 1901 Lord Norton had a severe illness, of which, however, he thought little, but henceforth he discontinued his daily ride at the age of 87.

Among notes for 1902 is a remark recorded with keen satisfaction :

" Birmingham Bishopric.   Hope *at last*! "—for the realisation of which he had so long been working and waiting.   When the prospects of the creation of the new See were at their darkest Lord Norton never lost heart, and through him a continuity of effort was maintained that facilitated the realisation of Bishop Gore's endeavours.   It was at once inspiriting and pathetic to those at that time associated with Lord Norton to witness his impatience of obstacles, his fertility of suggestion, his undaunted hopefulness and energy.

He was now busily engaged in writing an essay on colonial affairs, thirty-four years having passed since he published his work on the same subject in 1869.

1903

" Imperial Fellowship, or Self-Governed British Colonies," is the title of a short but valuable treatise which Lord Norton brought out in 1903 in his 90th year—surely a remarkable achievement. The Dedication runs : " To the Right Hon. Joseph Chamberlain, M.P., under the auspices of whose pre-eminent statesmanship a crisis in our colonial history, which first revealed to our full consciousness the warm sympathy and ready co-operation of our Colonies, has been made to rivet our attention on the aggregate power of *United British* Empire for the peaceful and prosperous commerce of the world."

Lord Norton is thus described by one who saw him in July 1903 : " Although of course his hair is grey [it was slightly so], he is not bald, and only quite recently shows any signs of his great age, being slightly deaf, but otherwise his faculties and his marvellous memory are perfectly unimpaired. . . . He never seems tired, and almost every day he still attends some meeting, board, or sessions, and is indefatigable as regards his duties as a guardian of the poor and a member of County Council." [1]   Lord Norton, when in London, was still, in all weathers, a regular attendant at the House of Laymen, the Bishop of London's Fund, and the Mendicity Society.   He went daily to the House of Lords, and frequently spoke.   It is said that he spoke at a later age than any peer had previously done. [2]

[1] *The World*, July 21, 1903, where Lord Norton appears among the series of "Celebrities at Home."
[2] The following is a list of subjects on which Lord Norton

A letter from Sir Arthur Godley to a friend, giving an account of a visit to Hams in October 1903, mentions an excursion with his host to Drayton Manor, where, over sixty years before, in the time of the great Sir Robert Peel, Lord Norton as a young man was frequently a guest. "It was delightful," wrote Sir Arthur Godley, "to see how, as we drove towards our destination, his mind began to work, and his recollections to revive, until he seemed to be twenty years younger than his real age. The house, built by the Prime Minister, is not beautiful, but contains some fine corridors and rooms for the exhibition of pictures. Of these a good many, chiefly old masters, have been sold, but a great number remain, mostly portraits of the great man's friends and contemporaries. There was an interesting portrait of Gladstone at the age of 32. It was a great historical show. Lord Norton could not see the pictures very well,

spoke in the House of Lords during the last eight years of his life, from the age of 83 to 90—the year before his death :

1897
Discharged Prisoners' Aid Society.
Elementary Education Act.
School Boards' Expenses Bill.
Secondary Education.
Sunday Bill.
Voluntary Schools Bill.

1898
Day Schools.
Day and Residential Colleges.
Floods Prevention Bill.
Overloading of Ships.
Poor Law Unions Association Bill.
Pupil Teacher System.
Secondary Education.
Workhouses, Religious Ministrations, Motion for Returns.

1899
Board of Education Bill.
Educational Measures.
Money Lending Bill.
Poor Law Acts Amendment Bill.
Reformatory Schools Amendment Bill.
Seats for Shop Assistants Bill.
Small Houses (Acquisition of Ownership).
Youthful Offenders Bill.

1900
Board of Education Act.
Education Bill.
Secondary Education Bill.
Shops (Early Closing) Bill.
Youthful Offenders Bill.

1901
Day Industrial Schools.
Education (Cockerton Judgment) Code of.
Intoxicating Liquor (Sale to Travellers).
Licensing Boards Bill.
Light Load-line Bill.
Reformatory and Industrial Schools.

1902
Light Load-line.
Teachers—Training of Elementary Teachers abroad.

1903
Bishoprics of Southwark and Birmingham Bill.

1904
Education (Transferred Schools) Bill.
Transvaal, Importation of Chinese Labour.

but for him the whole place was peopled with ghosts—above all, the great ghost of Sir Robert; and in every room, at every window, almost at every table, he poured forth anecdotes and reminiscences; some of them trivial, but all helping to form a picture of Peel and his surroundings. . . . The house, except for its ghosts, was empty. . . . When we were again in the carriage, driving homewards, Lord Norton was at first silent for several minutes, and then said, evidently with a good deal of emotion, 'I feel as if I had been spending half an hour with Peel!''

This was fifty-three years after the death of Peel; and it was to the years from 1837 to 1842 that Lord Norton's recollections of Drayton chiefly turned— to the time before Peel had even thought of repealing the Corn Laws!

NOTES FOR 1903

I correspond with Chamberlain on his return from South Africa.

September 28.—Chief visit of interest: Sir Redvers Buller and his wife came to Hams.

Birmingham Bishopric getting on.

Sad death of Wynne Finch immediately after visit to Hams.

Deaths of Maclagan, the only doctor who knew me, and Hanbury (Right Hon. Robert W.) after his great kindness to my grandson, Dick Crewe. Lord Salisbury, old Mrs. Dugdale aged 96 [sister of 1st Viscount Portman], and my brother Edmund.

1904

He was in his usual health, and spoke twice in the House of Lords. On the Licensing question he wrote to *The Times*, May 9, 1904 : "The public-house trade is a necessity, and, if kept to healthy supply of healthy demand, its extent can be of no more baneful influence than any other trade in the necessities of life." He was, however, in favour of greater penalties on abuses, "such as drunkenness, rioting, or adulteration of drink."

The notes now become more scattered, and chiefly refer to business. In his book of meditations he writes:

I look at all things passing away. Two books on the *after-life* engage me, and talks with Jim—who says *that* does not affect men's lives. Perfect sincerity and complete devotion, without reserve or shirking indolence, give confidence in God's love and bring one to Christ.

May 22.—Whitsunday at Hams. Felt cheerful thoughts of my coming end. God's mercy has followed me all the days of my very long life. Enjoyed these scenes in retrospect, and with no desire to retrace; but to anticipate the *scene beyond.*

August 2.—*Ninety years old.*

On the eve of his birthday he wrote the following touching letter to his brother-in-law, Lord Leigh, who was prevented from attending the birthday festivities at Hams :

My DEAR HENRY,
        I greatly grieve that I must lose you to-morrow, but I treasure your kindness in so heartily proposing to come. I hoped to be with you all the day, as it was my chief prospect of pleasure—you are becoming so scarce. My life is certainly near its end, or rather passage elsewhere. I am in the last room before the *Presence,* and peeping through the entrance to get acquainted with it, and confidence.

Not " happy returns," but " happy reflections " are for me to-morrow, and with none more than the links of affection past, connected with future hopes.

I should have enjoyed the day doubly with you here. I have Georgie [1] and Cholmondeley [2] just arrived.

[1] His sister-in-law the Honourable Mrs. Newdigate, Lord Leigh's sister. This lady, gifted with remarkable quickness of intellect and independence of character, combined with single-mindedness and generosity of feeling, died, deeply regretted, in August 1907.
[2] Rev. the Hon. Henry Cholmondeley, Lord Norton's brother-in-law.

I have the whole full band of Reformatory Boys to honour you with, as Arnold particularly wished.

Give me a visit as soon as you can, or I must rattle my old bones over to Stoneleigh to see you.

Ever your affectionate
NORTON.

Among the many who wrote congratulations on this occasion were two of his oldest friends, the Duke of Rutland and Gathorne Hardy (Lord Cranbrook). The latter was three months, and the Duke of Rutland four years younger than Lord Norton. The Duke, who, as Lord John Manners, was closely associated with Lord Norton's political life from its beginning, and who had been one of the little band of " Young England " in the early forties, wrote :

BELVOIR CASTLE,
August 2, 1904.

MY DEAR OLD FRIEND,
On this anniversary I cannot refrain from writing a few words of congratulation on its recurrence, and of heart-felt aspiration that, during the period leading up to its successor, Heaven's blessing may rest upon you.

Your attached friend,
RUTLAND.

Lord Cranbrook wrote :

August 4, 1904.

MY DEAR NORTON,
I am a couple of days too late, but accept my congratulations and good wishes on entering your tenth decade. With some envy, I have seen how you have been present in the House, and even taken part in debate. Long may you continue able to use your influence, and occupy your mind ! My country retirement suits my health, but the limits are laid down for me, and I keep within them, and they are an absolute obstacle to my undertaking duties in London.

Yours ever sincerely,
CRANBROOK.

Lord Norton's memoranda during the last year of his life show the interest he still took in the management of his property, as well as the continuance of his practice of self-communing, self-examination, and introspection.

In October he did not fail to give his annual address at Saltley College, and it was characterised by marvellous force and freshness.

Bishop Gore of Birmingham wrote: " He was full of energy, full of thought for the affairs of the Church, full of self-sacrifice both in the way of money and trouble. So wonderful an enthusiasm, freshness, and hopefulness I never witnessed in any one else of his great age. But it was not merely external activity or interest in outward things that distinguished him : underneath there was an intensity of spiritual life altogether wonderful. I think I never knew any one, priest or layman, who was more full of enthusiasm for the kingdom of God. This heart of enthusiasm was kept fresh to the end."

Early in 1905 he was ailing and the precautions enjoined by his physician were irksome to a man of his active habits.

He continued to write to his friends as usual. His correspondence of a life-time with eminent statesmen is suitably concluded by a letter from Lord Cranbrook, himself at this time a nonagenarian. Lord Cranbrook wrote :

February 9, 1905.

After long lives unusually prolonged, we may well have warnings how frail we are, and recognise that at ninety we must be riding at single anchor, ready for the call to cross the bar. May our Pilot bring us to the haven where we would be. That thought is in your heart. . . . I doubt if we shall meet again, as I see no prospect of going to London this year. May God bless and be with you is the prayer of
Yours ever sincerely,
CRANBROOK.

Seven weeks later Lord Norton "crossed the

bar," or, in the words of his own booklet, his " course " was run, and " the goal " reached on March 28, 1905.

It was well said : " When one thinks of a spirit so vigorous and so devout passing into the unseen world the thrill of a great triumph passes through one. Old age has no sense of failure and death no sting."

THE NORTON MEMORIAL HALL, SALTLEY, BIRMINGHAM.

Among many memorials dedicated to the beloved memory of Lord Norton the principal one consists of a Large Hall and Institute in Saltley for working men. It was subscribed to by a large number of friends, of all political parties and religious creeds, and cost the sum of £6,000. The architect was Mr. Holland Hobbiss. The foundation was laid by the Marquis of Salisbury. The Hall was opened by the Countess of Selborne and the Lord Mayor of Birmingham.

INDEX

Abercorn, Marquis of, 167 (*note*)

Abercorns, 1st Duke and Duchess of, 190

Aberdeen, Lord, Prime Minister, 125, 144

Acland, Lydia, 37

Acland, Sir Henry Dyke, 301

Acland, Right Hon. Sir Thomas, 10th Baronet, 12, 20, 47, 50, 157 (*note*); death of, 212

Acland, Right Hon. Sir Thomas Dyke, 11th Baronet, 20, 171; death of, 299

Acland, Sir Thomas Dyke, 12th and present Baronet, 301

Adams, Sir J., 278

Adderley, Anna Maria, 21

Adderley, Hon. Arden, 241, 242, 249

Adderley, Arthur, 233

Adderley, Hon. Charles, 201, 232, 241, 242

Adderley, Charles Bowyer (afterwards Lord Norton), his relation to his Parliamentary work, 1; refusal of a post in the Government early in his career, 2; his best work, *ib.*; his unofficial benefits to Cape Colony, *ib.*; his attitude to the future of British Colonies, 3; his formation of the Colonial Reform Association, *ib.*; his relations with New Zealand, *ib.*; his habit of making notes of the events of his life, *ib.*; how he was led to his Parliamentary career, 4; his shyness, *ib.*; his deep religious views, *ib.*; Dr. Gore's estimate of him, 6 (*note*); birth and ancestry of, 8–10; estates of, 8; early memories of, 11; death of his father, *ib.*; education of, 13; death of his mother, *ib.*; his Oxford days, 16; memorial to him at Saltley Church, Birmingham, 17 (*note*); travels through Scotland, 19; foreign travels of, 20; early days in London, 23–29; studies law, 28; urged by Sir Robert Peel to go into Parliament, 31; his friendship with J. R. Godley, 33; asked to enter Parliament, 35; elected for North Staffs, 39; his engagement, 41; his correspondence with Miss Leigh, 43–49; his early married life, 50–55; birth of his first child, 51; speaks against the Game Law, and Irish Colleges, 55; birth of a son and heir, 60; re-elected for North Staffs, 61; begins pedigree farming, 63; death of his daughter Julia, 65; contributes articles to *The Spectator* and *Morning Chronicle*, *ib.*; writes an essay, *ib.*; sends a report of a speech to *The North Staffordshire*, 67; put on the Ceylon Committee, 68; his interest in New Zealand, 69 *et seq.*; attacks Lord Grey's colonial policy, 73; the Cape Colonists' appreciation of him, 76, 77; his name given to a street in Cape Town, *ib.*; forms the Colonial Reform Society, 78 *et seq.*; his correspondence with Lord Lyttelton, 87; his pamphlet on "Transportation," 88, 93; his work on the Committee for the Australian Constitution, 88; his speech on the Prison Discipline motion, 94; sends families to the Canterbury settlement, 98; takes a house in Lowndes Street, *ib.*; moves for a Commission on the Kaffir question, 99; his Cape Motion, 103 *et seq.*; offered Secretaryship of Board of Control by Lord Derby, 110; his leaning towards the Peelites, *ib.*; busy with colonial schemes, 112; his Cape schemes, 115 *et seq.*; abandons *Protection*, 121; remains nominally a follower of Lord Derby, 125; his work at Saltley, 126 *et seq.*; introduces a Bill to establish Reformatory Schools,

Printed by Hazell, Watson & Viney, Ld., London and Aylesbury.

CPSIA information can be obtained at www.ICGtesting.com
Printed in the USA
BVOW03s1447070214

344280BV00013B/443/P

9 781407 749297